Among the Wild Tribes
of the
Afghan Frontier

Dr. Pennell

Among the Wild Tribes of the Afghan Frontier

A Record of Sixteen Years Close Intercourse with the Natives of the Indian Marches

by

T. L. Pennell

With an Introduction by

Field-Marshal Earl Roberts

Delta Book World

New Delhi-110002

Among the Wild Tribes of the Afghan Frontier:
A Record of Sixteen Years Close Intercourse
with the Natives of the Indian Marches
by T. L. Pennell

First Published in 1922
Edition 2022
ISBN: 978-81-955519-7-2

Published by
Delta Book World
G-4, Prahlad House
4832/24, Ansari Road, Darya Ganj
New Delhi-110002 (India)
Tel.: 011-4707 2321
E-mail: deltabookworld@gmail.com

PRINTED IN INDIA

INTRODUCTION

This book is a valuable record of sixteen years' good work by an officer—a medical missionary—in charge of a medical mission station at Bannu, on the North-West Frontier of India.

Although many accounts have been written descriptive of the wild tribes on this border, there was still plenty of room for Dr. Pennell's modestly-related narrative. Previous writers—*e.g.*, Paget and Mason, Holdich, Oliver, Warburton, Elsmie, and many others—have dealt with the expeditions that have taken place from time to time against the turbulent occupants of the trans-Indus mountains, and with the military problems and possibilities of the difficult regions which they inhabit. But Dr. Pennell's story is not concerned with the clash of arms. His mission has been to preach, to heal, and to save; and in his long and intimate intercourse with the tribesmen, as recounted in these pages, he throws many new and interesting sidelights on the domestic and social, as well as on the moral and religious, aspects of their lives and characters.

During a long career in India I myself have seen and heard a good deal about these medical missions, and I can testify to their doing excellent and useful work, and that they are valuable and humanizing factors and moral aids well worthy of all encouragement and support.

No one can read Dr. Pennell's experiences without feeling that the man who is a physician and able to heal the body, in addition to being a preacher who can "minister to a mind diseased" as well as to spiritual needs, wields an influence which is not possessed by him who is a missionary only.

As the author himself writes: "The doctor finds his sphere everywhere, and his hands are full of work as soon as he arrives (at his station). He is able to overcome suspicion and prejudice, and his kindly aid and sympathetic treatment disarm opposition, while his life is a better setting forth of Christianity than his words. There is a door everywhere which can be opened by love and sympathy and practical service, and no one is more in a position to have a key for every door than a doctor."

These few words fairly sum up the situation, and I fully agree with the view they express.

On such a wild frontier as that on the North-West Border of India the life of a doctor-missionary is beset with many perils. A perusal of Dr. Pennell's most interesting story shows that he has had his share of them, and that in the earnest and zealous discharge of his duties he has faced them bravely and cheerfully. I cordially recommend his book to all readers, and my earnest hope is that medical missions will continue to flourish.

ROBERTS, F.M.

December 19, 1908.

PREFACE

TO THE FIRST EDITION

After sixteen years of close contact with the Afghans and Pathans of our North-West Frontier in India, I was asked to commit some of my experiences to paper. The present book is the result. I have used the Government system of transliteration in vernacular names and expressions, and I beg the reader to bestow a few minutes' consideration on the table of corresponding sounds and letters given on p. xvi, as it is painful to hear the way in which Englishmen, who, with their wide imperial interests, should be better informed, mispronounce common Indian words and names of places which are in constant use nowadays in England as much as abroad.

Nothing is recorded which has not been enacted in my own experience or in that of some trustworthy friend. In Chapters XIII. and XIV. it would have been unwise to give the actual names, so I have put the experience of several such cases together into one connected story, which, while concealing the identity of the actors, may also make the narrative more interesting to the reader; every fact recorded, however, happened under my own eyes. In Chapter XXII., the night adventure of Chikki, when he met an English officer in disguise, was related by him to me of another member of his profession, and not of himself.

I wish to thank the Church Missionary Society for allowing me to reproduce some articles which have already appeared in their publications, notably Chapter XX. and part of Chapter IV. I tender my best thanks to Major Wilkinson, I.M.S., Major Watson, H. Bolton, Esq., I.C.S., and Colonel S. Baker, for some of the photographs which have been here reproduced; and to Dr. J. Cropper for his kindness in reading the proofs.

We are at present engaged in building a branch dispensary at Thal, a place on the extreme border mentioned several times in the text, where the medical mission will have a profound influence on the trans-border tribes, as well as on those in British India. This will be known as the "Lord Roberts Hospital," as that place was at one time of the 1879-80 campaign the headquarters of his column.

T. L. PENNELL.

P. and O. s.s. "China,"
Gulf of Suez,
September 24, 1908.

PREFACE

TO THE FOURTH EDITION

THE kind reception which has been afforded to the earlier editions of this book has induced the publishers to bring out the present edition at a price which will bring it within the reach of all. The Lord Roberts Hospital at Thal has profited considerably by the sales of the earlier editions, and I hope that now a still wider circle of friends will add their share to the carrying on of this beneficent Christian agency in one of the wildest corners of our North-West Frontier.

T. L. PENNELL.

BANNU,
May 24, 1911.

CONTENTS

CHAPTER I

THE AFGHAN CHARACTER

CHAPTER II

AFGHAN TRADITIONS

CHAPTER III

BORDER WARRIORS

CHAPTER IV

A FRONTIER VALLEY

CHAPTER V

THE CHRISTIAN'S REVENGE

CHAPTER VI

A DAY IN THE WARDS

CHAPTER VII

FROM MORNING TO NIGHT

CHAPTER VIII

THE ITINERANT MISSIONARY

CHAPTER IX

AFGHAN MULLAHS

CHAPTER X

A TALE OF A TALIB

CHAPTER XI

SCHOOL-WORK

CHAPTER XII

AN AFGHAN FOOTBALL TEAM

CHAPTER XIII

'ALAM GUL'S CHOICE

CHAPTER XIV

'ALAM GUL'S CHOICE (*continued*)

CHAPTER XV

AFGHAN WOMEN

CHAPTER XVI

THE STORY OF A CONVERT

CHAPTER XVII

THE HINDU ASCETICS

CHAPTER XVIII

SADHUS AND FAQIRS

CHAPTER XIX

MY LIFE AS A MENDICANT

CHAPTER XX

A FRONTIER EPISODE

CHAPTER XXI

FRONTIER CAMPAIGNING

LIST OF ILLUSTRATIONS

TABLE OF THE CHIEF SOUNDS REPRESENTED IN THE GOVERNMENT SYSTEM OF TRANSLITERATION

a = short *u*, as in "bun."
á = broad *a*, as in "mast."
i = short *i*, as in "bin."
í = *ee*, as in "oblique."
e = *a*, as in "male."
o = long *o*, as in "note."
u = short *oo*, as in "foot."
ú = long *oo*, as in "boot."
q = guttural *k*.
kh = *ch*, as in "loch."
gh = guttural *r*, not used in English.
' = the Arabic letter *'ain*, a guttural not used in English.

PRONUNCIATION OF THE PRINCIPAL ORIENTAL WORDS USED IN THIS BOOK

Afghán
Afghánistán
Afrídi
Alláhu Akbar
Amír
Badakshán
Baltistán
Bengáli
Bezwáda
Bhágalpur
Bukhára
Chenáb
Chilás
Chinárak
Chitrál
Deraját
Dharmsála
Ghulám
Hákim (ruler)
Hakím (doctor)
Hardwár
Hazára
Islám
Jahán
Jamála
Jelálábad
Kabír
Kábul
Káfir
Kálabágh
Kalám
Karáchi
Karím
Khalífa
Khorasán
Kohát
Laghmáni
Loháni
Majíd
Málik
Mirzáda
Mughál
Multán
Nának
Nárowál
Nezabázi
Nizám
Panjáb
Panjábi
Pathán
Patwár
Pesháwur
Qurán
Rám
Ramazán
Risáldár
Ríshíkes
Sádhu
Sanyási
Saragári
Sardár
Sarkár
Subadár
Sulíman
Tálib
Tamána
Tiráh
Waziristán

CHAPTER I

THE AFGHAN CHARACTER

Paradoxical ideas of honour—Blood-feuds—A sister's revenge—The story of an outlaw—Taken by assault—A *jirgah* and its unexpected termination—Bluff—An attempt at kidnapping—Hospitality—A midnight meal—An ungrateful patient—A robber's death—An Afghan dance—A village warfare—An officer's escape—Cousins.

THE East is the country of contradictions, and the Afghan character is a strange medley of contradictory qualities, in which courage blends with stealth, the basest treachery with the most touching fidelity, intense religious fanaticism with an avarice which will even induce him to play false to his faith, and a lavish hospitality with an irresistible propensity for thieving.

There are two words which are always on an Afghan's tongue—*izzat* and *sharm*. They denote the idea of honour viewed in its positive and negative aspects, but what that honour consists in even an Afghan would be puzzled to tell you. Sometimes he will consider that he has vindicated his honour by a murder perpetrated with the foulest treachery; at other times it receives an indelible stain if at some public function he is given a seat below some rival chief.

The vendetta, or blood-feud, has eaten into the very core of Afghan life, and the nation can never become healthily progressive till public opinion on the question of revenge alters. At present some of the best and noblest families in Afghanistan are on the verge of extermination through this wretched system. Even the women are not exempt. In 1905, at Bannu, there was a case where a man had been foully murdered over some disputed land. It was generally known who the murderer was, but as he and his relations were powerful and likely to stick at nothing, and the murdered man had no near relation except one sister, no one was willing to risk his own skin in giving evidence, so when the case came up in court the Judge was powerless to convict.

"Am I to have no justice at the hands of the *Sarkar?*" passionately cried the sister in her despair. "Bring me witnesses, and I will convict," was all the Judge could reply. "Very well; I must find my own way;" and the girl left the court to take no rest till her brother's blood, which was crying to her from the ground, should be avenged.

Shortly after this I was sitting in a classroom of the mission school teaching the boys. It was a Friday morning, when thousands of the hillmen come in to the weekly fair, and the bazaars are full of a shouting, jostling throng, the murmur of which reaches even the schoolroom. Suddenly a shot was heard, and then a confused shouting. Running out on to the street hard by, I found a Wazir, quite dead, shot through the heart. It was the murderer who had escaped the justice of the law, but not the hand of the avenger, for the sister had concealed a revolver on her person, and coming up to her enemy in the crowded bazaar, had shot him point-blank. She was arrested there and then, and the court condemned her to penal servitude for life. I met her some weeks later as she was on the march with some other prisoners to their destination in the Andaman Islands. Resignation and satisfaction were her dominant feelings. "I have avenged my brother; for the rest, it is God's will: I am content." Those were the words in which she answered my inquiries,

The officer who has most power with the Pathans is the one who, while transparently just, yet deals with them with a strong hand, whose courage is beyond question, and who, when once his mind is made up, does not hesitate in the performance of his plans. To such a one they are loyal to the backbone, and will go through fire and water in his train.

> "Tender-handed grasp a nettle,
> It will sting you for your pains;
> Grasp it like a man of mettle,
> Soft as silk it then remains."

This has its counterpart in a Pashtu proverb, and is no doubt a true delineation of the Afghan character.

Some years ago some outlaws had fortified a village a few miles across the border, and had there bidden defiance to the authorities while carrying on their depredations among the frontier villages, where they raided many a wealthy Hindu, and even carried off the rifles from the police posts. The leader of the gang was Sailgai. His father was Mian Khan, a Wazir of the Sparkai clan. When still a boy Sailgai showed great aptitude and skill in archery, and when about fifteen he commenced rifle-shooting, and soon became a noted marksman. This, however, led him to associate with the desperadoes of the clan, and before long he became the leader of a gang which used to go out at night-time to break into shops and into the houses of rich Hindus. When this occupation began to pall on him he became a highway robber, and lay in wait with his confederates in various parts of the Kohat-Bannu road to waylay and rob travellers both by day and night. The next step onward—or downwards, we should say—was to become the leader of a gang of dacoits. These men would enter a village, usually in the late evening, and hold up the inhabitants while they looted the houses of the rich Hindus at leisure. On these occasions they often cut off the ears of the women as the simplest way of getting their earrings; and fingers, too, suffered in the same way if the owner did not remove his rings quickly enough. At the same time Sailgai became a professional murderer, and used to take two hundred to four hundred rupees for disposing of anyone obnoxious to the payer.

Still, up to this time he had contrived to keep clear of the police, and had never been caught. If anyone informed against him he soon discovered who the informant was, and paid him a night visit, only leaving after he had either killed him or taken a rich ransom. Some eight years ago he took two hundred rupees for killing a Bizun Khel Wazir, and went to his house one evening with fifteen of his followers. The Wazir, however, got a warning, and made a bold stand, and Sailgai had to fire seven times before he despatched him, and by that time the brother of the deceased had fetched some police and followed up in chase of Sailgai. When, however, the police saw that they had a well-armed band to contend with, although about equal in number to the Wazirs, they beat a hasty retreat, with the exception of one man, who opened fire on the murderers at two hundred paces, but was hit and disabled, so that Sailgai and his party got away in safety. Government gave a reward to this, the one brave man, and put a price on Sailgai's head, so that he could no longer enter British territory except by stealth, and he retired to his fort at Gumatti, which he strengthened and made the base for marauding expeditions on Government territory.

These subsequently became so frequent and so successful that the Indian Government was finally constrained to send up a column under Colonel Tonnochy, who was in command of the 53rd Sikhs at Bannu, to destroy his fort once for all. Before the guns opened fire the Political Officer, Mr. Donald, walked up alone to the loopholes of his fort to offer Sailgai and his fellow-defenders terms. Knowing well the long list of crimes that would be proved against him, he replied that he had determined to sell his life as dearly as possible in the fort where he had been born and bred; and we must say, to his credit, that they restrained their fire till Mr. Donald got back to his own lines. Colonel Tonnochy brought the guns up to within sixty yards of the fort, and while directing their operations he was mortally wounded. When the tower was finally taken by storm, all Sailgai's companions were dead, and he himself wounded in four places. He, however, with a last effort took aim at the British officer, Captain White, who was bravely leading the assault, and shot him dead, and was almost at the same moment despatched by that officer's orderly. Wazirs from Gumatti, as well as from all the rest of the neighbourhood, are constantly coming to the mission dispensary, and some of them have been in-patients. The police *munshi* who made the bold stand above mentioned was himself treated for his wound in our hospital.

The Afghan has in some respects such inordinate vanity in connection with his peculiar ideas of *sharm*, and is so hot-headed in resenting some fancied insult, that he sometimes places himself in a ridiculous position, from which he finds it difficult to extricate himself without still further sacrificing his honour.

An instance of this occurred in December, 1898. The mission school athletic sports were in progress in the mission compound, and the political officers of the Tochi and Wano were engaged not far off in a *jirgah* of the representatives of the Mahsud and Darwesh Khel sections of the Wazirs. Suddenly the cry was raised, "The Wazirs have attacked us!" and for a short time all was confusion. Wazirs were seen rushing pell-mell into school, bungalow, and other buildings, and a great part of the spectators who had gathered to see the sports fled in confusion. It transpired, however, that, so far from the Wazirs desiring to do us any injury, they were the Mahsuds in flight from the Darwesh Khels, who were hot in pursuit, chasing them even into the mission buildings where they had sought refuge. The council had been proceeding satisfactorily, and with apparently amicable relations on both sides, when a Darwesh Khel *malik*, in the excitement of debate, gesticulated too close to the seat of the Political Officer. A Mahsud orderly, thinking he was disrespectful to the officer, pushed him back with needless force, so that the *malik* slipped and fell. The Darwesh Khels round him at once set on the orderly, saying he had done it of malice prepense, and began to beat him. In another moment the whole assembly were frantically attacking each other; but the Mahsuds, being very decidedly in the minority, found safety in flight, and, our mission compound being the nearest rallying-place, had come down upon us in this unceremonious manner, with the Darwesh Khels in hot pursuit. Fortunately, no serious injury resulted, and both parties were soon laughing at their own foolish hot-headedness.

Bluff is a very prominent characteristic of the Afghan, and this makes him appear more formidable than he really is to those who are not acquainted with his character. He is also a great bully and exults in cruelty, so that he becomes a veritable tyrant to those who have fallen into his power or are overawed by his bluff. At the same time, he has a profound reverence for the personification of power or brute force, and becomes a loyal and devoted follower of those whom he believes to be his superiors. It is often asked of me whether I carry a revolver or other arms when travelling about among these wild tribes. For a missionary to do so would not only be fatal to his chance of success, but would be a serious and constant danger. It would be impossible for him to be always on his guard; there must be times when, through fatigue or other reasons, he is at the mercy of those among whom he is dwelling. Besides this, there is nothing which an Afghan covets more, or to steal which he is more ready to risk his life, than firearms; and though he might not otherwise wish harm to the missionary, the possibility of securing a good revolver or gun would be too great a temptation, even though he had to shed blood to secure it.

My plan was, therefore, to put myself entirely in their hands, and let them see that I was trusting to their sense of honour and to their traditional treatment of a guest for my safety.

At the same time, I was rather at pains than otherwise to let them see that the bluff to which they sometimes resorted had no effect upon me, and that I was indifferent to their threats and warnings, which, as often as not, were just a ruse on their part to see how far they could impose on me. Once, when I was in a trans-border village, resting a few hours in the heat of the day, some young bloods arrived who had just come in from a raid, and were still in the excitement of bloodshed. Some of them thought it would be a good opportunity to bait the *Daktar Sahib*, and one of them, holding his loaded revolver to my chest, said: "Now we are going to shoot you." I replied: "You will be very great fools if you do, because I am of more use to you than to myself, and you would as likely as not poison yourselves with my drugs if I were not there to tell you how to use them." At this the senior man of the party rebuked them, and offered me a kind of apology for their rudeness, saying: "They are only young fellows, and they are excited. Do not mind what they say. We will see that no harm comes to you." On another occasion I came to a village across the border rather late at night. There were numerous outlaws in the village, but the chief under whose protection I placed myself took the precaution of putting my bed in the centre of six of his retainers, fully armed, in a circle round me, one or two of whom were to keep watch in turns. I had had a hard day's work, and was soon sound asleep, and this was my safety, because I was told in the morning that some of the more fanatical spirits had wanted to kill me in the night, but the others said: "See, he has trusted himself entirely to our protection, and because he trusts us he is sleeping so soundly; therefore, no harm must be done to him in our village."

Not long ago there was a notorious outlaw on the frontier

called Rangin, who had been making a practice of kidnapping rich Hindus, and then holding them to ransom. I was in the habit of visiting our out-station at Kharrak about once a month, and usually went alone and by night. Information was brought that Rangin, knowing of this, intended one day to kidnap me, and hold me to a high ransom. The next time I visited Kharrak, I purposely slept by the roadside all night in a lonely part, that the people might see that I was not afraid of Rangin's threats. Needless to say, no harm came of it; but the people there in the countryside spread the idea that, as there was an angel protecting the *Daktar Sahib*, it would be a useless act of folly to try to do him an injury.

Although the honour which an Afghan thinks is due to his guest has often stood me in good stead, yet sometimes the observance of the correct etiquette has become irksome. A rich chief will be satisfied with nothing less than the slaying of a sheep when he receives a guest of distinction; a poorer man will be satisfied with the slaying of a fowl, and the preparation therefrom of the native dish called *pulao*. On one occasion I came to a village with my companions rather late in the evening. The chief himself was away, but his son received me with every mark of respect, and killed a fowl and cooked us a savoury *pulao*, after which, wearied with the labours of the day, we were soon fast asleep. Later on, it appeared, the chief himself arrived, and learnt from his son of our arrival. "Have you killed for him the *dumba?*" he at once asked; and, on learning from his son that he had only prepared a fowl, he professed great annoyance, saying: "This will be a lasting shame (*sharm*) for me, if it is known that, when the Bannu *Daktar Sahib* came to my village, I cooked for him nothing more than a fowl. Go at once to the flock, and take a *dumba*, and slay and dress it, and, when all is ready, call me." Thus it came about that about 1 a.m. we were waked up to be told that the chief had come to salaam us, and that dinner was ready. It would not only have been useless to protest that we were more in a mood for sleep than for dinner, but it would also have been an insult to his hospitality; so we got up with alacrity and the best grace possible, and after a performance of the usual salutations on both sides, we buckled to that we might show our appreciation of the luscious feast of roast mutton and *pulao* that had been prepared for us.

On one occasion, in turning back to Bannu from a journey across the frontier, I had an escort of two villainous-looking Afghans, who appeared as though they would not hesitate at any crime, however atrocious. They, however, looked after us with the greatest attention, and brought us safely into Bannu. On arrival there, I offered them some money as a reward for their good conduct; they, however, refused it with some show of indignation, saying that to take money from one who had been their guest would be contrary to their best traditions. Consequently, I sent them over to rest for the night at the house of one of my native assistants, with a note to give them a good dinner, and send them away early in the morning. He gave them the dinner, but when he got up in the morning to see them off, he found that they had already decamped with all his best clothes.

Among the Afghans theft is more or less praiseworthy, according to the skill and daring shown in its perpetration, and to the success in the subsequent evasion of pursuit. Two years ago an Afghan brought his little daughter for an operation on her eye. The operation was successfully performed, and the day of discharge came. Meanwhile the eyes of the Afghan had lighted on my mare, and he thought how useful it would be to him on his travels, and the night following his discharge we found that he had come with a friend and taken the horse away. Unfortunately for the success of the undertaking, he had an enemy, who, when a reward was offered for the discovery of the thief, thought he might enrich himself and pay off an old grudge at the same time. The culprit had, however, by this time arrived with his capture safely across the Afghan frontier into Khost, and no laws of extradition apply there. Other members of the tribe, however, reside in British India, and would be going up with their families into the hills as the heat of summer increased. The Deputy Commissioner called for the chiefs of the tribe, and informed them that until they arranged for the return of the mare, he would be reluctantly compelled to issue orders that they were not to go up to the hills with their families. At first they protested that they had no control over the thief, whom they had themselves turned out of their tribe because he was a rascal; but when they found that the officer knew them too well to be hoodwinked by their bluff, they found it convenient to send up into Khost and bring back the mare. The man through whose instrumentality it was brought back has posed to me ever since as my benefactor, and expected a variety of favours in return. The theft was universally reprobated by the tribe, but chiefly because circumstances had doomed it to failure.

Notorious thieves and outlaws have frequently availed themselves of the wards of the mission hospital when suffering from some fever or other disease which has temporarily incapacitated them; but, of course, they come under assumed names, and otherwise conceal their identity. It is to be hoped, however, that they benefit all the same from the addresses and good counsel which they daily hear while under treatment. Sometimes, as in the case I am about to relate, their identity becomes known. A few years ago, in Bed 26—the "Southsea" bed—there was Zaman, a noted thief, who came in suffering from chronic dysentery, and continued under treatment for over two months. He lingered on, with many ups and downs, but was evidently past recovery when he came in. He paid much attention to the Gospel that was read to him, and sometimes professed belief in it, but showed no signs of repenting of his past career. But when told eventually that there was no hope of his recovery, he at once had a police officer summoned, so as to give him the names of some of his former "pals," hoping thereby not only to get them caught and punished in revenge for their having thrown him off when too weak and ill to join in their nefarious practices, but also to gain a reward for the information given. He gradually sank and died, professing a belief in Christ; but He alone, who readeth the heart, knoweth. I do not think he would have turned informer had not his confederates apparently deserted him in his distress.

No description of Afghan life would be complete which did not give an account of their public dances. These take place on the '*Id* days, or to celebrate some tribal compact, or the cessation of hostilities between two tribes or sections. It can only be seen in its perfection across the border, for in British India the more peaceful habits of the people and the want of the requisite firearms have caused it to fall into desuetude. Across the frontier some level piece of ground is chosen, and a post is fixed in the centre. The men arrange themselves in ever-widening circles round this centre and gyrate round it, ever keeping the centre on the left, so as to give greater play to their sword-arms. The older and less nimble of the warriors form the inner circles; outside them come the young men, who dance round with surprising agility, often with a gun in one hand and a sword in the other, or, it may be, with a sword in each hand, which they wave alternately in circles round their heads. Outside them, again, circle the horsemen, showing their agility in the saddle and their skill with the sword or gun at the same time. On one side are the village minstrels, who give the tune on drums and pipes. They begin with a slow beat, and one sees all the circles going round with a measured tread; then the music becomes more and more rapid, and the dancers become more and more carried away with excitement, and to the onlooker it appears a surging mass of waving swords and rifles. The rifles are as often as not loaded and discharged from time to time, at which the gyrations of the horsemen on the outside become more and more excited, and one wonders that heads and arms are not gashed by the swords which are seen waving everywhere. Suddenly the music ceases, and all stop to regain their breath, to start again after a few minutes, until they are tired out. The excitement and the intricate revolutions often bring the scene to the brink of a real warfare, and not infrequently it ends in bloodshed. In one instance, where a man fell, and in falling discharged his rifle with fatal effect into another dancer, the unintentional murderer would have had his throat cut there and then had not his friends hurriedly dragged him out and carried him off to his home, fighting as they went. In this way blood-feuds are sometimes started, which will divide a village into two factions, and not end till some of the bravest have fallen victims to it.

On one occasion I was seated with some Afghans in a house in the village of Peiwar in the Kurram Valley. Most of the houses were on either side of one long street running the length of the village, and I noticed that some little doors had been made from house to house all down the street, and on inquiring the object of this, I was told that some time before a great faction fight had been carried on in the village. One side of the street was in one faction and the other side in the other faction, and they were always in ambush to fire at each other across the street. The only way to get to the village supply of water was to go from house to house down to the bottom of the street, and in order to do this without exposure, doors had been made, while by common consent they had agreed not to shoot while getting their supplies from the stream at the bottom. My host went on to show me sundry holes in his door and in the wooden panels of the windows, which the bullets of his neighbours across the

A KHATTAK SWORD-DANCER

The men range themselves in circles, having a post in the centre. Round this they gyrate with surprising agility, with a sword in each hand, which they wave alternately in circles round their heads.

street had penetrated, and said: "It was behind that hole in the door there that my uncle was shot; that hole in the window was made by the bullet which killed my brother." Pointing to another Afghan who had come into the room and seated himself on the bed, he said: "That is the man who shot my brother." On my remarking upon the peace and goodwill in which they appeared to be living at the present time, he said: "Yes, we are good friends now, because the debt is even on both sides. I have killed the same number in his family." After a faction fight of this kind, the fatalities on both sides are added up, and if they can be found to be equal, both sides feel that they can make peace without sacrificing their *izzat* (honour), and amicable relations are resumed, it being thought unnecessary to investigate who were the real instigators or murderers. If, however, one side or the other believes itself to be still aggrieved, or not to have exacted the full tale of lives required by the law of revenge, then the feud may go on indefinitely, until whole families may become nearly exterminated. The avenger will go on waiting his opportunity for months or years, but he will never forget; and one will always remember the hunted look and the furtive expression and nervous handling of the revolver and cartridges which mark the man who knows that one or more such avenger is on his track.

A Political Officer in the Kurram Valley was once visiting a chief of the village of Shlozan, who, like all chiefs, had a high tower, in which he would seek security from his enemies at night. His host took him up into the tower, after carefully seeing that a window in the upper story was shut. The officer, thinking he would like a view of the country round, went to open it, but was hurriedly and unceremoniously pulled back by the chief, who told him that his cousin had been watching that window for months in the hope of having an opportunity of shooting him there. The officer made no further attempt to look out of the window, but some months later he heard that his friend the chief, having inadvertently gone to the open window, had been shot there by his cousin. So universal is the enmity existing between cousins in Afghanistan that it has become a proverb that a man is "as great an enemy as a cousin," the causes of such feuds being such as are more likely to arise between those who have some relationship. The causes of 90 per cent. of such feuds are described by the Afghans as belonging to one of three heads—*zan*, *zar*, and *zamin*, these being the three Persian words meaning women, money, and land; and disputes are more likely to arise between cousins than between strangers on such matters as these.

CHAPTER II

AFGHAN TRADITIONS

Israelitish origin of the Afghans—Jewish practices—Shepherd tradition of the Wazirs—Afridis and their saint—The *zyarat* or shrine—Graveyards—Custom of burial—Graves of holy men—Charms and amulets—The medical practice of a faqir—Native remedies—First aid to the wounded—Purges and blood-letting—Tooth extraction—Smallpox.

A CONTROVERSY as to the origin of the Afghans centres round the question as to whether they are the children of Israel or not; and there are two opposing camps, one regarding it as an accepted historical fact that they are descended from the lost ten tribes of Israel, and the other repudiating all Israelitish affinities except such as may have come to them through the Muhammadan religion. The Afghans themselves—at least, the more intelligent part of the community—will tell you that they are descended from the tribe of Benjamin, and will give you their genealogy through King Saul up to Abraham, and they almost universally apply the term "Bani-Israil," or children of Israel, to themselves. Wolff, the traveller, relates that an Afghan, Mulla Khodadad, gave him the following history: Saul had a grandson called Afgháná, the nephew of Asaph, the son of Berachiah, who built the Temple of Solomon. One year and a half after Solomon's death he was banished from Jerusalem to Damascus on account of misconduct. In the time of Nebuchadnezzar the Jews were driven out of Palestine and taken to Babylon. The descendants of Afghana residing at Damascus, being Jews, were also carried to Babylon, from whence they removed, or were removed, to the mountain of Ghor, in Afghanistan, their present place of residence, and in the time of Muhammad they accepted his religion.

To most observers the Afghan has a most remarkably Jewish cast of features, and often in looking round the visitors of our out-patient department one sees some old greybeard of pure Afghan descent, and involuntarily exclaims: "That man might for all the world be one of the old Jewish patriarchs returned to us from Bible history!" All Muhammadan nations must, from the origin of their religion, have many customs and observances which appear Jewish because they were adopted by Muhammad himself from the Jews around him; but there are two, at least, met with among Afghans which are not found among neighbouring Muhammadan peoples, and which strongly suggest a Jewish origin. The first, which is very common, is that of sacrificing an animal, usually a sheep or a goat, in case of illness, after which the blood of the animal is sprinkled over the doorposts of the house of the sick person, by means of which the angel of death is warded off. The other, which is much less common, and appears to be dying out, is that of taking a heifer and placing upon it the sins of the people, whereby it becomes *qurban*, or sacrifice, and then it is driven out into the wilderness. The Afghan, more than most Muhammadans, delights in Biblical names, and David, Solomon, Abraham, Job, Jacob, and many other patriarchs, are constant inmates of our hospital wards. New Testament names, such as King Jesus (Mihtar Esa) and Simon are occasionally met with. The ceremonies enacted at the Muhammadan "'Id-i-bakr," or Feast of Sacrifice, have a most extraordinary similarity to the Jewish Passover; but as these have a religious, and not a racial, origin and signification, and can be read in any book on Muhammadanism, it is unnecessary to describe them here. The strongest argument against their Jewish origin is the almost entire disappearance of any Hebrew words from their vocabulary; but this may be partly, at least, explained by their admixture at first with Chaldaic, and subsequently with Arab, races. The Wazirs have a tradition as to their origin, which, although its Biblical resemblance may be accidental, is yet certainly remarkable when found among so wild and barbarous a race. The tradition is that a certain ancestor had two sons, Issa and Missa (probably Jesus and Moses). The latter was a shepherd, and one day while tending his flocks on the hills a lamb strayed away and could not be found. Missa, leaving his other sheep, went in search of the lost one. For three days and nights he wandered about the jungle without being able to find it. On the morning of the fourth day he found it in some distant valley, and, instead of being wroth with it, he took it up in his arms, kissed it, and brought it safely back to the flock. For this humane act God greatly blessed him, and made him the progenitor of the Wazir tribe. Though it would seem to us more appropriate had this action been attributed to Issa instead of to Missa, yet this tradition has often given me a text for explaining the Gospel story to a crowd of these wild tribesmen.

Though all Afghans are fanatically zealous in the pursuit of their religion, yet some are so ignorant of its teachings that more civilized Muhammadans are hardly willing to admit their right to a place in the congregation of the faithful. The Wazirs, for instance, who would always be ready to take their share in a religious war, are not only ignorant of all but the elementary truths of Muhammadanism, but the worship of saints and graves is the chief form that their religion takes. The Afridis are not far removed from them in this respect, and it is related of a certain section of the Afridis that, having been taunted by another tribe for not possessing a shrine of any holy man, they enticed a certain renowned Seyyed to visit their country, and at once despatched and buried him, and boast to this day of their assiduity in worshipping at his sepulchre.

The frontier hills are often bare enough of fields or habitations, but one cannot go far without coming across some *zyarat*, or holy shrine, where the faithful worship and make their vows. It is very frequently situated on some mountain-top or inaccessible cliff, reminding one of the "high places" of the Israelites. Round the grave are some stunted trees of tamarisk or ber (*Zisyphus jujuba*). On the branches of these are hung innumerable bits of rag and pieces of coloured cloth, because every votary who makes a petition at the shrine is bound to tie a piece of cloth on as the outward symbol of his vow. In the accompanying photograph is seen a famous shrine on the Suliman Range. Despite its inaccessibility, hundreds of pilgrims visit this yearly, and sick people are carried up in their beds, with the hope that the blessing of the saint may cure them. Sick people are often carried on beds, either strapped on camels or on the shoulders of their friends, for considerably more than a hundred miles to one or other of these *zyarats*. In some cases it may reasonably be supposed that the change from a stuffy, unventilated dark room to the open air, and the stimulus of change of climate and scenery, has its share in the cure which often undoubtedly results.

Another feature of these shrines is that their sanctity is so universally acknowledged that articles of personal property may be safely left by the owners for long periods of time in perfect confidence of finding them untouched on their return. This is the more remarkable, remembering that these tribes are thieves by profession, and scarcely look upon brigandage as a reprehensible act. The inhabitants of a mountain village may be migrating to the plains for the winter months, and they will leave their beds, pots and pans, and other household furniture, under the trees of some neighbouring shrine, and they will almost invariably find them on their return, some

Ziarat or Shrine on the Takht-i-Suliman

These burial-places of holy men are frequently located in almost inaccessible spots on mountains. Yet bed-ridden sufferers are hauled up the precipitous sides in order that they may be benefited by contact with the holy place, as may be seen in the illustration.

months later, exactly as they left them. One distinct advantage of these shrines is that it is a sin to cut wood from any of the trees surrounding them. Thus it comes about that the shrines are the only green spots among the hills which the improvident vandalism of the tribes has denuded of all their trees and shrubs.

Graves have a special sanctity in the eyes of the Afghans, more even than in the case of other Muhammadans, and you will generally see an Afghan, when passing by a graveyard, dismount from his horse and, turning towards some more prominent tomb, which denotes the burial-place of some holy man, hold up his hands in the attitude of Muhammadan prayer, and invoke the blessing of the holy man on his journey, and then stroke his beard, as is usually done by the Muhammadans at the conclusion of their prayers. There are few graveyards which do not boast some such holy man or faqir in their midst; in fact, as often as not, the chance burial of some such holy man in an out-of-the-way part determines the site of a cemetery, because all those in the country round desire to have their graves near his, in the belief that at the Resurrection Day his sanctity will atone for any of their shortcomings, and insure for them an unquestionable entry into bliss. The graves always lie north and south, and after digging down to a depth determined by the character of the soil, a niche is hollowed out at one side, usually the western, and the corpse is laid in the niche, with its face turned towards Mecca. Some bricks or stones are then laid along the edge of the niche, so that when the earth is thrown in none of it may fall on the corpse, which in enveloped in a winding-sheet only, coffins being never used. The origin of the word "coffin" is possibly from the Arabic word *kafn*, which denotes the winding-sheet usually used by Muhammadans.*

Great marvels are related about the graves of these holy

* More probably from the Greek κοφινος.—J. C.

men, among the commonest being the belief that they go on increasing in length of their own accord, the increase of length being a sign of the acceptance of the prayers of the deceased by the Almighty. Near the mission house in Peshawur was one such grave, which went on lengthening at the rate of one foot a year. When it had reached the length of twenty-seven feet it was seriously encroaching on the public highway, and it was only after the promulgation of an official order from the district authorities that the further growth of the holy man should cease that the grave ceased to expand. This shrine is still famous in the country round as "the Nine-Yard Shrine," which numbers of devotees visit every year, in the expectation of obtaining some material benefit.

The use of charms or amulets is practically universal. The children of the rich may be seen with strings of charms fastened up in little ornamented silver caskets hung round their neck, while even the poorest labourer will not be without a charm sewn up in a bit of leather, which he fastens round his arm or his neck. These charms are most usually verses out of the Quran, transcribed by some Mullah of repute and blessed by him; others are cabalistic sentences or words, while some are mere bits of paper or rag which have been blessed by a holy man. On more than one occasion I have found my prescriptions made up into charms, the patient believing that this would be more efficacious than drinking the hospital medicines; in fact, one patient assured me that he had never suffered from rheumatism, to which he had previously been subject, after he had tied round his arm a prescription in which I had ordered him some salicylate of soda, although he had never touched the drug. In one instance I found that a man who had been given some grey powders, with directions how to use them, had instead fastened them up, paper and all, into a little packet, which he had sewn up in leather and fastened round his neck, with, he told me, very beneficial result. From this it can be readily understood that Mullahs and faqirs who pretend to have the power of making charms for all known diseases, and sell them to the people at large, are often able to enrich themselves far more rapidly than a doctor who confines himself to the ordinary methods of treatment.

Once, when I was in camp, I came across a mountebank who was making quite a large fortune in this way. He had travelled over a large part of South-Western Asia, but did not stop long in any one place, as no doubt his takings would soon begin to wear off after the first days of novelty. One of his performances was to walk through fire, professedly by the power of the Muhammadan *Kalimah.* A trench was dug in the ground, and filled with charcoal and wood, which was set alight. After the fire had somewhat died down, the still glowing embers were beaten down with sticks, and then the faqir, reciting the *Kalimah* with great zest, proceeded to deliberately walk across, after which he invited the more daring among the faithful to follow his example, assuring them that if they recited the creed in the same way and with sincerity, they would suffer no harm. Some went through the ordeal and showed no signs of having suffered from it; others came out with blistered and sore feet. These unfortunates were jeered at by the others as being no true Muhammadans, owing to which they had forfeited the immunity conferred upon them by the recitation of the creed. One young Sikh student, calling out the Sikh battle-cry, ventured on the ordeal, and came out apparently none the worse. The Muhammadans looked upon this as an insult to their religion, because Muhammadans oftener than not heard that cry when the Sikhs had been engaged in mortal combat with them, and this action of the young Sikh appeared to them to be a challenge as to whether the Muhammadan or the Sikh cry had the greater magic power. However, some of the more responsible persons present checked the more hot-headed ones, and the affair passed off with a little scoffing. Every morning and afternoon the faqir prepared for the reception of the patients, who were collected in great numbers on hearing of his fame. Each applicant had to give 5 pice to the assistant as his fee. He was then sent before the faqir, who remained seated on a mat. The faqir asked him one or two questions as to the nature of the illness, wrote out the necessary charm, and passed on to the next. Three or four hundred people were often seen at one sitting. This would give about 50 rupees (£3. 6s. 8d.) as a day's takings. Some days would, no doubt, be occupied in travelling, and others less fruitful; but his equipment and his method of travelling showed that it was a very profitable business. He was stopping in the rest-house, and invited me to dinner, which was served in English fashion. He entertained me with stories of his travels, and made no secret of the fact that he took advantage of the credulity of the people to run a good business. When dinner was nearly over an assistant came in to say that there were many people outside clamouring for charms. With an apology to me for the interruption, he took a piece of paper, tore it up into squares, quickly wrote off the required number, and gave them to the assistant to go on with. In some cases, especially those suffering from rheumatism or old injuries or sprains, he used rubbings and manipulations, much as a so-called bone-setter does, and these, no doubt, helped the charm to do its work.

The medical and surgical treatment of the faqirs is extremely crude. Sometimes Jogis and herbalists from India travel about the country and practise a certain amount of *yunani*, or Hippocratic medicine; but the native doctors of Afghanistan have extremely little knowledge of medicine. The two stock treatments of Afghanistan are those known as *dzan* and *dam*. *Dzan* is a treatment habitually used in cases of fever, whether acute or chronic, and in a variety of chronic complaints, which they do not attempt to diagnose. It consists in stripping the patient to the skin and placing him on a bed. A sheep or a goat is then killed and rapidly skinned. The patient is then wrapped up in the skin, with the raw surface next him and the wool outside. He is then covered up with a number of quilts. When successful, this treatment acts by producing a profuse perspiration, and when it is removed—on the second day in the summer and the third day in the winter—the patient is sometimes found to be free from fever, though very worn and weak from the profuse sweating. If the first application is not successful, it may be repeated several times. In a case of severe injury to one of the limbs, the same treatment is often applied locally. In the case of a fractured thigh, for instance, the sheepskin is tied on, a rough splint applied externally, and often left for a week or more. Where there has been an open wound, and the patient has been brought several days' journey through the heat down to our hospital in Bannu, you can usually anticipate the character of the case by seeing the men who have carried the bed in carefully winding their *pagaris* round their noses and mouths before proceeding to unbandage it for your inspection, and when it is at last opened all except the doctor and his assistant try to get as far away as possible. A surgeon can scarcely be confronted with a more complete antithesis to his modern ideas of aseptic surgery than a case like this, and many and prolonged applications of antiseptics and deodorants are required before the wound begins to assume a healthy aspect, even if inflammation and gangrene have not rendered amputation a necessity. In the case of a small wound, the whole or a part of the skin of a fowl is used in the same way, the flesh of the slaughtered animal being always a part of the fee of the doctor.

The other remedy, or that known as the *dam*, is akin to what is known in Western surgery as a "moxa." A piece of cloth is rolled up in a pledget of the size of a shilling, steeped in oil, placed on the part selected by the doctor, and set alight. It burns down into the flesh, and a hard slough is formed; this gradually separates, and leaves an ulcer, which heals by degrees. This remedy is used for every conceivable illness, a particular part of the body being selected according to the disease or the diagnostic ability of the doctor who applies the remedy. Thus, in people who have suffered from indigestion you will often see a line of scars down each side of the abdomen. For neuralgia, it is applied to the temples; for headache, to the scalp; for rheumatism, to the shoulders; for lumbago, to the loins; for paralysis, to the back; for sciatica, to the thighs; and so on indefinitely. I have counted as many as fifty scars, each the size of a shilling, on one patient as the result of repeated applications of this remedy. The Afghans have extraordinary faith in both these treatments, and I have sometimes sat in a village listening to an argument in which some young fellow, lately returned from a visit to a mission hospital, recounted the wonderful things he had seen there, to which some old conservative greybeard retorted: "What do we want with all these new-fangled things? The *dzan* and the *dam* are sufficient for us." As formerly in the West, so still in Afghanistan, the village barber performs the ordinary surgical operations, such as opening an abscess or lancing a gum.

The women all claim a greater or less knowledge of such surgery and medicine as they think necessary for them. After one of the village frays, when the warriors come back to their homes more or less cut and wounded, the women of the household at once set about their treatment. If there is severe hæmorrhage some oil is quickly raised to boiling-point in a saucepan, and either poured into the wound, or if, for instance, a limb has been cut off, the bloody stump is plunged into the oil. This, no doubt, acts as an effective, though somewhat barbarous, hæmostatic. If the bleeding is only slight, a certain plant gathered from the jungle is reduced to ashes, and these ashes rubbed on the wound. In the case of a clean cut the women draw out hairs from their own head, and sew it up with their ordinary sewing-needles, and I have sometimes seen flesh wounds which have been quite skilfully sewn up in this way. They are less skilful in the application of splints. In most neighbourhoods there is some village carpenter who prides himself on his skill in the application of splints to broken bones; but in most cases he bandages them too tightly, or with too little knowledge of the circulation of the limb, so that not a year passes in which we do not get one or more cases of limbs which have become gangrenous after quite simple fractures through this kind of treatment.

Almost the only drugs which are used to any extent in Afghanistan are purgatives, and especially those of a more violent and drastic nature. Nearly every Afghan thinks it necessary to be purged or bled, or both, every spring, and not unfrequently at the fall of the year too. Scarcely any illness is allowed to go to a week's duration without the trial of some violent purge. Sometimes the purge is given with so little regard to its quantity and the vitality of the patient that it results in rapid collapse and death. In other cases a latent dysentery is excited, which may result in an illness lasting many months, and leaving the patient permanently weakened thereby. The seasonal blood-lettings are performed, as in the West, from the bend of the arm, this position having, no doubt, come down to the practitioners of both East and West from the ancient Greeks; but in the case of illness, while the physicians of the West have had their practice revolutionized by modern ideas of anatomy and physiology, those of the East still follow the humoral and hypothetical pathologies of Hippocrates and his predecessors. These practitioners know the particular vein in the particular limb or part of the body which has to be selected for venesection in any particular illness. I have known a young doctor from England lose at once the confidence which the people might up to that time have had in his medical knowledge, because in a case of illness to which he was called he recommended venesection, and the patient's medical attendant who was to carry out the treatment made the, to him, very natural inquiry, "From what vein?" The English doctor said: "It does not matter." Both patient and medical attendant not unnaturally assumed that he was either a very careless doctor or an ignoramus, and, in either case, that they had better call in a fresh opinion.

Cataract is a very common complaint in Afghanistan, and from time immemorial there have been certain *hakims*, or native practitioners, who operate on this by means of the old process of couching. These men usually itinerate about the country from village to village, as in most cases the old men and the old women who are suffering from cataract are unable to undertake the journey to a town where one of these practitioners lives; or it may be that their relations are not willing to take the trouble for someone whose working days are apparently over. In some cases no doubt the operation results in good sight, but in the majority other changes which take place in the eye as a result of the operation lead before long to total blindness. As, however, the *hakim* seldom goes over the same ground again till after the lapse of several years, his reputation does not lose by these failures, as it would have done if he were always resident in one place. The tooth extracting of the village is usually entrusted to the village blacksmith, who has a ponderous pair of forceps, a foot and a half to two feet long, hung up in his shop for the purpose. Where the crown of the tooth is fairly strong and prominent the operation generally results in a short struggle, and then the removal of the aching tooth; but if the tooth is very carious, or not prominent enough for a good grip, the results are often disastrous, even to fracture of the jaw, and these ultimately come to the mission hospital for repair, several often turning up in one day.

At one time smallpox was terribly rife in Afghanistan, and

even now no village can be visited without seeing many who are permanently disfigured by it. When an Afghan comes to negotiate about the price of an eligible girl for marrying to his son, one of the first questions asked is, "Has she had the smallpox?" and if not, either the settlement may be postponed until she is older, or else some deduction is made for her possible disfigurement if attacked by the disease. Many times fathers have brought their daughters to the hospital with the scars left by smallpox in their eyes, begging me to remove them, not so much for the sake of the patient as because the market value of the daughter will be so much enhanced thereby. The custom of inoculation was at one time almost universal in Afghanistan. A little of the crust of the sore of a smallpox patient was taken and rubbed into an incision made in the wrist of the person to be inoculated. The smallpox resulting, though usually mild, was sometimes so severe as to cause the death of the patient, and the people have not been slow to recognize the great advantages which vaccination has over inocùlation. Only two circumstances deter the people from universally profiting by the facilities offered by the British Government. The first reason is that very often the vaccinators are underpaid officials, who use their opportunities for taking bribes from the people, and make the whole business odious to them. The other is, that they have a widespread superstition that the Government are really seeking for a girl, who is to be recognized by the fact that when the vaccinator scarifies her arm, instead of blood, milk will flow from the wound; she is then to be taken over to England for sacrifice, and the parents are afraid lest their girl should be the unlucky one.

CHAPTER III

BORDER WARRIORS

Peiwar Kotal—The Kurram Valley—The Bannu Oasis—Independent tribes—The Durand line—The indispensable Hindu—A lawsuit and its sequel—A Hindu outwits a Muhammadan—The scope of the missionary.

I WAS standing on a pine-clad spur of the Sufed Koh Range, which runs westwards towards Kabul, between the Khaiber Pass on the north and the Kurram Pass on the south. The snow-clad peaks of Sika Ram, which rise to a height of fifteen thousand feet, tipped by fleecy white clouds, were just behind me, while in front was the green valley of the Kurram River, spread out like a panorama before me, widening out into a large plain in its upper part, where numerous villages, partly hidden in groves of mulberry and walnuts, nestled among the lower spurs of the mountains, while farther down the hills on either side of it closed in and became more rugged and bare, and the river wound its circuitous path through defile and gorge, till it debouched on the plains of India. Immediately before me was the pine-covered Pass of Peiwar, which will always be memorable as the scene of the great battle fought between the forces of the Amir, Sher Ali, and the advancing column of Sir Frederick Roberts. There were the pines covering the crest where the Afghan batteries were ensconced, and one could trace without difficulty the circuitous path up the stony bed of the mountain torrent, through a deep ravine, and then winding up among the pine-woods, by which the gallant regiments of the advancing army stormed and finally captured the Afghan position.

Westward of the pass was a fertile valley, dotted over with villages here and there, forming part of the territory of the Amir of Afghanistan. A few miles below the top of the pass could be seen the fort where the soldiers of the Amir guarded his frontier. Turning eastward, some dozen miles off, could be seen the cantonments of Parachinar, the westernmost cantonments of British occupation, and the seat of administration of this trans-border valley. There was a fort garrisoned by the local levies of the Kurram Militia—Afghans from the villages round, who, under the training and influence of three or four British officers, have become part of the "far-flung battle line" of the defences of the Empire.

I had been spending some weeks among the people of this district, and the time had come for reluctantly leaving the shady groves and cool breezes of the Upper Kurram for the sweltering plains of Bannu, which even now I could see in the eastern distance covered by heat haze, recalling the punkahs and restless nights which were soon to be my lot instead of the bracing air of the Sufed Koh. Our tents and baggage had been loaded up on some mules, which we could see winding along the white road below us, while we were lingering behind to take a last leave of the hearty Afghans, who had been both our hosts and our patients. Three times had we to pitch our nightly camp before we crossed the border of British India and entered the border town of Thal, which is the first town in British India which a traveller from Afghanistan enters. From the time of crossing the Afghan frontier till now, he has been going through what is known as an "administrative area." Here was a fort, occupied by troops of the Indian Army, under command of a British officer.

Thirty-four miles still remained in a direct line between us and our destination in Bannu, and before accomplishing this special arrangements had to be made with the tribes occupying it for our escort; for this tongue of country running up between Thal and Bannu was not British India, nor even an administrative area, but independent, and owned by the marauding Wazir tribe, who owed allegiance to neither Amir nor Viceroy. A couple of ruffianly-looking Wazirs arrived to escort us down. Their rifles were slung over their shoulders, and well-filled cartridge belts strapped round their waists; a couple of Afghan daggers were ensconced in the folds of the dirty red *pagaris* which they had bound round their bodies, and they carried their curved Afghan swords in their hands. We had now left the fertile valley of Upper Kurram behind us, and wandered through a succession of rocky mountain defiles, over precipitous spurs, and along the stony bed of the river for more than thirty miles. The lower mountain ranges separating Afghanistan from India form by their intricacy and precipitate nature a succession of veritable *chevaux de frise*, which by their natural difficulties maintain the *parda* or privacy of the wild tribes inhabiting them, who value the independence of their mountain fastnesses more than life itself. Here and there is a patch of arable land in a bend of the Kurram River, overlooked by the walled and towered village of its possessors, who have won it by force of arms, and only keep it by their armed vigils, even the men who are ploughing behind their oxen having their rifles hung over their shoulders, and keeping their eyes open for a possible enemy. In some places a channel from the river has been carried with infinite labour on to a flat piece of ground among the mountains, where a scanty harvest is reaped. For the rest the hill seems to be almost devoid of animal or vegetable life. A few partridges starting up with a shrill cry from a tuft of dry grass in front of one are occasionally seen, and stunted trees of *ber* and acacia supply a certain amount of firewood, which some of the Wazirs gather and take down to the Friday Fair in Bannu.

THE KHAIBER PASS

A village in the Pass belonging to independent Afghans, showing tower and fortifications.

A CAVALRY SHUTUR-SOWAR OR CAMEL-RIDER

The Afghans will tell you that when God created the world there were a lot of stones and rocks and other lumber left over, which were all dumped down on this frontier, and that this accounts for its unattractive appearance. There is one more range of hills to surmount before we reach the plains of India. We have toiled up a rocky path, from the bare stones of which the rays of the summer sun are reflected on all sides, without any relief from tree or shrub, or even a tuft of green grass, till the ground beneath our feet seems to glow with as fierce a heat as that of the blazing orb above us. We have reached the summit, and the vista before us changes as if by magic. Five hundred feet below us is the broad plain of India, irrigated in this part by the vivifying waters of the Kurram River, which, liberated from the rock-bound defile through which they have wandered for the last thirty miles, now dashing over their stony bed, anon hemmed in by dark overhanging cliffs, are at last free to break up into numberless channels, which, guided by the skill of the agriculturist, form a labyrinth of silver streaks in the plain below us. As far as the life-giving irrigation cuts of the Kurram River extend are waving fields of corn, sugar-cane, maize, rice, turmeric, and other crops, spread in endless succession as far as the eye can reach.

Scattered among the fields are the teeming villages of the Bannuchies, partly hidden in their groves of mulberries and figs and their vineyards, as though Cornucopia, wearied by the barren hills above them in Afghanistan, had showered down all her gifts on the favoured tribes below. Such is India as it appears to the Pathans inhabiting the hills on our North-West Frontier, and when we see it thus after some time spent with them in their barren and rocky hills, we can readily understand that two thoughts are dominant in their minds. The one is: "Those rich plains have been put there, in contiguity to our mountains, because God intended them to be our lawful prey, that when we have no harvest we may go down and reap theirs; and when we are hard up, and have a big fine to pay to the British Government, we may lighten some of the wealthy Hindus of the money that they have accumulated through usury and other ways which God hates." The other thought is: "What possible reason has the British Government, the overlord of such rich lands, for coming and interfering with us in our mountain homes, which, though nothing but rocks and stones, are still our homes for all that, where we resent the presence and interference of any stranger?"

The reader will have observed that in the journey above described, from Peiwar down to Bannu, four different territories have been passed through. The first and the last—viz., Afghanistan and British India—are two well-defined, easily comprehensible geographical areas; but it is seen that betwixt the two are various other tribal areas, in varying relations with the Indian Government. A few words must be said to familiarize the reader with the political conditions obtaining there. The frontier of British India is well defined, but that of Afghanistan was more or less uncertain until the year 1893, when Sir Mortimer Durand was deputed by the British Government to meet the officers delegated by the Amir Abdurrahman, in order that the frontier might be delimited. This frontier is since known as the "Durand Line." The intervening area between the Durand Line and the British frontier is in varying relations to the Indian Government.

Some parts of this, such as Tirah (the country of the Afridis and Orakzais) and Waziristan (the country of the Wazirs and Mahsuds), are severely left alone, provided the tribes do not compel attention and interference by the raids into British territory, which are frequently perpetrated by their more lawless spirits.

These raids are no doubt disapproved of by the majority of the tribesmen, who recognize the fact that they must stand to lose in any conflict with the British Government; but such is the democratic spirit of the people that every man considers himself as good as his neighbour, and a step better if he has a more modern rifle. As in the interregnums of the days of the Israelitish Judges, each man does what seems good in his own eyes, and bitterly resents any effort of his neighbour, and even of the tribe, to control his actions or curtail his liberty. Thus it happens that it is really very difficult for the tribal elders to prevent their bad characters from perpetrating these raids. The raiders are usually men with nothing to lose, owning no landed property within the confines of British India, and guilty of previous murders or other crimes, which make it impossible for them to enter the country, except surreptitiously, as they would certainly be imprisoned, and perhaps hanged, if caught.

A great number in the tribe own lands on both sides of the border, and find it to their interest to take no overt part against the Government; while at the same time, unless they give asylum to the desperadoes, and conceal them on occasion, they are liable to be themselves the victims. Thus it happens that in nearly every frontier expedition there are some sections of the tribe which desire to be on good terms with the British, and are known as "friendlies." It is difficult for a military commander who has not previously known the people to appreciate this, and when he finds his camp being sniped from a supposed "friendly" village, he not unnaturally doubts the sincerity of the people. As likely as not, however, the recalcitrant sections of the tribe have been at pains to snipe from such points as to implicate the friendly sections and force them into joining the standard of war. On one occasion the exasperated General refused to believe the representations of the Political Officer that the villages from the neighbourhood of which the sniping came were friendly until he left the camp and went over to live in the (supposed) enemies' village himself! The well-disposed clans would welcome an administration of the country by which these lawless spirits could be kept in check.

Then, there are certain semi-independent States, such as Chitral and Dir, where there are rulers of sufficient paramount power to govern their own country and to render it possible for the British to maintain that amount of control of their external relations which is considered desirable, by means of a Political Agent attached to the court of the chief, while still leaving the latter free to manage his own internal affairs in accordance with the customs of his tribe and the degree of his own supremacy over the often conflicting units composing it.

Thirdly, there are what are known as "administered areas," such as the Upper Kurram Valley, above mentioned. These are inhabited by tribes over whom no one chief has been able to gain paramount authority for himself, where, as is so often the case among Afghans, the tribe is eaten up by a number of rival factions, none of which are willing to acknowledge the rule of a man from a faction not their own. The Government official, therefore, is unable to treat with one ruler, but has to hear all the members of the contending factions. So great is the democratic spirit that any petty landowner thinks he has as much right to push his views of public policy as the representative of an hereditary line of chiefs. This naturally greatly complicates official relations, and the Political Officer, however much he would like to refrain from interference in tribal home policy, finds that, amid a host of conflicting units, he is the only possible court of appeal. This results in an intermediate form of government: the Indian Penal Code does not obtain; tribal laws and customs are the recognized judicial guides, and there is a minimum of interference with the people; yet the Political Officer is the supreme authority, and combines in himself the executive and judicial administration of the area.

Notwithstanding the exclusiveness of the religion that

these people profess, they find it impossible to do their business or live comfortably without the help of the ubiquitous and obsequious Hindu. Just as much as the great Mughal Emperors of old found it best to have Hindus for the posts of treasurer, accountant, adviser, etc., so the frontier chief of to-day has his Hindu vassal always with him, to keep his accounts, write his petitions, and transact most of his written and judicial business. The majority of the shopkeepers also are Hindus. Even under the settled administration of British India the Muhammadan has never become such an adept at bargaining, petty trade, and shopkeeping as the more thrifty and quick-witted Hindu. Thus in every village of any pretension there are the Hindus, with their shops, who make their journeys to the big market-towns on the frontier—Peshawur, Bannu, and Dera Ismail Khan—and return with piece-goods, matches, looking-glasses, and a variety of Western trinkets, as well as the food-stuffs which the Afghan covets, but cannot produce himself, such as white sugar and tea. These Hindus are regarded as vassals by the Muhammadan community they supply, and each Hindu trader or shopkeeper has his own particular overlord or Muhammadan *malik*, who in return for these services guarantees his safety, is ready to protect him—by force of arms, if necessary—from rival Muhammadan sections, and to revenge any injury done to him as if it were a personal one to himself.

The Hindu supplies the brains and the Muhammadan the valour. The Hindu is ever ready to outwit his overbearing but often obtuse masters, and under British rule avails himself of the protection the law affords to do things he would not venture on across the border. Once when travelling across the border my guide was an outlaw, who had been obliged to fly from British territory after committing a murder. He told me that he had gone into partnership with a Hindu for an extensive contract for road-making: the Hindu was to supply the capital and keep accounts, and he was to recruit the coolies and do the supervision of the work. "While I," he said, "was broiling and sweating in the summer sun, that pig of a Hindu was comfortably seated in his office falsifying the accounts, and I never got an anna for all my labours. I thought I should get justice from the *Sarkar*, so I brought a civil action against him; but I was a plain man, and he learnt all about the ways of the law from some pleader friend of his, and I lost the case. Then I paid another pleader a big sum to take my appeal to the Sessions Judge, but he had manipulated the accounts and paid the witnesses, so that I lost that too. *Allahu Akbar!* The Judge gave his verdict before the shadow had turned [before midday], and before the time of afternoon prayers had arrived that son of a pig was as dead as a post. But then I had to come over here, and I can only pay an occasional night visit to my village now."

A story which he told me to illustrate the mercantile genius of the Hindu will bear repeating. A Muhammadan and a Hindu resolved to go into partnership. The Muhammadan, being the predominant partner, stipulated that he was to have the first half of everything, and the Hindu the remainder. The Hindu obsequiously consented. The first day the Hindu brought back a cow from market. He milked it, got the butter and cream, made the dung into fuel-cakes for his fire, and then went to call the Muhammadan because the cow was hungry and wanted grass and grain. The Muhammadan said he was ready to do his share if the Hindu did his. The Hindu blandly replied that he had already done his, while the stipulated "first half" of the cow included the animal's mouth and stomach, and fell clearly to the lot of the Muhammadan.

Now let us see what is the position of the missionary in each of these areas. In British India he has a free hand so long as he keeps within the four corners of the law. In Afghanistan there is an absolute veto against even his entry into the country, and there is no prospect of this changing under the present régime. A convert from Muhammadanism to Christianity is regarded within the realms of the Amir as having committed a capital offence, and both law and popular opinion would decree his destruction. In the intervening tribal areas there is no reason why a cautious missionary, well acquainted with the language and customs of the people, should not work with considerable success. A medical missionary who did not attack their religion with a mistaken zeal would undoubtedly be welcomed by the greater number of the people, though the Mullahs, or priests, would be an uncertain element, and certainly hostile at the beginning. The local political authorities have the final say as to how far the missionaries may extend their operations. I shall revert to this subject in the concluding chapter (Chapter XXV.), where I shall show that in no part of the country are medical missions more obviously indicated, not only for Christianizing the people, but equally so for pacifying them and familiarizing them with the more peaceful aspects of British rule.

CHAPTER IV

A FRONTIER VALLEY

Description of the Kurram Valley—Shiahs and Sunnis—Favourable reception of Christianity—Independent areas—A candid reply—Proverbial disunion of the Afghans—The two policies—Sir Robert Sandeman—Lord Curzon creates the North-West Frontier Province—Frontier wars—The vicious circle—Two flaws the natives see in British rule: the usurer, delayed justice—Personal influence.

AMONG the various tracts of border territory that have recently been opened up and brought under the influence of civilization by the frontier policy of the Indian Government, none is fairer or more promising than the Upper Kurram Valley, on the lower waters of which river Bannu, the head-quarters of the Afghan Medical Mission, is situate. The River Kurram rises on the western slopes of Sikaram, the highest point of the Sufed Koh Range (15,600 feet), and for twenty-five miles makes a détour to the south and east through the Aryab Valley, which is inhabited by the tribe of Zazis, who are still under the government of the Amir, and form his frontier in this part. The river then suddenly emerges into a wider basin, the true valley of Upper Kurram, stretching from the base of the Sufed Koh Range to the base of a lower range on the right bank, a breadth of fifteen miles, the river running close to the latter range, and the north-western corner of this basin being separated from the head-waters of the Kurram by the ridge of the Peiwar Kotal, where was fought the memorable action of December 2, 1879, by which the road to Kabul was opened. This wide valley runs down as far as Sadr, thirty miles lower down towards the south-east, being narrower, however, below. Here the valley narrows down to from two to four miles, and runs south-east for thirty-five miles to Thal, where it ceases to be in British territory, but winds for thirty miles among the Waziri Hills, until it emerges into the Bannu Plain, and flows through the Bannu and Marwat districts into the Indus at Isa Khel. Thus, with the exception of the head-waters and some thirty miles just above Bannu, the territory is all now subject to British rule, and is steadily becoming more peaceful and civilized.

Below the Zazis the valley down as far as Waziristan was originally possessed by the Bangash, a Sunni tribe of Pathans, who came themselves from the direction of Kohat. The Turis were a Shiah tribe inhabiting some districts on the eastern bank of the Indus near Kalabagh, who, being ardent traders and nomads, were accustomed to visit the cool regions of Upper Kurram every summer for trade, health, and pasturage. One summer, some two hundred years ago, a quarrel arose between them and the Bangash of a village called Burkha, and resulted in a battle, in which the Turis came off victorious, and, destroying or driving away the inhabitants of Burkha, made it their first settlement in the valley. Soon after this they attacked and possessed themselves of two of the most important villages of the valley, Peiwar and Milana, and to this day every Turi with aspirations to importance claims land in one of these three villages, though it may be only the fiftieth part of a field, as proof of his true lineage.

Year by year the Turis gradually strengthened their position, driving the Bangash farther down the valley, except in some cases, such as the inhabitants of the large and beautiful village of Shlozan, the Bangash of which, all becoming Shiahs, amalgamated with the Turis, and retained their lands.

Finally, having made their position secure, and realizing

the charms of the valley, the Turis ceased to return to the plain, and remained in the valley all the year round. Hence to-day we find the upper part of the valley inhabited only by Turis, while below this, as far as the Alizai, the Turis and Bangash are mingled, their villages being often side by side; and further down still the Bangash have the land all to themselves.

Since the people have realized the peace resulting from English rule, and have begun to beat their swords into ploughshares, many of the hill tribes bordering the valley have taken every opportunity of settling in allotments in the valley, and enjoying the larger produce of its richer soil. These are the Mangals and Makbals above, and the Zaimukhts below, thus introducing a fresh element into the population. Over and above these any worker in the valley has to count on dealings with the neighbouring tribes, who still cling to their mountain fastnesses, and sometimes still show their old disposition to loot the more peaceable inhabitants. These are the Ningrahars, Spinwars, and Paris on the north, and the Zazi-i-Maidan on the south; while the Afghan country of Khost being in close proximity, its people also would be easily reached. To make the enumeration of the inhabitants complete, it only remains to mention the Hindus, who, mostly of the Arora caste, are in large numbers in the valley, and retain most of the trade, and do much clerical and business work for the Muhammadans.

In the time of the Hindu Rajahs of Kabul they were probably in the ascendant here, and the little archæology which the valley presents is all of Hindu origin. Apart from the variety of tribes who are thus brought into close proximity in the valley, it has a special interest and importance from its being one of the two routes from Kabul to India (the other being the Khaiber). Hence many nomads from Afghanistan frequently visit and temporarily inhabit the valley. Prominent at present among these are the Hazaras, numbers of whom have been driven out from their own lands by the Amir, and have come here to labour on the roads.

The Khorotis and Ghilzais also frequent the valley. It is owing to this peculiarly central and cosmopolitan position, and partly to the character of the people themselves, that this district presents so many advantages as a centre of mission work and influence. There is a great opportunity for mission work among the Turis. These, as above mentioned, are Shiahs, while all the tribes round belong to the orthodox sect of Sunnis; consequently, previously to the English occupation in 1891 they were subjected to persistent, relentless persecution at the hands of the Amir, and to frequent inroads from their Sunni neighbours. They naturally, therefore, look on the Christians as deliverers from the throes of Sunni rule and persecution, and are *ipso facto* inclined to look on Christianity favourably, since it has brought them so much peace and freedom from oppression. And still, as a wordy warfare is carried on by their respective Mullahs, both sides endeavour to find in Christianity points of resemblance by which they can magnify their own sect, rather than, like the Muhammadans of Bannu, to be constantly cavilling at every word from a Christian tongue or a Christian book.

This has resulted in a wonderful (wonderful, at any rate, to a missionary from bigoted Bannu) openness to conversation about the Christian Scriptures, and readiness to receive Christian teaching. For instance, in Bannu a well-inclined Mullah dare not read a Bible except in secrecy, while in Kurram I have frequently seen Mullahs publicly reading and commenting on the Holy Word to large groups of Khans and other men.

Again, in Bannu mention of such doctrines as the Sonhood, the Crucifixion, or the Sinlessness of Christ, or the Fatherhood of God, is as often as not the signal for an uproar; while here the same doctrines, even if not partially accepted, may yet be freely talked about, with the certainty of nearly always getting a fair hearing.

The first summer during which I spent some time among these people I nearly everywhere had a hospitable, not to say cordial, reception. This, of course, was partly attributable to the medical benefits they received, but it was markedly different from the reception often accorded to the bearer of Gospel tidings in Hindustan. At no place was there any open opposition from the Mullahs, and most of them came to see me, and had long talks about the Injil (Gospel), and asked for and gratefully accepted copies of it, which I have reason to believe they preserved carefully and read regularly; while the people often besought us to partake longer of their hospitality or to visit them again next year, or, better still, to start a dispensary in their midst.

A reference to the map shows how intimate are the relations of this valley with Afghanistan, and relics of Afghan rule frequently present themselves to the doctor when going about their villages—men who have been crippled for life as a punishment for some crime, or it may be merely because they incurred the displeasure of someone of influence, who manufactured a case against them. I have seen men who have had their right hand cut off for robbery, and others whose feet were completely crippled by long-continued incarceration in the stocks, or by a torture often inflicted to extract evidence, in which the foot is tied with cords to a piece of wood like a magnified tent-peg fixed in the ground. This peg has a cleft in it, and a wedge is then hammered slowly into this cleft, thus gradually tightening the cords till they cut into the foot and cause its mortification.

In every village there are one or more *matamkhanas*, where the Shiahs hold their annual mournings for the martyrs of Kerbela (Hasan and Huseïn) at every Muharram. Under Afghan (Sunni) rule these ceremonies were often interdicted, or at least restricted; but now they are able to carry them on unhindered, and pray for the continuance of British rule in consequence. These places form convenient centres for the men to gather together and talk, and in them many of my religious discussions have been held. They are all the more ready to accept the Christian account of the Crucifixion and its meaning (which is such a stumbling-block to the Sunnis), because they look on the martyrdom of the two brothers at Kerbela as having a vicarious efficacy for those who perform the memorial rites, and regard 'Ali, the fourth Khalifa from Muhammad, as being indeed a saviour.

If we could have visited this valley in the days long before the Christian era, when the first Aryan immigrants were passing down from Central Asia into the Panjab, we should have seen it covered with their settlements, and seen them engaged in the simple Nature-worship depicted in the Vedas, which record this stage of Aryan civilization. This region was probably much better watered and more fertile in those days than it is now. Not only does geological evidence point to a greater rainfall and vegetation, but as these early immigrations were mostly of large bands of pastoral people, moving with their flocks and herds, their families and household possessions, and as they probably only gradually moved down the valley into the plains below, they must have found more pasturage than the desolate frontier ranges would now afford.

The Kurram Valley above described serves as a good example of an administered area fairly well advanced in the civilizing effects of a settled and just Government.

The independent tribes, on the other hand, go down the scale till you find tribes, such as some sections of the Wazirs and Afridis, who are utter barbarians, entirely devoted to a nomadic life of systematic highway robbery.

A Political Officer was once seated, with a number of

the head men of some of these independent tribes, on the top of one of their rugged mountains, from which you look down on Afghanistan to the west and India to the east. They had been touring with him as his escort for some days. He had fed them well, and could chat familiarly with them in their own lingo, so that they had learnt to talk with him without reserve about even their tribal secrets.

"Now, tell me," said the officer, "if there were to be war —which God forbid—between Russia and England, what part would you and your people take? whom would you side with?"

"Do you wish us to tell you what would please you, or to tell you the real truth?" was their naïve reply.

"I adjure you only tell me what is the 'white word'" (meaning the true statement).

"Then," said an old greybeard among them, voicing the feelings of all present, "we would just sit here up on our mountain-tops watching you both fight, until we saw one or other of you utterly defeated; then we would come down and loot the vanquished till the last mule! God is great! What a time that would be for us!"

No doubt he spake truly, but such is the discord of the Afghan tribes that no doubt the spoil would scarcely be gathered in before they would begin to fight among themselves over the division of it. These tribal jealousies and petty wars are inherent among the Afghans, and greatly diminish their formidableness as foes. If you ask them about it they will acknowledge this defect in their character, and tell you how that one of their ancestors displeased the Almighty, who, to punish him, wove the strands of discord in the web of their nature from that time onwards. Hence the saying, "The Afghans of the frontier are never at peace except when they are at war!" For when some enemy from without threatens their independence, then, for the time being, are their feuds and jealousies thrown aside, and they fight shoulder to shoulder, to resume them again when the common danger is averted. Even when they are all desirous of joining in some *jihad*, they remain suspicious of each other, and are apt to fail one another at critical moments; or else one tribe will wait to see how it fares with those already in it before unsheathing their own swords. Thus it was in the frontier rising of 1897 that the difficulty of quelling the rising would have been immensely greater had it not been that the tribes rose seriatim instead of simultaneously, and the rising in one part of the frontier had been put down before another broke out.

Two policies have at various times been advocated with equal warmth by their respective partisans. The earlier policy, which was supported by Lord Lawrence in the days of his Viceroyalty, was generally known as the "policy of masterly inactivity." Later on the "forward policy" received more general approbation, its chief exponent being Sir Robert Sandeman. Those who advocate the former point out the great expenditure involved in all interference with the internal tribes across our border, and that almost inevitably we become sooner or later involved in wars with them. They would therefore have the British Government strictly abstain from all trans-frontier politics, and leave the tribes severely alone, so long as they give no trouble to us on our side of the border. The "forward" party, on the other hand, point out the danger of having this extensive area on the most vulnerable part of our Indian Empire outside our own control, and they advocate a system of controlling all the political affairs of the trans-border tribes, while leaving their internal policy in the hands of their own chiefs, who, though guided by our political officers, would be free to maintain the ancient tribal customs.

Sir Robert Sandeman is, perhaps, the most remarkable instance of the power which a single officer has been able to exercise over these border tribes, and it was through him that the large tract on the border between Quetta and the Deras was organized under our Political Officers, working through the tribal chiefs. Allowances are made to the tribes, in return for which they guarantee the safety of the British posts on the highroads, and become responsible for any misdemeanours on the part of other members of their tribe. Tribal levies are organized under young officers of the British Army, who train them in military discipline, drill, and marksmanship. The pay received by these soldiers becomes a valuable asset to the tribe, and a strong inducement to give up their more predatory habits, in favour of the *pax Britannica.* Still, it was found necessary to place regular troops of the Indian Army in some of the more important and critical situations. The frontier is, for the most part, composed of intricate, and in many parts inaccessible, mountain ranges, which form an absolute barrier to the passage of troops; but piercing through these are the passes, of which the best known are the Khaiber and the Bolan, which from time immemorial have formed the highways through which hostile armies have invaded India, and it would be through them that any enemy of the future would endeavour to bring its forces. It is therefore a paramount necessity to the British Government that these passes should be securely guarded, and therefore each one of them forms part of one of the areas administered by British officers, and guarded either by native troops or tribal levies.

It is through these passes, too, that the great merchant caravans pass down from Afghanistan and Central Asia into British India. In former times the merchants had to subsidize the tribes through which they passed, who would otherwise have blocked the passes and stolen their goods; and it is partly to make up to the tribes for the loss of this income that the tribal subsidies were arranged. Near where each of these passes debouches on to the trans-Indus plain is a city, which forms an emporium for the merchandise brought

THE KHYBER PASS

A Khyber rifle sepoy on the watch in the Pass

down, and a military station for the protection of the pass. While Peshawur serves this purpose for the Khaiber, Kohat commands the Kurram, Bannu the Tochi, and Dera Ismail Khan the Gumal.

When Lord Curzon assumed the Viceroyalty, the frontier districts formed part of the Panjab, and the Lieutenant-Governor of that province was in administrative control of them. Lord Curzon wished to bring them more directly under his own control, so in 1901 a new province, composed of five frontier districts of the Panjab, was constituted, and called the North-West Frontier Province. The five districts composing this province are Hazara, Peshawur, Kohat, Bannu, and Dera Ismail Khan. These are all beyond the Indus, except Hazara, which is to the east of that river.

A Chief Commissioner was appointed over the whole province, directly responsible to the Viceroy, and he had his headquarters and the centre of government at Peshawur.

Lord Curzon's next move was to advance the railway systems of the Panjab along the frontier, bringing their termini to the mouths of the Khaiber and Kurram Passes. As this enabled a rapid concentration of troops at any point along the frontier, he was able to withdraw the regiments of the Indian Army which garrisoned the more outlying districts, and to replace them by tribal levies.

No doubt it is the desire of the Government not to make any further annexations of this barren, mountainous, and uninviting border region; but it is not always equally easy to avoid doing so, and it is a universal experience of history that when there are a number of disorganized and ill-governed units on the borders of a great power, they become inevitably, though it may be gradually and piece by piece, absorbed into the latter. There are, however, financial considerations which induce the Government to refrain from annexing a country which has few natural resources, can pay little in taxes, and must cost a great deal to administer.

But these frontier tribes form some of the finest fighting material from which the Indian Army is recruited, and it may be that years of regular and peaceful administration will destroy the military qualities of these people, as has been the case in South India. The many opportunities afforded by the frontier to the Indian Army for active service, and the training that they get in the little frontier expeditions, may also be looked upon by some as a valuable asset.

The usual sequence of events is as follows: First, the more unruly sections of the tribes carry on a series of raids on the frontier villages of India, as has been their custom from time immemorial. Sometimes the miscreants are captured and meet their fate; more often they escape, and, in accordance with the system of tribal responsibility, a fine is put on the tribe from which they come. These fines go on accumulating, the tribe running up an account with the Government for its misdeeds.

Thus we come to the second stage, when the patience of the Government is exhausted. The tribal heads are called in, and an ultimatum offered to them. They must pay so much in fines and deliver the criminals demanded, or an expedition will be organized. Much time—it may be many months—is occupied in councils, while the tribe is endeavouring to gain time or to make the terms more favourable.

The third stage is when the tribe fail to meet the Government's conditions, and a punitive expedition is organized against them. This expedition enters their hills, raises their *parda*, burns their villages, fights a few actions—usually of the nature of ambuscades or rearguard actions—realizes more or less of the fine, confiscates a number of rifles, and comes back again.

The tribe is now free to commence its depredations afresh with a clean sheet, and to begin to run up a new account, and, in order more effectually to prevent this and keep a greater control over them, the Government find themselves compelled to enter on the fourth stage, which is that of annexing some points of vantage where military posts can be erected, which will overawe and control them.

It is thus that a gradual, though it may be reluctant, annexation of territory becomes inevitable.

Then, it must be remembered that there is always a section of the tribe, and often a majority, who are favourable to annexation, for the more settled and peaceful rule of the British brings many advantages in its train. While before they were not able to cultivate their crops at any distance from the village, and even then only when fully armed, now they are able to till the ground in peace even miles away from their habitations, and land which was before unculturable becomes of great value. They are able to trade and carry on the ordinary avocations of life with a security to which they have been hitherto strangers. They learn the value of money, and begin to amass wealth.

There are always, however, two parties in the tribe who are opposed tooth and nail to British rule, and as they have got power far in excess of their more peacefully disposed brethren, they are usually able to terrorize the more peace-loving majority into a false acquiescence in their own opposition. These two parties are the outlaws and the Mullahs.

The outlaws have made their living by raiding and robbery for generations, and have no inclination to give up their profession for more peaceable but less exciting and less profitable employment.

Not only have the Mullahs an antipathy to those whom they consider *kafirs*, or infidels, but they know that under the changed conditions of life, their influence, their power, and their wealth must all suffer.

Besides this, there are two elements in our rule which are equally repugnant to all. One is the protection which we give to the money-lender, and the other is the dilatory nature of our justice. Usury is unlawful to the Muhammadans, but as they are spendthrift and improvident, the Hindus are able to make a living among them by lending them money in times of necessity. The Hindu was formerly prevented from charging too high a rate of interest or running up too long an account, by the fact that if he did so, his Muhammadan masters, who held the sword, would come one night and burn his house over his head, and let him start afresh. Under British régime, however, the usurer is protected. He is able to recover his debts from the impecunious Muhammadan by a civil action, and may get the latter thrown into prison if he does not pay; while if the Muhammadan tries to burn his account-books, he will find himself an inmate of His Majesty's gaol.

The justice which the Muhammadan of the frontier appreciates is a rapid and appropriate justice, such as used to be meted out by officers in the days of Nicholson, when the offender might find himself accused, arrested, judged, and visited with some punishment appropriate to the crime all within the course of a few days. At the present time he can, if rich enough, call in a pleader, and get any number of false witnesses, and his case is inevitably dragged out by the magistrate by successive postponements for getting the attendance of these witnesses, or through some technicality of the law; and even when he does—it may be after the lapse of some months—get a judgment, the losing party in the suit is at liberty to bring an appeal to the Sessions Judge, and from him another appeal can be lodged at the High Court of Lahore, which has so many cases on its lists that it may be his case will not be taken till after the lapse of two or three years.

The real strength of our administration on the frontier is the *personnel* of our officers, for it has always been the man, and not the system, that governs the country; and there are names of officers now dead and gone which are still a living power along that frontier, because they were men who thoroughly knew the people with whom they had to deal, and whose dauntless and strong characters moulded the tribes to their will, and exerted such a mesmeric influence over those wild Afghans that they were ready to follow their *feringi* masters through fire and sword with the most unswerving loyalty, even though they were of an alien faith.

As an example of this, it is related that on a certain frontier expedition the regiments were passing up a defile on a height, above which some of the enemy had ensconced themselves in ambush behind their *sangars*. The Afghans had been soldiers in the Indian Army, who had now completed their service and retired to their hills, and were, as is often the case, using the skill which they had learnt in their regiments against us. They were about to fire, when one of them recognized the officer riding at the head of the regiment as his own Colonel. He stopped the others, and said: "That is our own *Karnal Sahib*. We must not fire on him or his regiment." That regiment was allowed to pass in safety, but they opened fire on the one which succeeded.

CHAPTER V

THE CHRISTIAN'S REVENGE

Police posts *versus* dispensaries — The poisoning scare — A native doctor's influence—Wazir marauders spare the mission hospital—A terrible revenge—The Conolly bed—A political mission—A treacherous King—Imprisonment in Bukhara—The Prayer-Book—Martyrdom—The sequel—Influence of the mission hospital—The medical missionary's passport.

I WAS once urging on a certain official the need of a Government dispensary in a certain frontier district. "There is no need there," he replied; "the people are quiet and law-abiding. Now A——, that is a disturbed area: there we ought to have medical work"—an unintentional testimony to one result of the doctor's work, though rather hard on the law-abiding section of the populace that they should have no hope of a hospital unless they can organize a few raids, or get a reputation for truculence.

Which will be better—a punitive police post or a civil dispensary? This seems a not very logical conundrum, yet it is based on sound reasoning, and a well-managed establishment of the latter kind will often remove the necessity of setting up the former. The doctor is a confidant in more matters than one, and the right man will often smooth down little frictions and mollify sorenesses which bid fair to cause wide-spread conflagrations.

A medical mission is a pacific, as well as an essentially pioneer, agency.

There was a little missionary dispensary on the frontier, in charge of a native doctor, a convert from Muhammadanism, who had gone in and out among the people till he was a household friend all down the country-side.

One day he was sitting in his dispensary seeing out-patients, when he heard the following conversation:

Abdultalib. "The *Sarkar* has sent out agents to kill the Mussulmans by poisoning their drinking-water."

Balyamin. "*Ma'uzbillah!* how do you know that?"

A. "Mullah D. arrived last night, and, sitting in the *chauk*, he told how he had seen a man throwing pills into the well at Dabb village. He went after him, but as soon as the man saw him he ran away."

B. "What is to be done?"

A. "First we must tell the women not to draw water from the wells—they have certainly been poisoned in the night—but they can take their pitchers to the tank in the big mosque; no one would interfere with that."

B. "If we can catch the miscreant, we will show him plainly enough who is the Mussulman and who the infidel."

As the news spread through the village, the excitement grew; women who had already filled their pitchers from the wells hurriedly emptied them and started off afresh to the mosque tank. Guards were placed at the well, both to warn the faithful and to give short shrift to any hapless stranger on whom suspicion might fall. The men about the bazaar had procured thick sticks, and seemed only waiting for the opportunity of using them, and things looked black all round. News was brought to the police-station, and, without waiting to don his uniform, the inspector buckled on a revolver, and, taking a constable with him, hurried off to the most disturbed portion of the village.

The men there were sullen, and would give no information, and two or three of the more truculent seemed inclined to hustle the police-officer. Just then the native doctor appeared on the scene, and recognized the gravity of the situation at once. One rash act, and the police might have to use their firearms in self-defence. The people, however, trusted the doctor. Had he not often championed them when subjected to little police tyrannies, and had they not often sought counsel from him in their village quarrels, and always found his advice had helped them to come to an amicable settlement? So now, when he quietly slipped his arm into that of the inspector, and led him out of the dangerous quarter, chatting the while, till he got him safely into a house without loss of official dignity, not even the most truculent tried to resist his passage. Then he returned and reasoned with them on the groundlessness of their suspicions. Had any of them ever seen anyone throw anything into the wells? Had anyone even got a stomach-ache from drinking the water? Did any King ever want to kill off all his own subjects? If so, whom would he rule, and where would be his kingdom? Finally, he bantered them out of their war-like intentions: the sticks were returned home, business resumed, the inspector came back as though his authority had never been questioned, and a very ugly situation was successfully negotiated.

In the year 1879 the tribe of the Wazirs had been incited by their Mullahs to rise, and they came down suddenly with their *lashkar* on the little frontier town of Tank. There was a mission hospital there, in charge of an Indian doctor, the Rev. John Williams. Before the authorities could summon the troops the Wazir warriors had overrun town and bazaar, and were burning and looting. Some young bloods went for the mission hospital, but they were at once restrained by the tribal elders, who forbade them to meddle with the property of "our own *Daktar Sahib*," as they called him. Had they not often been inmates of his hospital and partakers of his hospitality? Not a hair of his head was to be injured. They at once set a guard of their own men on the mission hospital, who warned off any excited tribesmen who might have done it injury, and that was the only place in the bazaar that escaped fire and sword and pillage. Some of his surgical instruments had been carried off before the posting of the guard; but upon this being made known, search was made through Waziristan, and the friends of the doctor were not satisfied until all were returned to him.

Revenge is a word sweet to the Afghan ear, and even a revenge satisfied by the culminating murder is the sweeter if the fatal blow, preferably on some dark night, is so managed that the murdered man has a few minutes of life in which to realize that he has been outwitted, and to hear the words of exultation with which his enemy gluts his hatred. In one case that came to my knowledge, after strangling his victim, but before he was quite gone, the murderer dealt his victim a terrific blow on his jaw, shattering the bone, with the taunt: "Do you remember the day when I told you I would knock out your teeth for you?"

In the autumn of 1907 a fine stalwart Wazir was brought to the Bannu Mission Hospital in a pitiable state: both of his eyes had been slashed about and utterly blinded with a knife. His story was that his enemies came on him unexpectedly in his cottage one day, beat his wife into insensibility, tied him to a bed, and then deliberately destroyed his eyes with a knife. His wife came to hospital with him, suffering from severe contusions and some broken ribs, and we put them both into one of our small "family wards"—so called because father, mother, and children, if there be any, can all stop together for treatment. It was painful to have to tell him that he would never see again, and still more painful to hear him as he piteously said: "Oh, Sahib, if you can give me some sight only just long enough to go and shoot my enemy, then I shall be satisfied to be blind all the rest of my life." It could not be. His lot would probably become that of the numerous blind beggars that throng Eastern bazaars; for who would plough his land now or speak for him in the village council? Yet of pure pity we kept him a few weeks, that he might hear the story of the Gospel of goodwill and forgiveness; but he would shake his head and sigh. "No, that teaching is not for us. What I want is revenge—revenge!" Then, because a concrete case will sometimes accomplish what a mere statement cannot effect, I told him the story of the Conolly bed. Over each bed is a little framed card denoting the benefactor or supporter of that bed and the person commemorated thereby, and over this particular bed is written:

Conolly Bed.

In Memory of Captain Conolly, beheaded at Bukhara.

As long ago as 1841 this brave English officer was sent on a political mission to Bukhara, which was then an independent State, and not under the rule of Russia, as now. The Muhammadan ruler, Bahadur Khan, affected to be suspicious of his intentions, and threw him into prison, where another English officer, Colonel Stoddart, had already been incarcerated. It was in vain for them to protest and to claim the consideration due to a representative of the British Government; they were met by the answer that no letter had come from the Queen in reply to one sent by the Amir, and that therefore they had certainly come to stir up Khiva and Khokand to war against the Amir of Bukhara. Their effects were confiscated; even their very clothes were taken from them, till they only had their shirts and drawers left, when a filthy sheepskin was given to Captain Conolly as some protection against the winter cold of Bukhara. Their servants were thrown into a horrible dungeon called the Black Well, into which each man had to be lowered by a rope from the aperture at the top, and was then left to rot in the filth below.

Captain Conolly managed to secrete a small English Prayer-Book about his person, and this was a daily source of comfort to him and his companion in prison, and he marked verses in the Psalms and passages in the prayers from which they derived comfort. On the fly-leaves and the margins he wrote a diary of their sufferings; month succeeded month, and their hearts grew sick with hope deferred, and their bodies worn with fever, wasting and wounds. On February 10, 1842, he writes: "We have now been fifty-three days and nights without means of changing or washing our linen. This book will probably not leave me, so I now will, as opportunity serves, write in it the last blessing of my best affection to all my friends." Again, on March 11, he writes: "At first we had viewed the Amir's conduct as perhaps dictated by mad caprice, but now, looking back upon the whole, we saw indeed that it had been the deliberate malice of a demon, questioning and raising our hopes and ascertaining our condition, only to see how our hearts were going on in the process of breaking.

"I did not think to shed one more tear among such cold-blooded men, but yesterday evening, as I looked upon Stoddart's half-naked and much lacerated body, conceiving that I was the especial object of the King's hatred, because of my having come to him after visiting Khiva and Khok, and told him that the British Government was too great to stir up secret enmity against any of its enemies, I wept on, entreating one of our keepers to have conveyed to the chief my humble request that he would direct his anger upon me, and not further destroy by it my poor broken Stoddart, who had suffered so much and so meekly here for three years. My earnest words were answered by a 'Don't cry and distress yourself.' He, alas! would do nothing, so we turned and kissed each other and prayed together, and we have risen again from our knees with hearts comforted, as if an angel had spoken to us, resolved, please God, to wear our English honesty and dignity to the last, within all the misery and filth that this monster may try to degrade us with."

Again, on March 28: "We have been ninety-nine days and nights without a change of clothes."

One of the native agents of the mission, Salih Muhammad by name, subsequently escaped to India, and thus relates the closing scene of the tragedy.

"On Tuesday night (June 14, 1842) their quarters were entered by several men, who stripped them and carried them off, but I do not know whether it was to the Black Well or to some other prison. In stripping Colonel Stoddart a lead pencil was found in the lining of his coat and some papers in his waist. These were taken to the Amir, who gave orders that he should be beaten with heavy sticks till he disclosed who brought the papers, and to whom he wrote. He was most violently beaten, but he revealed nothing. He was beaten repeatedly for two or three days. On Friday the Amir gave orders that Colonel Stoddart should be killed in the presence of Captain Conolly, who should be offered his life if he would become a Muhammadan. In the afternoon they were taken outside the prison into the street, which is a kind of small square. Their hands were tied across in front. Many people assembled to behold the spectacle. Their graves were dug before their eyes.

"Colonel Stoddart's head was then cut off with a knife. The chief executioner then turned to Captain Conolly and said: 'The Amir spares your life if you will become a Mussulman.' Captain Conolly answered: 'I will not be a Mussulman, and I am ready to die!' saying which he stretched forth his neck, and his head was then struck off. Their bodies were then interred in the graves which had been dug."

For a long time the fate of these two officers was unknown in England, and, indeed, overshadowed by the greater disaster in Kabul. Then a missionary, the Rev. Joseph Wolff, undertook a journey to Bukhara, and after many sufferings and dangers, ascertained that they had been murdered two years before. He did not, however, come across the little Prayer-Book, which appears to have been lying about in some shop in Bukhara for seven years after the officers' death, when a Russian officer, passing through the bazaar, happened to light on it. He picked it up, and, observing its interesting nature, purchased it from the shopkeeper. For another fourteen years the little book was lying on his table at St. Petersburg, when a visitor who knew Captain Conolly's relations saw it, and obtained leave to take the precious relic and place it in the hands of the relatives of the deceased; and thus, twenty-one years after her brother's death, Miss Conolly obtained the full account of his sufferings, written with his own hand.

So far no vengeance had been exacted for the Amir's atrocity; now the murdered man's sister thought she would like to have her revenge, so when the Bannu Mission Hospital was inaugurated, she wrote out to the medical missionary, expressing her desire to support a bed in memory of her brother, and that bed has been supported in his name ever since, and we tell the Afghans in it that that is THE CHRISTIAN'S REVENGE. When I sit by the bedside of some sick or wounded Afghan in that bed, and tell him and the others round him that it was their co-religionists who killed this officer because he would not forsake Christianity for Islam, and that now his sister is paying for them to be nursed and tended, and praying for them that they may learn of the Saviour who bid us forgive our enemies, and do good to those who despitefully use us and persecute us, then it is easy to see that the story has set them thinking. And when it is further brought home by their experiences in the mission hospital, where they have been lovingly tended by the very native converts whom they have abused and perhaps maltreated in the bazaar, they return to their Afghan homes with very different feelings towards Christians.

It is thus that the medical missionary gets his passport

to all their villages, not only in British India, but across the border among the independent tribes. While visiting a Wazir chief once in his border fort, he said to me: "You can do what we cannot possibly do. I cannot go into that village over there, because I have enmity with the people there. The chief of that tribe across the river a few miles off has a blood-feud with me, and I have always to go armed and with a guard lest he should waylay me; at night I cannot leave my fort, but have to sleep ready armed in my tower. And I am like most of us in this country: we all have our enemies, and never know when we may meet them. But you can go into any of our villages and among all the tribes, although you have not even got a revolver with you, and, more than that, you get a welcome, too."

In some parts of the country across the border it is necessary to take a fresh guide every few miles, as the various villages are on bad terms, and might injure the traveller on the lands of the opposing village merely in order to get their enemies involved in a feud, or into trouble with the Government. These guides are called *badragga*, and within the tribal boundary any member of the clan, even a child, is often sufficient protection, as that is sufficient to show that the traveller has received the sanction of the tribe to move about within their boundaries. If, however, marauding bands are known to be about, or if the tribe is at feud with a neighbouring one, then they will send a fully-armed *badragga* of several men with you. I have, however, seen a traveller consigned to the care of a boy of nine years or so, and, no doubt, with perfect security.

On one occasion when it had been arranged that the *badragga* of a certain clan was to meet me at a prearranged rendezvous, I arrived at the appointed time and place under the care of the *badragga* of the clan through whose territories I had just passed, but no one was forthcoming. We waited an hour or so, but still no one came; my *badragga* then accompanied us a little way forward till we came in view of the first village of the next clan. Here they stopped and said: "We can go no farther. If we were to go into that village, there would very likely be bloodshed, as there is enmity between us and them; but we will sit at the top of this knoll here and watch you while you go on to the village, and if anyone interferes with you on the way we will shoot." I went on with an Indian hospital assistant who was with me, and when nearing the village a man came up and shook hands with great heartiness, saying: "Don't you remember me? I brought my brother to your hospital when he was shot and his leg broken, and we were with you for two months." He brought me to the village and to his brother, who hobbled out on a crutch to meet us, and was very pleased. They insisted on our stopping while they called some of the other villagers, who were anxious to see the doctor, and finally sent us forward on our journey with a fresh escort and a hearty "God-speed."

CHAPTER VI

A DAY IN THE WARDS

The truce of suffering—A patient's request—Typical cases—A painful journey—The biter bit—The conditions of amputation—"I am a better shot than he is"—The son's life or revenge—The hunter's adventure—A nephew's devotion—A miserly patient—An enemy converted into a friend—The doctor's welcome.

As I have already said, the Afghans never forget their tribal feuds except in the presence of foes from without. Then they may put them aside for a while, especially if their foe be not Mussulman in faith, but only for a while. The feuds begin again as soon as the danger is past.

But in the wards of the mission hospital all this is changed, and here may be seen representatives of all the frontier tribes chatting fraternally together, who as likely as not would be lying in ambush for one another if they were a few miles off across the frontier. But it is generally recognized among them that feuds are to be forgotten in hospital; and accordingly the doctor gets an audience from half a dozen different tribes in one ward when he is drawing out the conversation from the land of feuds to the Prince of Peace, and when he contrasts the Gospel of loving your neighbour with their rule of "shoot your neighbour and get his rifle." They say in a half-apologetic tone: "True; but God has decreed that there shall always be discord among the Afghans, so what can we do?" Sometimes a patient will say: "I want to be in a ward that has no windows, because I am afraid that one of my enemies may come at night when the lamp is burning in the ward and shoot me through the window by its light."

Great as is the variety of physiognomy, of dress, and of dialect, even more diverse are the complaints for which they come. Eye diseases form more than a quarter of the whole, and few cases give so much satisfaction both to surgeon and patient as these, in many of which the surgeon is able to restore sight that has been lost for years, and to send the patient back to his home rejoicing and full of gratitude. Here is a Bannuchi *malik* suffering from consumption, a not uncommon complaint in their crowded villages; next him is a Wazir lad from the hills, Muhammad Payo by name, suffering from chronic malarial poisoning. He is an old acquaintance, as he returns to his home when he feels strong enough, and then, what with coarse fare and exposure (for he is a poor lad), soon relapses and comes back to us at death's door, as white as a sheet, and has to be nursed back again to vigour. Just now he is convalescent, and is going about the ward doing little services for the other patients, and telling them what to do and what not to do, as though he had been in the hospital all his life. Poor fellow! he has lost both his parents in a village raid, and would have been dead long ago himself but for the open door of the mission hospital.

In another bed is a fair-haired, blue-eyed boy of twelve from Khost, suffering from disease of the bones of his right leg, which he has not been able to put to the ground for two years. His home is eighty miles away across the mountains, and he had no one to bring him to Bannu, though he had begged some of the traders to let him sit on one of their baggage camels; but who was going to inconvenience himself with a friendless boy like that? He had heard such wonderful stories of the cures effected in the Bannu Hospital from a man in his village who had been an inmate for six weeks for an ulcer of the leg, that he determined to get there by hook or by crook, and he had accomplished the greater part of the journey crawling on his hands and knees, with an occasional lift from some friendly horseman, and had been six weeks on the road, begging a dinner here and a night's lodging there from the villages through which he passed. When he arrived, his state can be better imagined than described: the weary, suffering look of his face; the few dirty rags that covered him; the malodorous wound on his leg, full of maggots, bound round with the last remains of his *pagari;* while now there is no brighter, happier boy in the hospital, with his white hospital shirt and pyjamas, clean, gentle face and pleasant smile, as he moves about from bed to bed with his crutch, chatting with the other patients.

Passing on, we see a big swarthy Afghan, with fine martial features, in which suffering is gradually wearing out the old truculent air. He had gone armed with a friend one night to a village where there was a Militia guard. He maintains that they had merely gone to visit a friend, and had been delayed on the road till night overtook them; but to be out armed at night is of itself sufficient to raise a *prima-facie* case against a man on the border, and when the Militia soldiers challenged him, and instead of replying he and his friend took cover, it was so clear to the former that they must be marauders, that they opened fire. The friend escaped, but our patient received a bullet through the left thigh, which shattered the bone. He was not brought to the mission hospital for some time, and when we first saw him it was obvious that unless the limb were speedily removed, his days were numbered. He, like all Afghans, had an innate repugnance to amputation, but finally consented on condition that the amputated limb should be given to him to take back to his home, that it might ultimately be interred in his grave; only thus, he thought, would he be safe from being a limb short in the next world. Once I tried to argue an Afghan out of this illogical idea, and when other arguments failed, I suggested that the unsavoury object might be buried in a spot in the mission compound, and he might leave a note in his grave specifying where it might be found. He answered at once: "Do you suppose the angels will have nothing better to do on the Resurrection Day than going about looking for my leg? And even if they would take the trouble, they would not come into this heretic place for it."

So the limb was removed and carefully wrapped up and stored away somewhere, so that he might on recovery take it back with him to his village. His wound is nearly healed now, and he has sent off his sister, who was in hospital to nurse him, to his home to fetch a horse on which to ride back the forty miles to his village, where he will wile away many a long winter's night with stories of his experiences in the Bannu Mission Hospital, and how kind the *feringis* were to him.

Among Afghans a man's nearest relations are often his deadliest enemies, and "he hates like a cousin" is a common expression. Thus it came to pass that one day a wounded Afghan was brought to the mission hospital on a bed borne of four, and examination showed a serious condition. He had been shot at close quarters the night before while returning to his house from the mosque after evening prayers. The bullet had passed completely through the left side of the chest, the left lung was collapsed, and the patient was blanched and faint from the severe bleeding that had occurred. A compress of charred cloth and yolk of egg had been applied, through which the red stream was slowly trickling. He believed he had been shot by his uncle, with whom he had a dispute about the possession of a field, but had not seen his face clearly. A room was got ready, the patient's blood-saturated garments were replaced by hospital linen, and the wound was cleansed and dressed.

For a long time he hovered between life and death, constantly attended by two brothers, who, if they had been as instructed as they were assiduous, would have made two very excellent nurses. Gradually, however, he recovered strength, and the wound healed; and one day when visiting his ward I found him sitting up with a smile on his face, and after the usual greetings, he said: "Please come to me, Sahib; I have a request to make." I sat by his bedside, and asked what I could do for him. He drew me closely to him, and said in a subdued voice: "Sahib, I want you to get me some cartridges; see, here are four rupees I have brought for them." "Why, what do you want them for?" said I. "Look here," said he, pointing to the wound in his chest; "here is this score to pay off. I am stronger now, and in a few days I can go home and have my revenge."

I said to him deprecatingly: "Cannot you forego your revenge after all the good counsels you have been hearing while in hospital? We have, after so much trouble and nursing, cured you, and now, I suppose, in a few days we shall be having your uncle brought here on a bed likewise, and have to take the same trouble over him." "Don't fear that, Sahib," was the prompt reply; "I am a better shot than he is." Well, we never did have to deal with that uncle, though I never gave him the cartridges; probably he got them elsewhere.

Another day a similar *cortège* came to the hospital. This time the man on the bed was a fine young Pathan of about twenty summers, and his father—a greybeard, with handsome but stern features, and one arm stiffened from an old sword-cut on the shoulder—accompanied the bearers, carefully shielding his son's face from the sun with an old umbrella. His was a long-standing feud with the *malik* of a village hard by, and he had been shot through the thigh at long range while tending his flocks on the mountain-side. It had happened four days ago, but the journey being a difficult one, they had delayed bringing him; and meanwhile they

THE RESULT OF A BLOOD FEUD

An old woman in the Peshawur Hospital describing how her grandson was shot in Tirah as the result of a blood feud. He was the last male representative of a clan which had been exterminated owing to the vendetta.

A TRANSBORDER AFGHAN BRINGING HIS FAMILY TO THE HOSPITAL

had slain a goat, and, stripping the skin off the carcass, had bound it round the injured limb with the raw side against the flesh. Under the influence of the hot weather the discharges from the wound and the reeking skin had brought about a condition of affairs which made bearers and bystanders, all except the father and the doctor, wind their turbans over their mouths and noses as soon as the hospital dresser began to unfold and cut through the long folds of greasy *pagari* which bound the limb to an improvised splint and that to the bed. It was a severe compound fracture of the thigh-bone, with collateral injuries, and I called the father aside and said: "The only hope of your son's life is immediate amputation. If I delay, the limb will mortify, and he will certainly die." The old man, visibly restraining his emotion, said: "If you amputate the leg, can you promise me that he will recover?" "No," I said; "even then he might die, for the injury is severe, and he is weak from loss of blood; but without amputation there is no hope." "Then," said the father, "let it be as God wills: let him die, for, by our tribal custom, if he dies as he is I can go and shoot my enemy; but if he dies from your operation then I could not, and I want my revenge." After this they would not even accept my offer of keeping the wounded lad in the hospital to nurse, but bore him away as they had brought him, so that he might die at home among his people, and then—well, the mind pictured the stealthy form crouching behind the rock; the hapless tribesman of the other village with his rifle loaded and slung on his shoulder right enough, but who was to warn him of his lurking enemy? And then the shot, the cry, and exultation.

A man of the Khattak tribe was out on the hills with a friend after mountain goats; he tracked one, but in following it up passed over into the hills of a section of the Wazir tribe. He was passing along one of those deep gorges which the mountain torrents have worn through the maze of sandstone ridges, where the stunted acacia and tufted grass afford pasturage to little else than the mountain goats, when his practised eye descried two heads looking over the ridge four hundred feet above him. Seeing they were observed, the two Wazirs stood up and challenged them.

"Who called you to come poaching in our country?" "I shall come when I choose, without asking your permission," retorted the Khattak. "Swine! has your father turned you out because there was no maize in your corn-bin?" The Khattak retorted with something stronger, and each proceeded to impugn the character of the other's female relations, till the Wazir, thinking he had excited the Khattak to give him sufficient provocation, sent a bullet whistling past his head. The Khattak made a jump for the cover of a neighbouring rock, but before he had time to gain shelter a second bullet had struck him in the leg, bringing him headlong to earth. His companion had got the shelter of a rock and opened fire on the Wazirs; but the latter, thinking they had sufficiently vindicated the privacy of their stony hills, made off another way.

The Khattak could do no more than lift his friend into the shelter of a cliff, stanch the bleeding with a piece torn from his *pagari*, and make off in hot haste for his village to sound a *chigah* and bring a bed on which the wounded man might be carried home. The *chigah*, of course, came too late to track the Wazirs, but they bore the wounded man home, and next morning brought him to the mission hospital. He lay there for three months, carefully tended by his father and a brother, and there all three were attentive listeners to the daily exposition of the Gospel by the doctor or catechist; but the wounded man got weaker and weaker, and when it became clear to all that his recovery could not be hoped for, they took him off to his home to die.

The next day a Wazir of the same tribe that had shot him

was brought in suffering from an almost identical gunshot wound, and we thought at first it had been the work of an avenger, but it proved to have been received in another feud about the possession of a few *ber*-trees (*Zizyphus jujuba*). This Wazir submitted to amputation, and is now going about the hills the proud possessor of an artificial limb from England, which his father sold a rifle to buy, and which is the wonder and admiration of his neighbours.

The devotion shown in some cases by relations who have accompanied some sick or wounded man to hospital is very touching, and in pleasing contrast to their frequent enmity. One case that imprinted itself on my memory was that of a man from Kabul, who had been a sufferer for several years from severe fistula; his nearest relation was a nephew, and he was a *talib* (student). Both were poor, but the man sold up some little household belongings and hired a camel-driver to bring him down on his camel. The journey to Bannu occupied fourteen days, and the sick man suffered much from the constraint and jolting of the camel-ride. An operation was performed, but it was some months before the patient was cured and discharged, and during all that time he was assiduously nursed by the *talib*, who sat day and night by his bedside, attending to his wants and reading to him either the *Suras* of the Quran or some Persian poet, only leaving him to go into some mosque in Bannu, or in a village near, where some charitable Muhammadans would give him his morning and evening meal.

To save the patients from the danger of having their money stolen by other patients or visitors, we advise them on admission to give up their money into our charge, to be kept safely until they get their discharge, when it is returned to them. Usually they readily agree to this, but sometimes we have some wary characters, usually Kabulis or Peshawuris, whose experience of the world has led them to trust no one, and these refuse to let their possessions out of their own keeping, usually securing their money in a bag purse tied round their waist under their clothes. One such Kabuli came into the hospital terribly ill with dysentery. Fearing, I suppose, we might take his money by force, he swore, in answer to the usual question, that he had not a single anna on him, and all through his illness he begged a few pice from us or from other patients to buy some little delicacy he fancied to supplement the regular hospital diet. He said he had no relations or friends living; "all had died," and certainly none ever came to inquire after him. His disease resisted all our efforts to cure it—he had been worn out with exposure and hard living—and at last, one morning, we found him dead in his bed; he had passed away quietly in the night, without even the patient in the bed next him knowing of it. We then found a bag containing eighty rupees bound round his waist; he had kept it carefully concealed from everyone throughout, and now died leaving behind him what might have purchased him so many little delicacies. There being no claimant for the money, we made it into a fund for helping indigent patients to get back to their more distant homes.

There was once a Mullah in Bannu who was particularly virulent in his public denunciations of the mission and everything connected with it. He would frequently give public lectures which were tirades against all Christians, and missionaries in particular, telling the people that if they died in the mission hospital they would assuredly go to hell, and all the mission medicine they drank would be turned into so much lead, which would drag them relentlessly down, down to the bottomless pit—and very much more in that strain. We were therefore somewhat surprised when one fine morning we beheld four white-robed *talibs* bringing a bed to the hospital, on which was a form covered by a white sheet, and on lifting the sheet, there was this very Mullah! We did not ask him awkward questions, but admitted him at once, and I think our Christian assistants throughout his long and dangerous illness showed him particular attentions, and nursed him with special care. They never taunted him with his former attitude to us, but strove, by the exhibition of Christian forbearance and sympathy, to give him a practical exposition of what Christianity is. When he left the hospital he thanked us in the presence of his disciples, offered a prayer for blessing on the hospital, and is now one of our staunchest friends.

Here is a very sad case in Bed 18, called "the Gleaners' Bed," because it is supported by the Gleaners' Union of Lambeth: A young man of twenty-five or thirty, blind from his birth, and yet brought to the hospital cruelly slashed in several places with sword and knife; one cut on the right shoulder went through the muscle down to the bone. And this was done only to rob him of the few things he possessed. Had the culprit known that the man was blind, let us hope he would not have been so brutal, but poor Mirzada was on the ground asleep, covered up with a sheet, as is the custom with the natives, and had been attacked in this way before he could escape or beg them to spare him. It was so sad to see him stretched moaning on his bed, with eyes that had never seen the light or the beauty of God's creation, heart that had never felt, ear that had never heard of the "Light of Life" or the "glory that shall be revealed." Our Christian assistants sat beside him day by day, and told him of Christ and His love; but he never, so far as we could judge, seemed to grasp the truth for himself, and, when his wounds were healed, left us to beg by the wayside. We pray for Mirzada, "who sitteth by the wayside begging," that he may yet find the Light! He at least has learnt to bless the mission hospital and the Christian friends in England, through whose charity he can say: "I was a stranger, and ye took me in; sick, and ye visited me."

The doctor or his assistants may go a long journey up and

down the frontier and both sides of the border without coming to a village where they will not get a hearty welcome from some old patient. He will be made to sit down for a little good cheer in the village *chauk*, that the grateful patient may call his acquaintances round to shake hands with the *Daktar Sahib*, whose patient he was while in the mission hospital, and with stories about whom he has so often regaled them in the winter evenings.

CHAPTER VII

FROM MORNING TO NIGHT

First duties—Calls for the doctor—Some of the out-patients—Importunate blind—School classes—Operation cases—Untimely visitors—Recreation—Cases to decide.

An Eastern day begins early. As the first streak of dawn lightens the Eastern sky the slumberers are awakened by the long-drawn-out chant of the Muezzin calling to prayer from all the mosques in the city. "God is great, God is great. I give witness there is no God but God. I give witness that Muhammad is the prophet of God. Come to prayer; prayer is better than sleep." And forthwith every pious Muslim hastily rises, performs the necessary ablutions, and commences the day with ascription of praise to the Creator. The Hindus follow suit: little bells tinkle in their temples as their priests rouse the slumbering Gods, or as the Puritanical Arya Samajist offers his early sacrifice of "Hawan," or incense. Meanwhile, the church bell calls the little Christian community together for early morning worship, and they unite in prayer and praise before separating, each to his or her own sphere of work for the day. If the missionary desires a morning "quiet time" he must get up early enough to get it in before this, as after morning service the busy round of duties leaves him little leisure till the evening shades close in.

Darya Khan, the "Lord of the Rivers," the hospital cook, is waiting for the day's supplies, and reports fifty patients on full diet, twenty on middle, and fifteen on milk diet. So many cases have left the hospital, so many admitted; such a one died last night. And so the supplies for the day are measured out and weighed, and orders given for the purchase of fresh goods as needed.

Then come the ward clerks, with their tale of soiled linen and case sheets to be checked, and clean towels, bandages, bed-linen, and clothes for the in-patients have to be dealt out according to the needs of each one.

This over, the head gardener, 'Alam Khan, or the "Lord of the World," is standing by with the day's supply of vegetables and flowers, and these have to be apportioned to the patients in the hospital and to the various members of the staff whose families reside on the premises. He follows with a string of questions, each of which requires due consideration, such as, "Are the mulberries to be shaken yet?" "Where are the young Pipul tree saplings to be planted?" "Some oranges were stolen in the night; would I come and see the footmarks?" "A hostel boy ('Light of Religion') was caught among the plum-trees with some fruit in his pocket. Would I punish him?" And so on, as long as one has leisure to listen and adjudicate.

The clock strikes eight, leaving just half an hour to visit the wards before out-patients begin. There is the abdominal section operation of yesterday to examine; the house-surgeon has come to report that the case of tubercular glands has had a hæmorrhage during the night. We are just hurrying over to see them, when up comes 'Alam Gul, the "Flower of the Earth," to say his brother was coming down from the roof that morning, when his foot slipped on the ladder; he fell on his head, and was lying unconscious. Would I go and see him? The serious cases seen, and 'Alam Gul's brother visited, the out-patient department is demanding our attention. The verandahs are full of patients, the men in one and the women and children in another, and while the catechist is preaching to the former, a Bible-woman is similarly engaged with the latter. Outside are some patients lying on the native beds, or *charpais*, and a variety of other equipages which have all brought patients—palanquins, camels, oxen, asses, and so on.

Let us see some of these. Here is a Wazir shepherd from the mountains. He has been shot through the thigh while tending his flocks, and eight rough-looking tribesmen of his have bound him securely on a bed and carried him down, journeying all night through, and they have left their rifles, without which they could not have ventured out, at the police post on the frontier. Another of those on the beds is a man of about fifty years, suffering from dropsy. He has been carried sixty miles on this bed from Khost, a district in Afghanistan. A third, who has been brought from another transfrontier village on an ox, is suffering from a tumour of his leg, which will require amputation. And so on with some half-dozen others. After this brief examination, saying a word of welcome to the travel-stained Afghans who have borne their precious burdens in with so much labour, and even danger, and with a word of comfort and reassurance to the sick ones themselves, the doctor enters his consulting-room, and the patients are brought in one by one to be examined. Those requiring in-patient treatment are sent off to the wards, and the remainder get the required medicines, or have their wounds dressed and leave for their homes.

A great number of the out-patients are cases of eye disease, and sometimes four or five blind men will come in a line, holding on to each other, and led by one who is not yet quite blind. Very likely they have trudged painfully upwards of a hundred miles, stumbling over the stones in the mountain roads, and arriving with wounded feet and bruised bodies. They sit together, listening, perhaps for the first time in their lives, to the Gospel address, and eagerly awaiting the interview with the doctor, when they will hear if they are to receive their sight there and then, or to undergo an operation, or what. For the stories they have heard of the power of Western skill lead them to believe that if the doctor does not cure them on the spot it must be that he is too busy or they are too poor. When, therefore, as sometimes happens, the doctor sees at the first glance that the case is a hopeless one, and that the sight is gone never to be brought back, it is a painful duty to have to explain the fact to the patient, and often the doctor needlessly prolongs the examination of the eye lest the man should think that it was want of interest in his case that makes the doctor say he can do nothing. And then the beseeching, "Oh, sahib, just a little sight!" "See, I can tell light from darkness; I can see the light from that window there." "I have come all the way from Kabul because they said the *feringi* doctor could cure everything. Why do you not cure me?"

One man refused to budge till I had taken him to see my mother; she might be able to do something—she must have more skill than I, for from whom had I learnt? Another went to her to beg her to intercede with me for him, because he was sure it was want of will, not want of power, that prevented him gaining his end. At last, when they are convinced that nothing can be done, it is touching to see them as they resignedly say, often with tears rolling down their cheeks: "It is God's will. I will be patient." Then they may begin their weary trudge home again, or stop in the Bannu bazaar for a few days to beg some money to get them a lift on a camel for part of the long journey.

A commotion at the door, and a Bannuchi boy of about seven is carried in on the shoulders of his father, with his hand tied up in the folds of a turban. "We were crushing sugar-cane in our press, when my beloved Mir Jahan got his hand in the cogs of the wheel, and it was all crushed before we could stop the buffalo. Oh! do see him quick—he is my only son, a piece of my liver!" And the father bursts into tears. Mir Jahan is chloroformed at once, the bandages unbound, and a terrible sight we see; the hand has been crushed into a pulp, but the thumb is only a little cut. That will enable him to pull the trigger of a rifle when he grows up, and that is what his father and he consider of great importance. So the thumb is saved, and the mangled remains of the other fingers removed, and a shapely stump fashioned. It is fortunate that the Bannuchis have not much machinery. This sugar-press is almost the only piece they have, and we get several crushed hands every year as a result, usually because they let their children play in dangerous proximity to the wheels, and then leave them to "Qismet" (Fate).

Meanwhile, perhaps, some big chief has come in with several attendants. He wants to have a special consultation with the doctor, and has to be treated with as many of the formalities of Oriental courtesy as the doctor can find time for. He gives some fee for the hospital, or perhaps may send one or two ox-burdens of wheat or Indian corn as his contribution to the hospital stores.

The patients are still coming, when a schoolboy comes to say that it is time for the doctor to take his classes in school. It is not every mission station that can provide a distinct European missionary for the school, and Bannu is one of those where the supervision of the school is one of the duties of the medical missionary, who takes the senior classes in Scripture, English, and Science. So the consulting-room is changed for the class-room, and the missionary finds himself surrounded by a class of twenty to twenty-five intelligent young fellows preparing for the matriculation at the Panjab University, and waiting to be initiated into the mysteries of optics, or chemistry, or mechanics, or to practise English composition, or he may have them attentively listening while he goes with them through the ever-fresh stories from the life of our Lord, hearing and asking them questions as its inimitable teachings are brought home to them by precept and by illustration. Class-work over, a visit of inspection is paid to the other class-rooms, where the remainder of the school staff are at their work, which the school principal must criticize and supervise, giving some advice here, some correction there, and seeing generally that everything is kept up to the mark.

Now we must go to see what progress has been made with the new ward which is being built in the hospital. The beams must be selected and tested. Here a carpenter has been putting some bad work into a lintel, thinking it will not be noticed; there the bricklayers have been idle, and have not finished the stipulated number of layers. The foreman has a complaint to make of some of the coolies, who went away from work without his permission. "We only went to say our prayers. Surely you would not have us miss them?" they plausibly urge. Put them on piecework, and their prayers are got over very quickly; but pay them by the day, and even the ablutions seem interminable! But such is human nature, and they have such an air of injured innocence it is difficult to be angry with them. They are Mahsud Wazirs from over the border, and work hard when well managed, so are let off with a warning this time.

This done, a visit must be paid to the mission press. Here not only is printing in vernacular and in English carried on for the mission's own requirements, but work is executed for the various offices and merchants in the city. Accounts have to be checked, bills have to be made out, proofs have to be corrected, and directions given for the day's work.

Now it is time to visit the hospital wards, and perform the day's operations.

Usually, patients are operated on the same day that they are admitted. If this were not done, not only would the wards become hopelessly congested, but in many cases the courage of the patients would ooze out of their fingers' ends, and, instead of finding them ready for the ordeal, one would be greeted by "I have just heard that my father has been

BANNU MISSION
A group of Patients.

A GROUP OF OUT-PATIENTS AT THE MISSION HOSPITAL, BANNU

taken seriously ill. If I do not go home at once, I shall never see him again." Another: "I quite forgot to arrange for my donkey to get hay during my absence. I will go home and make arrangements for it, and return in two days." Of course, one knows that these stories are pure fabrications, but it would be useless to tell them so, or to argue; one can only return them their own clothes, take back the hospital linen, and let them go. Sometimes they come back later on, and tell more fibs about their father or their donkey in justification of themselves; more often they are not seen again.

While the operation cases are being prepared by the house-surgeon, the doctor goes the round of the wards, examining, prescribing, and saying words of cheer from bed to bed. This done, he is just about to commence operations, when a man comes running up to say that his brother was out shooting when his gun exploded, blowing off his hand; would the doctor see him at once lest he bled to death? and close behind him is the wounded man brought up on a bed. The doctor examines him, sets a dresser to apply a temporary dressing, and perhaps a tourniquet, so that the case may safely wait till the conclusion of the other operations.

The operation cases to-day are representative of an average day in the busy time of the year: they begin with five old men and three women suffering from cataract, then two cases of incurved lids, then an amputation, the removal of a tumour, and two cases of bone disease. These over, the man with the injured hand is chloroformed and the wound stitched up, except for two fingers, which were so damaged that they had to be removed altogether.

The schoolboys are out now in the field playing football, and the doctor, after refreshing himself with a cup of tea, thinks that nothing would be more invigorating than a good hour's exercise with them; but he has scarcely got his togs on before the servant comes to announce that a certain big *malik*, or chief, has come to make a call. One would like to put him off with an excuse for a more convenient time; but then it was he who gave us lodging and hospitality when itinerating in his neighbourhood six months ago, and this would be a poor return for his courtesy; so he is ushered in, with four or five of his retainers, and some minutes are spent in formal courtesies and talking about nothing in particular. Then, just as one is going to suggest that as one has something to do the interview might terminate, he comes to the point and object of his interview. He has got a lawsuit on in one of the local courts against a neighbouring *malik*. His case is an absolutely just one; but as the other party have some relationship with the head-clerk of the Judge's office, he fears he will not get justice, unless—unless—— Would I just write a few lines to the Judge, asking him to give his case full consideration? It would be no trouble to me, and would confer a benefit on him which he will remember to his dying day. One launches into an explanation, which is wearying because one has so often given it in similar cases before, that the Judge would be very angry if I adopted such a method of influencing his case, that if his case is a just one there is no need of such measures, that he must rely on the integrity of his witnesses, and so on; no, he cannot or will not understand why you profess friendship with him, and yet refuse so very humble a request as the writing of a note. By the time the visitor has departed only half an hour is left for the game of football, and there is a man waiting to take you to a case of pneumonia at the other side of the bazaar, and two other calls have to be made on medical cases in the city.

It is evening now, and once more the church-bell collects the little Christian community together for the evening hymn of praise and worship, and the pastor gives some words of instruction and encouragement, specially intended for the catechumens and inquirers who are present.

At last, however, these duties accomplished, dinner is negotiated, and then the doctor can sit down to his newspaper and his correspondence. He is not, however, long left free from interruption. The first to come is the superintendent of the boarding-house; he reports that some of the Hindu boarders have been cooking meat in the school saucepan, and now the vegetarian party refuse to eat food cooked in that vessel, which has *ipso facto* become unclean.

The arguments of both sides are heard, and the case decided, that the meat party are to provide their own saucepan. Then the house-surgeon comes in with his nightly report of the wards, stating the condition of the operation cases or of any other serious cases, and taking the orders for the night. Following on him comes a catechumen who has a quarter of an hour's instruction every night; then three of the senior boarders, to ask some questions about the English composition for the morrow, and get some hints for their essays. Lastly, the night-watchman comes to report that, as there is a gang of Wazir marauders about, special precautions must be taken for the security of the compound; but he thinks that if I get him a new pistol and some cartridges all will be safe.

A day such as I have described is not at all above the average during the busy months of the year, and the doctor may consider himself lucky if the soundness of his slumbers is not disturbed by any calls during the night.

CHAPTER VIII

THE ITINERANT MISSIONARY

The medical missionary's advantage—How to know the people—The real India—God's guest-house—The reception of the guest—Oriental customs—Pitfalls for the unwary—The Mullah and the Padre—Afghan logic—A patient's welcome—The Mullah conciliated—A rough journey—Among thieves—A swimming adventure—Friends or enemies?—Work in camp—Rest at last.

There is this difference between the medical missionary and the preacher pure and simple: that while the latter has to seek his congregation, the former will have his congregation come to him, and often in such numbers that, like our Lord and His disciples, he will not have leisure even so much as to eat. But even a doctor, who finds his time at headquarters fully and profitably occupied, will be committing a great mistake if he never itinerates. For it is in camp and in village life that the missionary gets to know and understand the people, and by travelling from village to village, and living with them as their guest, he gets to know their real inner life in a way that otherwise he never would, and for a missionary, at least, such an experience is indispensable.

There are two methods of itineration. On the one hand, he may carry tents and a full camp equipment, and pitch his camp near some large village, or in the midst of several small ones, and may receive his patients and do his daily work there, while visiting the villages after his day's work is done. By this plan he is independent, and can work at his own time, and can stay or move as his fancy dictates. On the other hand, he may become the guest of one of the chief men of the village, who will put his guest-house at his disposal and give him hospitality. By this plan he is brought into much closer contact with the people and will see more of them, but he will forfeit his independence, will be obliged to consult his host in all his plans, and must be prepared to put himself and his time at the disposal of his host and the villagers, both by day and night.

Both methods have their advantages. For a new district, and where the people are suspicious, the latter plan, though more exacting, is probably the better; when the missionary has become well known and has much work to do, the former is preferable.

The traveller who has spent a winter in touring India, but has only visited the large towns and show places, and has never lived in an Indian village, remains altogether a stranger to the deep inner life of the Indian. The real India is not seen in the Westernized bazaars of the large cities, but in the myriads of villages, wherein more than 80 per cent. of the population of India dwell. Moreover, a much better and more attractive side of Indian life is seen in the villages than in the towns, and it is among their less sophisticated population that the missionary spends his happiest hours.

When travelling without camp equipment, we generally follow the Bible precept. We arrive at a village, and, "inquiring who within it is worthy, abide there till we depart thence." This is usually some *malik*, or head man, who possesses that great institution of Afghanistan, a *hujra*, or guest-house. We are shown to this house, usually a mud building with a low door and a few small apertures in the walls in the place of windows, and a clean-swept earthen floor, which may be covered by a few palm-mats. Hearing of our arrival, the owner of the guest-house comes to receive us in the Oriental fashion so familiar to readers of the Old Testament.

Thus, on one occasion I came rather late at night to one such guest-house. The host had already retired, but rose from his bed to receive me. I inquired if that was his *hujra*. He answered: "No; it is God's, but I am in charge of it." Such expressions are not mere form, as was shown by the cheerful and unostentatious way in which the owner put himself out in order to insure my comfort. Once I arrived about midnight at a village, the head man of which I did not know personally, though it appears he knew me well. He was not satisfied until I consented to occupy his bed, which he had just vacated for me, while he went off to make himself a shift elsewhere. The acceptance of such an offer might not always prove very attractive among those Afghans whose ideas of cleanliness are not the same as ours, but to refuse it would—at least, on the part of a missionary—be an act so discourteous as to injure the attainment of those relations with the people which he should desire.

The head man will at once call for some of his attendants, who, except at the busy time of sowing and harvest, are probably lounging about the *chauk*, and they at once bring a number of the plain wooden bedsteads of the country, which are almost universally used, even by the richer classes, in preference to chairs. Rugs and pillows are brought, and perhaps a carpet may be spread on the floor. Tea is then ordered, and an attendant brings in a tray on which is a very large teapot and a number of very small saucerless cups, called in these parts *balghami*, and used all over Central Asia for tea-drinking. The whole is covered by an embroidered cloth, which is removed by the attendant. Sugar is added to the teapot to a degree which to many Western palates appears nauseating. Cardamoms, and sometimes other spices, are also added. The milk, too, is usually added to the teapot, although some hosts, who have learnt by experience the peculiarity of Western taste, leave the milk and the sugar to be added by the guests themselves. Tea is poured out and

TWO METHODS OF TRAVEL

Travelling by riding camel.
Itineration with camp equipment by means of ekkas and mules.

handed round, and drunk usually very hot; and if the guests drink it with very loud smackings of the lips, it is supposed to indicate that they particularly appreciate it. The cups are filled repeatedly, and when the guest wishes to indicate that he has had enough he turns the cup upside down.

By this time the news of our arrival has spread through the village. There are probably a number of old patients there, who have once or oftener been inmates of the base hospital, and they help to collect all the blind, the halt, the maimed, and the sick of the village, and we proceed to unpack our medicines and commence prescribing and physicking.

Then will come the Mullah of the village, with his Quran under his arm and his rosary in his hand, and with a very sanctimonious and superior kind of air. He has come to see that the faith of the flock is not endangered, and is followed by a number of his *talibs*, or students, whose great desire is to hear a wordy battle between the *Padre* and the Mullah, and to see the former ignominiously defeated.

Eastern ideas are cast in such a very different mould to Western, and their system of logic and habit of mind are so unlike ours, that the young missionary may consider himself fortunate if he is not frequently held up to ridicule by some ignorant Mullah, who on such an occasion as this, before an audience who are naturally inclined to side with him, and can appreciate his language and arguments very much better than ours, has all the advantage on his side. It is no doubt better to avoid such discussions as far as possible. But this cannot always be done, as the refusal to answer questions would be assumed to imply inability to do so, and would be taken by the audience to indicate defeat. What really impresses the people would not usually be our arguments, but the patience and courtesy with which we meet, or ought to meet, the endeavours of our opponent to make us lose our temper. According to Eastern ideas, the mere stroking of the beard is supposed to indicate irritation arising from the inability to answer the questions, and if the inexperienced disputant incautiously puts his hand to his beard, his opponent will most probably show off his advantage by pretending to apologize to him for having made him lose his temper.

On one occasion, while touring among the frontier villages, I was spending the night at a *hujrà*, and after dark a Mullah had come in for discussion, and a great number of the men of the village, attracted by the hope of an interesting conflict between their champion and the *Padre Sahib*, had collected to listen.

It was winter, and there was a fire of twigs burning in the middle of the room, which was filling the place with its smoke, as there was only one quite inadequate aperture in the centre of the room by which it could find its exit. Round all four sides were a number of the native beds, on which both disputants and audience were seated cross-legged or reclining at their ease.

As the fire burnt low a boy would bring in some crackling thorns and branches which were piled outside the room, and throw some on the fire, which would blaze up and illuminate the faces of all around; for the only other light was the little earthen oil lamp in a niche in one corner, which only served to make the darkness visible.

The Mullah was evidently bent on making a display of his own dialectic skill at my expense, and began in a rather condescending tone to ask if I knew anything about theology; and on my replying that I had come to the country in order to teach the Christian religion, he turned to the audience, and said somewhat contemptuously:

"I do not suppose these *Padres* know much, but we will see." He then turned to me and said: "Can you tell me the colour of faith?"

Rather puzzled by the question, I asked what he meant. He said:

"Why, is it white, or green, or red, or what colour?"

I replied that, as an abstract idea, it did not possess the quality of colour.

MULLAH: "Then can you tell me what shape it is? Is it round, or square, or what?"

I: "Neither has it any shape. It is only an abstract quality."

MULLAH: "It is evident that he does not know much about theology, seeing he cannot answer such simple questions as the colour and shape of faith."

At this time I did not know that the Muhammadans ascribed such concrete qualities to all their abstract religious ideas.

MULLAH: "Do you know anything about astronomy?"

I thought that here at least my knowledge might not be far inferior to that of this Mullah, and said:

"Yes, I think I can answer you any questions on that subject."

MULLAH: "Tell me, then, what becomes of the sun when it sinks below the horizon every evening?"

I then proceeded to as simple and lucid an explanation as I could of the revolutions of the earth on its axis, but could see from the looks and ejaculations of the audience that they thought the idea rather a mad one.

The Mullah himself made no effort to conceal his contempt, and said:

"That, then, is all you know about it?"

A little nettled, I said:

"Well, what explanation do you give?"

"We all know that the fires of hell are under the earth. The sun passes down there every night, and therefore comes up blazing hot in the morning."

I rather had my breath taken away by this explanation, which met with ejaculations of approbation from the men around me, and I incautiously asked the Mullah if he could explain the seasons.

Mullah (turning to the people) · "It is evident that I shall have to teach him everything from the beginning."

To me: "It is in the spring that the devil makes up his fires, and piles on the firewood. Therefore the fires get very hot in the summer, and cool down later on. That is why the summer sun is so hot."

Needless to say, the explanations of the Mullah appeared to the audience as rational and lucid as mine were far-fetched and incomprehensible, and they had no doubt as to which of the disputants had won the day.

From this it can be seen that if a young missionary thinks that a mere knowledge of Western learning and Western logic will enable him to cope with the very limited learning of the Afghan Mullahs on their own ground, he is vastly mistaken, and will before long be put to ridicule, as I was on the above occasion, which was one of my earliest experiences on the frontier.

Since then I have learnt how to argue with Afghan logic, and from the Afghan point of view.

If it happens that the Mullah, or some friend of his, is in need of medical or surgical advice, his attitude to you will undergo a great change, and you will have much greater facilities for carrying on your work among the people. Sometimes, when he sees the benefits accruing to the poor people who had no other prospect of getting medical relief, his attitude becomes unexpectedly friendly, as his better feelings prevail over his religious animosity.

Once, having set out on an itineration, some Pathans came to tell me I might as well save myself the trouble of going in that direction because a certain Mullah, who had much influence in those parts, had gone before us, warning the people not to accept our treatment, listen to our preaching, or even come near us. I answered by the remark which appeals to the Muhammadan mind under almost every conceivable circumstance: "Whatever God's will has ordained will be," and told him we should adhere to our original plan.

On the first two days the people certainly seemed suspicious, and very few came near us. While we were on the march on the third day, passing not very far from a village, a man who had apparently noticed us from the village, which was situated on an eminence above the road, came running down to us, and, after the usual salutations, said: "There is an old patient of yours here who is very anxious to see you; please turn aside and come to the house." On arrival we found that it was a woman who, a year before, had been an inmate of the Bannu Hospital for malignant tumour on the leg, which had required amputation. Before she left the hospital we had made her a rough wooden pin leg, on which she now appeared hobbling along to greet us. She showed great delight at unexpectedly meeting us, and had apparently been telling her fellow-villagers wonderful stories of what she had seen and heard in the mission hospital, and of the unaccountable love and sympathy which had been shown her there, for others of her neighbours came crowding into her little courtyard, and among them, though unknown to us, the Mullah who was supposed to be preaching a crusade against us. He had apparently come in on the quiet to see for himself what we and our work were like, and was greatly struck at the undisguised delight with which we were greeted by our old patients; for when the woman of the house begged us to stop while she prepared us a meal, he came forward and disclosed himself, saying: "No; my house is in the next village, and it is my prerogative to entertain the *Padre Sahib*. He must come on to my house." At the same time he took up some Pashtu Gospels which we had been giving away, but which the people, for fear of theological displeasure, had been afraid to take openly, and said: "This is *Kalam Ullah* [Word of God], and is a good book." Thus, in a moment, by this providential presence of the Mullah, the whole attitude of our reception was changed. Word was passed on from village to village that we had become the guests and eaten the bread of the Mullah himself, and that he had pronounced in favour of our books, telling the people that we were *Ahl-el-Kitab*, or people of the Book, the term which Muhammadan theologians apply to Christians and Jews when they wish to speak of them in a friendly spirit.

We were not always equally fortunate, especially in our earlier years on the frontier.

About two years after I first went to Bannu I went out on a short itineration with my assistant Jahan Khan, an account of whom is given in Chapter XVI.

We came to one village where the Mullahs had been exciting the feelings of the people against us, and telling them that any food or vessel we touched was thereby defiled. We found it difficult to get food or drinking-vessel even on payment, and some of the patients who came to us were induced to go away, and in some cases to throw away the medicine they had already received.

With some difficulty we got a lodging for the night, and early next morning we started off to look for a village where we might get a more hospitable reception. But the minds of the people had already been poisoned against us.

We went into the courtyard of the *Patwar-Khana* (village bailiff), and sat down and opened our medicines. Some Hindus came for treatment, and we got one of them to bring us some food; but the Muhammadans were universally hostile, and stationed one of their number at the gate to prevent any Muhammadan communicating with us. They then apparently became annoyed with the Hindus, that they should be participating in benefits from which they had excluded themselves, and stones began to fall into the courtyard where we were seated; and as the Hindus in these villages are not only in a small minority, but live in dread of the fiercer Muhammadans, even they who had already come to us disappeared, and we were left alone. It seemed useless to stop in a village where we were not welcomed, so we saddled our animals and departed.

Many years have passed since this experience. Patients from both these villages frequently come to the Bannu Hospital, and now I and my assistants get a welcome and hospitality whenever we visit them.

At other times the difficulties of itineration are not so much from the people as from the hardships of travelling among the frontier mountains, where the roads are nil, and the bridle-tracks such that it is often impossible to get a loaded camel through.

I will therefore give a short account of a journey from Bannu across the Wazir Hills to Thal, which we made in the summer of 1904.

As our route lay chiefly through independent territory, it was difficult to procure camel-men for so trying a journey.

The men with the first camels we hired ran away when they found we were going into the hills, as not only is the road very difficult for laden animals, but they are afraid of being attacked by Wazir robbers, the Wazirs having the worst reputation of all the tribes of Afghans who live on the border. With some difficulty we got four more camels, and as their owners were themselves Wazirs, we prevailed on them to accompany us. We loaded up our tents, medicines, and bedding, and about 9 a.m., when the sun was already very hot, we finally started. Besides the two camel-men, there were a hospital assistant, two servants, a Muhammadan inquirer, whom I was taking along for the sake of instructing him, and one of the schoolboys, who had persuaded me to let him accompany us, so that we were quite a large party. After toiling for some hours along a mountain defile we came to Gumatti Post, one of those frontier forts that line the North-West Border. This was built close to an old Wazir fort, in capturing which, two years ago, Colonel Tonnochy and Captain

White lost their lives, as described in Chapter I. We passed through the wire entanglement, and spent the heat of the day talking to the native officer and soldiers in charge. In the afternoon we set out again, and marched along the bed of the Kurram River, which we had to ford six times, so that before we reached our night camp it had become quite dark. Taking advantage of the dark, some light-fingered Wazir thieves managed to steal the tent carpet off the back of a camel without our catching sight of them. Our camp was in a Wazir village, built on a cliff overhanging the river. The people were rather excited, as another Wazir clan had been up during the day and made off with twenty head of cattle. However, there were some old patients among the people, so we got a hearty welcome. They made us some tea, and set some of their number to watch round our beds with their Martini-Henrys ready loaded in case enemies should come during the night. The Mullah of the place came and had a talk with us, and then we were soon all fast asleep.

Next morning we were up betimes, and I found my bed surrounded by a number of women with squalling babies. One mother wanted me to see her baby's eyes, another the stomach of hers, another the ears; in fact, all the babies seemed to have made common cause to delay my departure as long as possible. However, after doling out various lotions and pills, and giving the mothers many instructions, which, I fear, were only heard to be forgotten, we managed to get the camels loaded and started. Now, however, a new difficulty confronted us. During the night there must have been heavy rain higher up the valley, for the river was in flood and unfordable. I knew by experience how strong yet deceptive the currents of the river are when it is in flood, for a few weeks before I had been out on a bathing excursion with some of our schoolboys in another part of the same river. I had dived into a deep pool, when I found myself in a return current, which was carrying me back under a small waterfall, where the water was sweeping over an obstruction like a mill-race, with a fall of about four feet. As soon as I got to the fall I went down, down, down, till I thought I was never coming up again. However, I did come up, only, however, to be pulled back at once under the waterfall and down into the depths again. The third time I came up I got a momentary glimpse of two of the boys trying to throw me the end of a *pagari*. They were, however, much too far away for me to reach it, and I was pulled under again before I had time to get even one good breath. As I went down I wondered if I should ever see the boys again, and how many times I should come up before it was all over. Then all at once it struck me that I was very foolish trying to get out at the surface, where the current was beyond my strength, and I must change my tactics; so I turned over and dived down till I felt the boulders at the bottom, and then crept along the bottom with the aid of the current—which there, of course, was flowing downstream—as long as I could. When I could do so no more, and had to strike upwards, I found, to my delight and thankfulness, that I was out of the eddy and going downstream. So it was clearly impossible to keep along the river, even if we had not had laden animals with us. We were obliged, therefore, to make a long détour through the hills, which took us nearly all day. So rough and precipitous was the path that we had the greatest difficulty in getting the camels along, and had several times to unload them in order to get them over bad places.

During the afternoon we saw a party of fifteen or sixteen armed Wazirs hastening towards us. At first we thought they were coming to loot us, and one of the Wazirs with us told us to stop, while he went forward and called out, "Are you friends or enemies?" When they replied "Friends" he went up to them, and then called us on to join him, when I found that they were a party of outlaws who had fallen foul of the Government, and, therefore, had made their escape across the frontier. They got me to sit down with them in the shade of a rock and write down a list of their grievances for them, so that they might propitiate the Political Officer and obtain permission to return to British India. I was very happy to render them this service, and we parted good friends. I noticed, however, that the Wazirs with us seemed uncomfortable, and kept their rifles ready cocked till they had disappeared behind a turn in the defile. I make it a principle never to carry any arms myself, and think I am much safer on that account, but the villagers who accompany me always go well armed; in fact, across the border few Afghans can go out of their houses without their rifles on their shoulders ready for use, so terribly prevalent are the blood-feuds and village quarrels. We spent that night in a Wazir village, where we saw a number of patients and made fresh friends. The head man of the village apologized next morning for not accompanying us more than half a mile. He said that he had blood-feuds with most of the villages round, and could not, therefore, venture farther. The fame of the Bannu Mission Hospital, however, was our best escort, and passport too, and we got a welcome at almost every village we passed, through the mediation of numerous old patients, who had recounted in all the villages the kind treatment they had received at the hands of the *feringis* (Europeans) in Bannu.

Progress was somewhat delayed by frequent calls to visit a sick person in one or another village, but openings for the Gospel were at the same time secured, and the lessons of the parable of the Good Samaritan imparted. By midday we reached Thal, which was for some days to be our field hospital. Here we pitched our tents, under the shade of some willows, by a small stream outside the town, and early the next morning started work. A large crowd of sick and their friends had collected from Thal itself and the villages round. I first read a passage out of the Pashtu Testament, and explained it to them in that language. The Gospel address over, I wrote out prescriptions for each one in order, which my assistant dispensed to them. After a minor operation or two, a fresh crowd had collected, another address was given, and they, too, were seen and attended to. In this way five lots of patients were treated, and about 200 or 300 people heard the Gospel story in their own language. Then, as evening was drawing on, we shut up our books and our boxes, washed off the dust of the day's work in the brook hard by, and proceeded to interest ourselves in the operations which the cook was conducting over an improvised fireplace, made of a couple of bricks placed on either side of a small hole in the ground. Dinner over, we had family prayers, and then fell soundly asleep.

An interesting town where we have sometimes stopped in our itinerations is that of Kalabagh. It is situated on the right bank of the River Indus where it finally breaks forth from the rocky gorge that has hemmed it in with high, often precipitous, sides, which rise at Dimdot to a sheer height of four hundred feet above the surging river, on to the boundless alluvial plain of the Panjab. In some of the bends between Attock and Kalabagh, it rushes at a great speed over rapids, where the boatmen warily guide their heavy river boats, lest they be drawn into some whirlpool, or dashed against the precipitous sides; at others there are deep, silent reaches where the bottom is two hundred feet from the surface. During the hot weather, when the river is in flood, it is an exciting experience to be ferried across its dark grey surging stream. At Kalabagh there are extensive quarries of salt of a beautiful pink and white colour and great purity; these bring in a considerable revenue to the Government. The town itself is built on the side of a hill of red salt marl, some of the houses being quarried out of the salt itself, so that the owner has only to chip off a bit of his own wall in order to season his cooking-pot. It is a standing grievance with the inhabitants that their own walls are Government contraband,

and they are subject to a fine if they sell a brick from their wall without paying duty on it. The streets are narrow and winding, and being, many of them, roofed and even built over, are very dark, and in the hot summer nights insufferably close and hot, and at all times distinctly insanitary and malodorous.

The people are pale and anæmic, and nearly all suffer from goitre in a greater or less degree. They form a great contrast to the hardy mountaineers of the Bangi Khel Khattak tribe on the hills behind them. These form one of the great recruiting grounds of the Pathan regiments of the frontier, while from Kalabagh itself it would be hard to find a score of men who could pass the recruiting officer. In the sultry summer weather the inhabitants spend the day under a number of large banyan - trees (*Ficus Indica*) which are scattered along the edge of the river. Here, too, the civil officers of the district hold their courts, and I was encamped under a spacious banyan. Its spreading branches not only sheltered me and all the sick and visitors who thronged around me, but also the Deputy Commissioner of the district and his court, together with the crowd of suitors and applicants that always followed in his train; and the District Judge, with his court, and a crowd of litigants, pleaders and witnesses — and this all without incommoding one another.

The land away from the river is pulsating with the fervid heat of the summer sun, and the town itself is like an oven; but there is nearly always a cool breeze blowing on the bank of the river, and, when heated and dusty with the day's work, one can throw off one's clothes and cool oneself with a swim in the river, where the young men of the place are disporting themselves all their leisure time. They use the inflated skin of a goat or of a cow, and, supporting themselves on this, can rest on the deep, cool bosom of the river as long as they like without fatigue. The river is too rapid for them to

THE INDUS RIVER

The boy is travelling down the river on a "kik" or inflated skin. The men on the bank are carrying theirs up the river as they can only be used when travelling with the stream.

FERRYING ACROSS THE RIVER INDUS

The rapids between Torbela and Attock

travel upstream, but when business takes them downstream, they simply fasten their clothes in a bundle on their heads, lie across their inflated skin, and quietly drift downstream at about four miles an hour as far as they desire. On returning, they simply deflate their skin, and sling it over their shoulders.

We were usually thronged with patients here from morning to evening, and I have seen as many as three hundred in one day, the work including a number of operations. One day a noted Muhammadan Sheikh visited the place. He was a convert from Hinduism, and was travelling about the country preaching Islam and decrying the Christian and Hindu religions. He sent us a challenge to meet him in a public discussion on the respective merits of the Cross and the Crescent. I was reluctant, as such discussions are seldom conducted fairly or sincerely; but, finding my reluctance was being misunderstood, I consented, and we met one evening, a Muhammadan gentleman of the place being appointed chairman. It was arranged that we were each in turn to ask a question, which the other was to answer. He was given the first question, and asked how it was that we had not miraculous powers, seeing that the Bible said that those who believed in Christ should be able to take poison or be bitten of snakes without suffering injury. The catechist with me gave so lucid and categorical a reply that the Muhammadan disputant and chairman changed their tone, and said that, as the time was getting late, it would be better to postpone my question till another time. Needless to say, that more convenient time never came, and we were not again challenged to a discussion at Kalabagh, and the Sheikh left for fresh pastures a few days later.

CHAPTER IX

AFGHAN MULLAHS

No priesthood in Islam—Yet the Mullahs ubiquitous—Their great influence—Theological refinements—The power of a charm—Bazaar disputations—A friend in need—A frontier Pope—In a Militia post—A long ride—A local Canterbury—An enemy becomes a friend—The *ghazi* fanatic—An outrage on an English officer.

Here we are met by an apparent paradox. There is no section of the people of Afghanistan which has a greater influence on the life of the people than the Mullahs, yet it has been truly said that there is no priesthood in Islam. According to the tenets of Islam, there is no act of worship and no religious rite which may not, in the absence of a Mullah, be equally well performed by any pious layman; yet, on the other hand, circumstances have enabled the Mullahs of Afghanistan to wield a power over the populations which is sometimes, it appears, greater than the power of the throne itself. For one thing, knowledge has been almost limited to the priestly class, and in a village where the Mullahs are almost the only men who can lay claim to anything more than the most rudimentary learning it is only natural that they should have the people of the village entirely in their own control. Then, the Afghan is a Muhammadan to the backbone, and prides himself on his religious zeal, so that the Mullah becomes to him the embodiment of what is most national and sacred.

The Mullahs are, too, the ultimate dispensers of justice, for there are only two legal appeals in Afghanistan—one to the theological law, as laid down by Muhammad and interpreted by the Mullahs; the other to the autocracy of the throne—and even the absolute Amir would hesitate to give an order at variance with Muhammadan law, as laid down by the leading Mullahs. His religion enters into the minutest detail of an Afghan's everyday life, so that there is no affair, however trivial, in which it may not become necessary to make an appeal to the Mullah. Birth, betrothal, marriage, sickness, death—all require his presence, and as often as not the Afghan thinks that if he has called in a Mullah to a sick relation there is no further necessity of calling in a doctor. Thus the Mullah becomes an integral part of Afghan life, and as he naturally feels that the advance of mission work and of education must mean the steady diminishing of his influence, he leaves no stone unturned to withstand the teaching of missionaries and to prejudice the minds of the people against them.

The great religious fervour of the Afghans must be evident to anyone who has had even a cursory acquaintance with them, whether in their mountain homes or as travellers through India. I remember once sitting in a village *chauk* while a religious discussion was going on which threatened to launch the two opponent parties into making bodily attacks on each other, and the whole of the matter under discussion was whether prayers said by a worshipper on the skin of a jackal were efficacious or not. According to the tenets of Islam, if a worshipper were to perform his genuflections on the bare ground they would be of no effect, because the ground might certainly be assumed to be ceremonially polluted. Ordinarily, the worshipper will spread a piece of clean cloth, or mat, or skin on the ground, and, removing his shoes beforehand, will perform his prayers thereon. It might be contended, however, that even though the skin of the jackal were absolutely clean, yet the unclean nature of the animal still attached to it, and rendered the prayers ineffective. The matter in this case was referred to a renowned Mullah who lived some way off, and to whom both parties had to send deputations several days' journey.

Then, in the mission hospital the question has frequently been raised by the Afghan patients as to whether it was lawful to say prayers in the clothes provided by the mission for the patients, even though these may have come direct from the washing; and we have been unable to persuade patients to put on clothes, however clean, which might possibly prevent them from saying their prayers until they have brought the case before some Mullah who was willing to give an *ex cathedrâ* pronouncement in our favour. Mullahs sometimes use the power and influence they possess to rouse the tribes to concerted warfare against the infidels, as they tell them that the English are; and often a prelude to one of the little frontier wars has been some ardent Mullah going up and down on the frontier, like Peter the Hermit, rousing the tribes to come down and fight. Often they lay claim to magical powers whereby those who submit themselves to their incantations become invulnerable, so that they are able to stand up before the bullets of the English troops unscathed. Before the war of 1897, a Mullah, known as the Mullah Povindah, was reputed to have this power; and many of the Afghans I met maintained that they had put it to the test, and seen with their own eyes the bullets fall harmless off the people to whom he had extended his protection. It was useless to say that they were trying to impose upon them, for they thoroughly believed it themselves, as was shown in many cases by the reckless daring with which they charged down on the British troops. Even those who may be supposed to be free from the superstition of the ignorant believe with equal fervour in this power of the Mullahs and holy men. An instance of this occurs in the Memoirs of the late Amir Abdurrahman, who relates that once during a military review a soldier deliberately shot at him as he was sitting in a chair,

The bullet passed through the back of the chair, and wounded a page-boy standing behind. He attributes his escape entirely to a charm written on a piece of paper which a holy man had given to him when a boy. He says: "At first I did not believe in its power to protect; I therefore tried it by tying it round the neck of a sheep, and though I tried hard to shoot the animal, no bullet injured her."

One of the commonest experiences of the open-air preacher on the borders of Afghanistan is the wordy warfare in which he is obliged to engage with some bellicose Mullah. The Mullah has heard that the missionary has begun to preach, and he regards it as his duty to come down and champion Islam. He brings a big volume of the Quran ostentatiously under his arm, and is followed by four or five students, or *talibs*, ready to applaud all his thrusts, while ridiculing in a very forcible way the replies of the preacher. Such arguments can hardly be expected to bear any reasonable fruit, because the object of the Mullah is not to ascertain what your views on any doctrine really are, but only to gain a strategical victory and hold you up to ridicule; but it is equally impossible to refuse the challenge, for then not only would the audience conclude that you had no answer to give, but the Mullah would take care that no one remained to listen to you. Frequently the object of the Mullah is to egg the people on to acts of open violence, and then, when they see that the row is well started, they suddenly make themselves scarce, and leave their flock to take the risk of any subsequent police investigations which may result.

On one occasion I had a providential deliverance from an unpleasant incident. On proceeding to the place in the market where I usually preached, I found a Mullah in possession preaching to a scowling crowd of townsmen. As we had always preached in that particular place for years, I saw it was only a ruse to oust us from preaching first there and then anywhere else where we might go, so I promptly took my place by the Mullah's side, and commenced preaching to the same audience. The Mullah vociferated, and the audience scowled more and more, and then the Mullah, turning to me, said: "Look here, you had better get out of this, as these people here are up to mischief, and it may go hard with you." I felt much like Micah when the Danites said to him: "Let not thy voice be heard among us, lest angry fellows run upon thee." But I told the Mullah that I held him responsible for the acts of his followers, and I did not intend to forsake the place to which long custom had given us a right. Just as the storm seemed about to break, and I momentarily expected to be pitched across the street, a stalwart smith, a well-known Muhammadan, himself respected by the people, pushed through the crowd, and, taking the Mullah by the arm, said: "Now, *Mullah Sahib*, you know the *Padre Sahib* never interferes with you in your place, and that this is not your proper preaching-place. Why do you want to make a row and injure him?" So saying, he took the rather unwilling Mullah off to his usual place, and the more unruly portion of the crowd, after hurling a few imprecations at me, followed him, too. Our friend the smith was an old hospital patient, so this, too, may be set down, under the overruling providence of God, to the mollifying influence of a medical mission.

One of the most influential Mullahs on the British side of the Afghan border is the Mullah Karbogha, so called from the village which forms his Canterbury. In some respects his influence was directed towards the moral improvement of the people, while in others his religious schools became hotbeds of fanaticism. Thus he set his face steadily against the evil practice, which is so prevalent among the frontier Afghans, of selling their daughters in marriage to the highest bidder. Not long ago a Mullah of considerable power, who had himself sold his daughter in marriage, had to make the most abject profession of repentance lest the Mullah Karbogha should excommunicate him, and he should have to fly the country. He regards the smoking of tobacco as one of the works of the devil, and when the Mullah makes his visitation to some village there is a general scramble to hide away all the pipes; for not only would any that he found be publicly broken, but the owner would incur his displeasure. As the Afghans do not confine themselves to the soothing weed, but mix it up with a number of intoxicating and injurious substances, such as Indian hemp or *charras*, this attitude of the Mullah may be regarded in the light of a reform. Unfortunately, he regards it as a heinous sin for any Muhammadan to take service with, or to receive pay from, the British Government. Often on the frontier a grave crisis has threatened to result from the refusal of one of his underlings, or Sheikhs, as they are called, to grant the rites of marriage or burial to some unfortunate Pathan who has enlisted in one of the regiments of the Indian Army. The missionaries, of course, are regarded by him and his Sheikhs as the embodiment of the heresies of an infidel Government.

For many years the Mullah Karbogha apparently ignored me, but finally I had information that his attitude was going to become more distinctly hostile. I thought it better, therefore, to act on the Biblical adage to "agree with thine adversary quickly, whilst thou art in the way with him," and to seek to modify his attitude by a personal interview. It was one hot August day that found me and an Indian medical assistant riding to this frontier Mecca. It was a part of the district notorious for deeds of violence, and after riding some ten miles, when the hot summer sun made us feel the need of some refreshment, we came to one of those villages where is posted a guard of some twenty Militia Sepoys, who represent the army of the Government in their midst. It was only a roughly-built house, loopholed and strengthened in some parts to simulate a fort, and the soldiers themselves were only removed by a few months' military training, a simple uniform, and the salt of the

Sarkar, which they had eaten, from the families of brigands and highwaymen from which they had been enlisted. There had been a double murder that morning in a village a few miles off, and most of the soldiers were scouring the country round in quest of the marauders; but, as usually happens, the murderers had got a good start, and were already probably well across the frontier. When the soldiers who remained in charge found that it was the Bannu *Daktar Sahib* who had come so suddenly upon them, they were all attention. Tea was brewed, and milk and unleavened cakes were fetched from the village, while men suffering from ague and women bringing their children suffering from various ailments to which Afghan children are liable soon came crowding in, and a little store of medicines that we had carried on our saddles was in great request.

After refreshing ourselves with their simple hospitality, and chatting with them on the various subjects which come most naturally to travellers and to missionaries, we tightened our saddle-girths, which had been loosened to give the horses a feed, mounted, and rode on. The road lay through a wide and picturesque valley. A small river was dashing into silver spray over the boulders on some steep descent, and elsewhere deepening into some pool overshadowed by acacias and oleanders, where the fish could be seen disporting themselves on the shingly bottom. The sides of the valley rose up to right and left in rough escarpments, where the olive and the gurguri-berry gave a clothing of green to the bare rocks, while here and there the hills receded sufficiently to enable the thrifty husbandman to clear a little piece of land from stones and to plant it with millet, which in good seasons would supply his household with bread through the winter months.

After a couple of hours of such riding, we approached the watershed of the valley, northward of which the streams flowed in the opposite direction towards the Miranzai and the Kurram. It was one of those wide stony plains called in Afghanistan *raghzas*, covered for the most part with stones stained black by oxides of iron and manganese, and called by the people *dozakhi kanrai*, or "hell-stones," from their tradition that they were thrown there in some ancient conflict between the devils and the angels. The coarse grass springs up in tufts between the stones, and affords a pasturage to the flocks of hardy goats and sheep. Shepherds may be seen here and there guarding and attending them, while in parts there may be sufficient soil to give in a rainy season a fair crop of millet or of barley. Before long we descried four tall minarets rising up beyond an undulation of the plain. This was our first view of the famed cathedral of this Canterbury of the frontier where the Mullah Karbogha held his court and issued his decrees and excommunications, which carried dismay into any hapless chief's home or village against whom they had been fulminated. As we drew near we met various other travellers, who had come, it may be, to bear the Mullah their respects and some votive offerings, or it may be to bring some long-standing dispute for settlement. We wondered within ourselves what the result of our pilgrimage would be.

As we drew near we got a fine view of the really beautiful and artistic mosque which the offerings of the faithful had enabled the Mullah to build at no little cost in this wild region, where both skilled labour and building material were at a premium. There was a beautiful tank of clear limpid water, supplied by a fountain in the hill above, and here the faithful performed their ablutions before worship. Some of the *talibs* and Sheikhs were sitting round the tank and in the courtyard of the mosque, and appeared not a little surprised to see the Bannu *Daktar Sahib* come to their own Mecca. We were informed that the Mullah himself had gone to a neighbouring village to decide some dispute, but two of the sons came out to receive us, and led us into a verandah, where we were soon surrounded by the curious of the place. They led our horses away with the promise to look after their needs, and inquired as to the reason of our unexpected arrival.

We told them how the fame of the Mullah Karbogha had reached Bannu, and how we had long been desirous of ourselves making his personal acquaintance. After some hesitation, the Mullah's eldest son, who was the chief in authority during his absence, asked if he should bring us refreshments. This was what we wished, not so much because the hot August sun had made us both tired and thirsty, but because it had a deeper signification; for, after having once offered us hospitality and broken bread with us, we should be recognized as guests of the Mullah, and any opposition which he might have been contemplating against us would be seen at once by the observant Afghans around to have been laid aside in favour of the reception due to an honoured guest. We therefore accepted the offer without demur, and tea sweetened with plenty of sugar and flavoured with cardamoms was brought, with biscuits, for our refection. Our repast over, and various questions asked and answered, we were left for a time to ourselves, for in the hot summer days of India the noonday hours are as sacred to retirement and repose as those of midnight.

After a few hours' interval, wherein we were left to rest ourselves, the Mullahs returned and commenced conversation somewhat more affably. They had no doubt found themselves between the horns of a dilemma, for their outward rejection of our advances might have led to acts of open violence on the part of the fanatical inhabitants of the town, the responsibility for which would ultimately have come home to themselves in a way far from pleasant; while, on the other hand, our reception as guests broke down their attitude of hostility, as at once it would be noised all down the countryside that the great Mullah had broken the bread of friendship with the *Daktar Sahib* from Bannu, and among the Afghans the relationship between host and guest is inviolable. Thus, it came about that on our host making inquiries as to where we intended to spend the night, and finding that we had no other plans, he insisted on our stopping as his guests, and there and then sent his servants for the preparation of our lodging and our evening repast. The ice thus broken, we were able to proceed from general topics to the more abstruse theological speculations, in which his reverence excelled, and, like a summer shower, this friendly interchange of ideas washed away the dust of many old prejudices and misunderstandings, and as the evening hours drew on our talk continued under the starlit canopy of the glorious Eastern night, and we were vowing mutual friendship, and he promising on his own behalf and on that of his father himself to become our guests on the next occasion of a visit to Bannu. When at last we lay down to rest, we first thanked God, who had so prospered our journey, and broken down the great barrier of prejudice, and opened a way for us to carry on our work in the villages round.

Many of the people still looked askance at us, and spoke of us as "infidels" and "blasphemers," and would, no doubt, have been led to proceed further at a hint from the Mullahs; but our mission had been accepted, and we knew it was only a matter of time that we should be actually welcomed. Even now, grown bolder by the attitude of the Mullah, some old patients appeared, and insisted on our accompanying them to various houses in the village where there were patients in need of medical help and advice. One cannot overestimate the religious influences emanating from a place like Karbogha. Numbers of religious students are attracted there by the fame of the Mullah even from distant places on both sides of the border, and the offerings of the faithful enable the Mullah to give a free-handed hospitality to one and all, and in Afghanistan there is no quicker road to influence than the ability to do this. It was a tradition in the villages round that when the Mullah daily prepared his saucepans of rice and cakes of unleavened bread in his kitchens, the amount was always found to be sufficient for the pilgrims of that day, even though hundreds might come in before night, unexpected and unprepared for.

After imbibing not only his theological teaching, but his religious and political ideals, these students are scattered far and wide from Kabul to Peshawur, and from Zwat to Waziristan, where they become his staunch adherents against rival Mullahs or against a materialistic Government. The more fanatical of these Mullahs do not hesitate to incite their pupils to acts of religious fanaticism, or *ghaza*, as it is called. The *ghazi* is a man who has taken an oath to kill some non-Muhammadan, preferably a European, as representing the ruling race; but, failing that, a Hindu or a Sikh is a lawful object of his fanaticism. The Mullah instils into him the idea that if in so doing he loses his own life, he goes at once to Paradise, and enjoys the special delights of the *houris* and the gardens which are set apart for religious martyrs. When such a disciple has been worked up to the requisite degree of religious excitement, he is usually further fortified by copious draughts of *bhang*, or Indian hemp, which produces a kind of intoxication in which one sees everything red, and the bullet and the bayonet have no longer any terror for him. Not a year passes on the frontier but some young officer falls a victim to one of these *ghazi* fanatics. Probably the *ghazi* has never seen him before in his life, and can have no grudge against him as a man; but he is a "dog and a heretic," and his death a sure road to Paradise.

One summer afternoon in Bannu I went out with some of our schoolboys who were training for the mile race in the coming school tournament. I was accompanying them on my bicycle as they were running round the polo-ground, where some officers of the garrison were enjoying a game of golf. Suddenly a young Afghan of some eighteen summers, who had been able to arm himself with no more formidable weapon than a sharp axe, rushed up to one of the officers, and, before he could realize what was coming, dealt him a violent blow across the neck. The officer partly shielded himself with his golf-club, and probably thereby saved his life, for the axe came within a hair-breadth of severing the main arteries, and before the fanatic could deal another stroke he was felled to the ground by a blow from another officer with his golf-club. He was only a village youth, with little knowledge of the world, but had been incited to this act of suicidal fanaticism by a Mullah, who, without the grit to become a martyr himself, thought it an act of piety to incite the ignorant boy to the murder of an innocent fellow-creature at the sacrifice of his own life. In this case it became known who the Mullah in question was, and which was the mosque in which he had given this teaching, and while the boy himself suffered the extreme penalty of the law, the Mullah and the mosque were not exempted from its operation. The former was transported to the Andamans and the latter dismantled. Still, it is well known that other Mullahs are daily engaged in the same teaching on both sides of the frontier, and other young bloods are equally desirous of obtaining the sweets of martyrdom.

CHAPTER X

A TALE OF A TALIB

Early days—The theological curriculum—Visit to Bannu—A public discussion—New ideas—The forbearance of a native Christian—First acquaintance with Christians—First confession—A lost love—A stern chase—The lost sheep recovered—Bringing his teacher—The Mullah converted—Excommunication—Faithful unto death—Fresh temptations—A vain search—A night quest—The Mullahs circumvented—Dark days—Hope ever.

MUHAMMAD TAIB was born in the village of Thandkoi, in the Peshawur district. His father was a small farmer, a good example of the better sort of Muhammadan of the Yusufzai tribe, thoroughly religious, yet not fanatical, and honest withal. He was careful not only to bring up Muhammad Taib in a knowledge of his religion, but to preserve him from the vices which are rife among the youth of the Pathan villages. Taib's inclinations were towards study, and he showed a great aptitude for books. His father, however, was of the old school, which looked with suspicion on the education of the *feringis*; so it happened with him as with most young men in Afghanistan who desire to cultivate their minds: he became a religious student, or *talib*.

There happened to be a Mullah in the village known as the Khani Mullah, who took a great fancy to young Taib, so he was placed under his tutelage, and passed his days studying Arabic and Persian in the village mosque, while at the same time all the tenets and rites of the religion of Islam were inculcated and explained. A *talib* could, however, never attain the knowledge and experience expected of a Mullah if he were to remain in his own town; he must travel and sit at the feet of several at least of the Mullahs most renowned for their sanctity and learning. So, when young Taib was fifteen years of age, he tied up his few books in a shawl, and set out from home to sit at the feet of the renowned Manki Mullah. The learned man himself would not condescend to teach so immature a pupil, but he was surrounded by his Sheikhs, who acted as his staff, and taught the *talibs* who flocked there from all parts of the country. Besides, here Taib met with Mullahs from Delhi, Lucknow, Bukhara, Kabul, and other far-famed seats of learning, contact with whom could not fail to widen the horizon and enlarge the experience of the pupils who sat around them, and listened to their arguments and dissertations on the various schools of thought, and engaged in wordy polemics, which practised the budding Mullahs in the art of drawing fine theological distinctions on the interpretation of a Hadis or the difference of a vowel point in the Quran.

Of a night the *talibs* would wile the hours away by telling tales of their respective countries or capping verses from the Persian poets. But Taib must travel and visit other Mullahs, too; so it happened that, when seventeen years old, he visited Bannu, and lodged in the mosque of a noted Mullah near the bazaar. One day, when passing down the Bannu bazaar, he saw a crowd, and, going up, he found an animated discussion going on between two Afghans. While one was obviously a Mullah, the other seemed not to be; but with him was a companion dressed as a Mullah, whose face struck Taib as not quite that of any of the Afghan tribes he knew. He began to listen to see if the enigma would be solved, but was still more surprised to find that the argument was as to whether the Injil (Gospel) and Tauret (Pentateuch) should be read by Muhammadans or not. The Mullah was arguing that the books had been abrogated by the mission of Muhammad and the descent of the Quran on that Prophet, saying that, though it was right to read them till Muhammad came, since then it was only lawful to read the Quran. The stranger, on the other hand, pointed out that Muhammad himself expressly referred his followers to the perusal and study of the "former Scriptures," and clinched his argument by quotations from the Quran itself.

Finally, the Mullah, finding himself getting into a dilemma, obtained a release by the artifice with which we are very familiar by now. "It is time for afternoon prayers. I must hurry off, or my prayers will lapse by default," he said; and, folding up his Quran in his shawl, hurried off. Finding their champion gone, another in the crowd called out: "All who are Mussalmans go away; he is no true Mussalman who stops to listen to these *kafirs*. There is no God but God, and Muhammad is the Prophet of God." And then with one voice all the crowd took up the last sentence, and shouted in unison: "La ilaha illa 'llahu, Muhammad rasulu 'llah!" till the bazaar echoed with the sound; and then, with jeers and curses at the two preachers, in which Taib thought it the proper thing to join, the crowd dispersed.

"Who were those two *kafirs?*" said Taib to a Bannuchi *talib* who was walking away with him.

"The one in the dress of a Mullah is a *feringi* whom we call the *Padre Sahib*. He has built a hospital here, where he preaches to the people about *Hazrat 'Esa*, and he has, indeed, misled many; in fact, the other *kafir* who was with him was led astray by him: he is an Afghan from Laghman, and has brought disgrace on the Prophet. May God destroy them both!"

Taib thought here would be good opportunities for acquiring the art of theological polemics, so he came regularly every day with other *talibs* to support the Muslim champion and jeer at the Christians if they appeared at all discomfited. He could not help, however, being struck by the forbearance of the Laghmani, who preserved an equable temper, though the *talibs* tried to excite him by all the opprobrious epithets with which their repertory is so well supplied. He saw, too, that the more difficult their champions found it to answer his arguments, the more they resorted to the expedient of crying him down with derisive shouts and jeers, and he began to have a feeling of sympathy, if not admiration, for him.

Then one day he waited behind till the *talibs* with him had gone, and the Afghan preacher, seeing him lingering, took him by the arm and entered into conversation with him. They went on talking till they reached the mission compound, and Taib accepted the invitation of the preacher to stop the night with him. Instead of finding him a reviler of the Prophet and a miscreant, as he expected, he found that all he said was quite reasonable and free from the rancour which his *talib* friends always introduced into their theological arguments. Then the peace and comfort of a Christian home, where the wife, instead of being a chattel or a drudge, was a real helpmate, opened up new trains of thought in his mind. The Laghmani, too, was a Pathan, like himself, with the same Afghan prejudices and predilections, and yet there was an undefinable something in him, a spirit of self-control and self-abnegation and inward peace of mind, that he did not remember having met with in any Pathan before. In short, Taib, instead of being the guest of one night, as he had at first, not without misgiving, consented to be, stopped on to learn more of the new doctrine and discover the secret of the change that had been effected in the Afghan preacher.

Taib proved an apt pupil, and the natural gentleness and fairness of his character made Christianity all the more attractive to him, and he applied himself with assiduity to the study of the Christian Scriptures, and attended the Christian worship. There were struggles without and doubts within to contend against. His former *talib* companions came in a body to see whether the *Padre Sahib* had kidnapped him, and when they found him stopping in the mission compound of his own freewill abused him and threatened him, but did not succeed in getting him away. One of the chief Bannu Mullahs came and argued with him for hours, telling him he was guilty of mortal sin in even allowing himself to entertain doubts about the truth of Islam. But Taib had become fascinated with the Scriptures, and especially with the teaching of the Gospels, as is often the case with those who have never read them till adult life, and he had no intention of forsaking his host till quite decided one way or the other.

Ultimately he decided that the Prophet Christ must indeed be the Son of God, the very Saviour that He claimed to be, and he asked for baptism. It was thought better to let him wait a few months till he had a maturer knowledge of the doctrines of Christianity, and had shown his sincerity by standing some of the fire of persecution. There was no lack of the latter. When he accompanied us to the bazaar preaching, the foulest abuse was showered on him, and sometimes stones were thrown, and on one occasion, when he was caught alone, he received a beating from some *talibs* and others.

The Bishop of Lahore visited the station about that time, and Muhammad Taib was baptized under the new name of Taib Khan, and was radiant with delight at having been at last admitted to the Christian Church. I was going on a long medical itineration about that time, and he accompanied me, and was zealous in his new-found faith, taking every opportunity of drawing Mullahs and others into conversation about the claims of Christ and the witness of the Quran to Him. Those were perhaps the happiest days he ever experienced.

Then came a new trial. Taib had been betrothed to a girl in his village, and his relations, having heard of his baptism, came to Bannu. In nothing is the honour and *sharm* of the Pathan more nearly touched than in his marital relation, and the taunt that he had lost the *sharm* which every Pathan so dearly loves, came nearer home to him than persecution or loss of land and patrimony. One morning I found that Taib had disappeared. No one knew exactly when or how, but he had been seen with the people from his village the night before, and nothing more was known. I assumed that by inducement or force they had taken him away to his village, and therefore would have gone by the Kohat road; but they had already had at least eight hours' start, and the sun was now declining. However, no time was to be lost, so I got an *ekka*, or native pony-cart, and, taking with me a young Bannuchi convert, Sahib Khan by name, started off in pursuit.

For a long time we could get no news of the fugitives; then, at a village thirty-five miles from Bannu, I was told that some Pathans answering to the description of Taib and his captors had said their afternoon prayers in the mosque there and then gone on. Our pony was too tired to go farther; it was already midnight; the next stage was eleven miles on, and they would certainly leave there before day-break. What was to be done? While we were debating this, we heard the bugle of the tonga with the mails. This runs between Bannu and Kohat every day in the winter and every night in the summer, and accommodates three passengers. If the seats had not been taken, we might go on in this. It so happened that two seats were vacant, so we got in, and soon arrived at the next stage, a village called Banda.

Here we alighted. It was 1 a.m. The village was silent and dark except for the light of the half-moon. On the side of the hill above the village was the village mosque, and we knew that was the most likely place for travellers to lodge; so we passed through the silent village, and, removing our shoes, entered the courtyard of the mosque. Thirteen men were stretched on the ground fast asleep and covered with their *chadars*, the sheet or shawl which an Afghan always carries about him and uses as a girdle or shawl during the day, and wraps himself up in cap-à-pie at night. As Afghans always sleep with their heads covered in their sheet or quilt, we could not recognize the object of our search, and to wake all would mean certain defeat. But the Bannuchies are at home in any night-work requiring stealth, so by the light of the setting moon my companion lifted the corner of the sheet from off the faces of the sleepers without waking any of them, and the last one was Taib himself.

A touch on his shoulder and he was roused, and recognized us. I merely said to him: "Will you come back with me to Bannu?" He answered, "Yes, Sahib," and got up, wound on his turban, and left with us without another word. We had to walk back to Khurram, the village where we had left our pony-cart, and, finding it still there, drove back to Bannu with the lost sheep, found none too soon.

Months now passed in study and in learning the work of a ward assistant in the mission hospital, so that he might be able to earn his own living, and use the opportunities of the mission hospital in working among the Afghans attending it. There was a Mullah in a village not far from Bannu, where he acted as the *imam* and village schoolmaster. At one time Taib had himself been his pupil, and was much attached to him. He had long been desirous of getting this Mullah, his quondam teacher, or *ustad*, to study the claims of Christ, and one day he had visited him with this object. When the Mullah mentioned that he had been suffering from some deafness for some months past, "Come to the mission hospital," said Taib; "the *Padre Sahib* there will certainly cure you."

The Mullah hesitated at first when he heard that every day an address on Christian doctrine was given to the assembled out-patients before they were treated. He thought it hardly seemly that he, a Mullah and an *ustad*, should sit and listen to heretical teaching without being able to protest. However, tales of others who had been under treatment and recovered won the day, and he decided to go. "After all," he said, "I need not listen, and I can say extra prayers to atone for any sin there may be in my going."

He came regularly till the cure was complete, but he did not keep up his intention of not listening to the preacher; in fact, some things that were said riveted his attention, and made him go home and search his Quran, and his curiosity was aroused, and he talked over many things with Taib Khan, and finally came to me to ask me if I would read the Gospels with him. He was careful to say that he had not any intention of becoming a Christian, but merely desired to read them because every Muhammadan regarded them with veneration as the word of God.

The Sermon on the Mount entranced him, and he used to kiss the book and place it on his head, as Muhammadans do with their Quran. He would read by the hour, but as I had not much time to devote to him, he used to betake himself to the room of Taib Khan, and sit there half the day studying the Scriptures. This could not go on, of course; the people of the village heard of it, and said that they must have an *imam* who was free from the suspicion of heresy; he lost his pupils, and at last a Synod of the chief Mullahs of Bannu formally excommunicated him.

He then came to live in the mission compound, and spent some happy months in study, while supporting himself as custodian of the mission bookshop. Seldom have I seen so remarkable a growth of the Christian graces in the character of any of our converts as in this man, and it was a great delight to see him admitted to Christian baptism, already more mature in Christian character than many who had been in the visible Church for years. He bore the most scurrilous abuse with exemplary forbearance, and even when struck, as happened several times when going through the bazaar, forbore to retaliate, which for an Afghan is the acme of self-control.

He was a Seyyid—that is, one who claims descent from Muhammad—and when he came with us to the bazaar preachings, and stood by our side, the people were furious with him, saying that it was bad enough that he, a Mullah and a Seyyid, should have become a Christian, but to parade it there in the bazaar in that shameless way was too much, and if he did not desist they would certainly kill him. I recommended him to abstain from accompanying us to the bazaar preachings, because I feared that the people would indeed put their threat into execution, but he would not hear of it. He had read, he said, that our Lord said He would be ashamed of those who were ashamed of Him before the world, so how could he refrain from showing publicly that he had become a Christian? He would think it an honour if he could obtain the crown of martyrdom for the sake of the Saviour in whom he had believed.

One morning he found an Afghan dagger lying outside his door. We thought perhaps his enemy had come in the night, but had been startled by the night watchman and escaped, dropping his weapon; or it might be that it had been left there to scare him, as much as to say, "That is what is waiting for you if you do not desist." As a precaution I told him not to sleep there any more, but gave him a bed in the house of a native Christian near where I slept myself; for it was summer, and we were all sleeping in the open. Three nights later I was awakened about one o'clock in the morning by the report of a gun, and, running over instinctively to Seyyid Badshah, found the enemy had indeed come and shot him through the stomach.

Everything possible was done for him, but the wound was mortal, and that evening he passed away, his last words being: "O Lord Jesus, I am Thy servant!" There were many moist eyes as we carried Seyyid Badshah to his last resting-place in the little cemetery at Bannu. His had been a very lovable character, and in his short Christian life he had been the means of influencing more than one Afghan towards Christ. One in particular was a Mullah from the Yusufzai country, Abdullah by name; and we sometimes spoke of the "four generations," as in these few years Taib had been brought by the Afghan preacher from Laghman, whose story is given in Chapter XVI.; then Taib had been the instrument in bringing Seyyid Badshah; and through Seyyid Badshah's influence this other Mullah believed.

Taib Khan continued in the work of the mission hospital, but fresh trials were about to test and sift him more severely than ever. The old friend of his boyhood, the Khani Mullah, and some relations came down to Bannu, and while pretending at first to acquiesce in his having become a Christian, recalled to him the memories and associations of his boyhood. He became violently homesick. The old village scenes, his patrimony there only waiting for him to claim, the girl to whom he had been engaged, and whom her parents were, they said, still keeping unmarried in hopes that Taib would recant and claim her—all these old scenes and ideas came to him with such irresistible force that he came to me one day and asked for a month's leave, that he might revisit his village. I well knew the dangers to which he would be exposed, but I sympathized with his homesick state of mind, and knew it would be futile to expect him to stifle it, so I gave him leave, and, warning him of the specious nature of the suggestions and temptations which would be offered to him there, reluctantly parted from him. At the same time I told him that if he did not return at the expiration of the month, I should conclude that something was wrong, and go in search of him.

The month passed, and Taib did not appear, so I started

for Peshawur, and thence to Thandkoi, to get news of him. I took as my companion Azizuddin, an Afghan, who but for his conversion to Christianity would have been a distinguished Mullah, but now was a simple mission catechist. It was a long walk of about seventeen miles from the station to the village, and we were caught in a tropical thunderstorm. Watercourses that had been all but dry an hour before were now surging up to our armpits, and could only be forded with difficulty. We reached the village like drowned rats, and the people were kind to us and dried our clothes and gave us breakfast; but all inquiries as to Taib Khan were fruitless, though someone indeed told us that he had gone to the Akhund of Swat in company with the Khani Mullah. We had to return to Peshawur after a bootless search.

A fortnight later, while on tour in the Kohat district, news was brought me that Taib was again in his village. This time I took a convert from Islam with the very Muhammadan name of Muhammad Hoseïn. Though children born of Christian parents are never given names distinctive of Islam, yet when converts have such names, and are not desirous of changing them, we do not advocate a change of name, because we wish them to feel that the change is a spiritual and not a material one. So Muhammad Hoseïn and I set off, but resolved to proceed more warily than in my previous visit; so, instead of going straight into the village, we sat down by a well outside the neighbouring town of Zaida, and my companion, leaving me there, went into the town to make inquiries. Zaida is a larger and more important place than Thandkoi, and contains many mosques, while the overlord is a well-educated Muhammadan nobleman, an *alumnus* of the Peshawur mission school. He was led to believe that Taib was secreted in one of the mosques there, but would not be allowed to appear except perhaps at night.

He returned to me at the well, and by this time it had

become known who we were, so there was less hope than ever of Taib being allowed to show himself. As evening drew on we made as though we would return to Peshawur, but on reaching the first village on the Peshawur road I let my friend go on alone, while I returned for a night quest. At the same time I told him to wait for me till morning at the ferry over the Kabul River, fifteen miles distant. I bound my turban over my face, as is the custom with Pathans when they wish to be incognito, and, throwing my *lungi*, or shawl, over all, returned to Zaida. I entered the mosques one by one, and finally discovered Taib seated with some Mullahs in one of them. I was still far from the attainment of my object, as to have made myself known to Taib under such conditions would, of course, have been fatal; so I betook myself to the chief of the village above mentioned. He, being in Government service, was away, but his brother received me, and I told him that I had reason to believe that Taib Khan was being kept there against his will, and wished him to call the young man and inquire from him whether he wished to return to Bannu with me or no.

The chief, who had received me with the greatest good-nature, even though he had been roused from his sleep for the purpose, acceded to my request and sent a messenger to have Taib and the other Mullahs called. Taib was much astonished, and apparently ashamed too, when he saw me; but when the chief addressed him, saying, "Do you wish to stop here as a Muhammadan or return with the *Padre Sahib*?" he at once replied: "I will go with the *Padre Sahib*." There was a great clamour from the Mullahs, on the one hand urging Taib not to leave, and reviling him when he persisted, and on the other insisting to the chief that Taib was really a true Muhammadan, and did not want to go, but the eye of the *Padre Sahib* had a mesmeric influence on him, and he should not, as a true Mussulman himself, allow Taib to go away with me.

Both Taib and the chief, however, stood firm, and the chief, turning to me, said: "Now take him away with you, and look better after him in the future; but make haste, and do not loiter on the way. I will see that no one leaves the village for half an hour; after that you must look out for yourselves."

I thanked him for his courtesy, and Taib and I wasted no time on the road, and reached the Kabul River at dawn, just as Muhammad Hoseïn was about to cross over.

Some years passed, and Taib Khan became one of our valued mission workers, and I hoped that he was mature and strong enough to stand any vicissitudes; but often one finds that, while a convert in his first enthusiasm will suffer much for the Gospel's sake, afterwards an inordinate idea of his own power and importance grows upon him, and he falls a victim to the blandishments of false friends who seek his downfall.

So it turned out with Taib Khan: he, like most of the Afghan converts, would not have shrunk from martyrdom, and, in fact, he had already undergone great hardships and sufferings for the Gospel's sake. He was put in joint charge with another Indian Christian of a rather remote dispensary. The Muhammadans of the place became very friendly, and pointed out how needless it was for him to forsake his village, his relations, and the graves of his forefathers just because he wished to be a Christian; let him be a Christian if he liked—it was no doubt written in his fate that he should be so—but let him go and live in his village. With the knowledge that he had acquired of medicine he could easily earn enough to support himself and his wife and child, and besides that he could claim the piece of land that was his by right, if he took the trouble to prove his title to it.

Then followed a spiritual decline. Hypercritical objections to Christianity, which had never troubled him before, were made into excuses for returning more and more to his original

Muhammadan position. Finally he went to live in his village, conforming himself outwardly at least to the Muhammadan standard, though, no doubt, professing in some respects still to have an attachment to the Christian religion. Who is to judge? Even through perverts Christian doctrine continues to permeate the great mass of Islam, and God will undoubtedly bring back His own at the last. So, "undeterred by seeming failure," we work and pray on, leaving the result with Him who knows the hearts of men.

CHAPTER XI

SCHOOL-WORK

Different views of educational work—The changed attitude of the Mullahs—His Majesty the Amir and education—Dangers of secular education—The mission hostel—India emphatically religious—Indian schoolboys contrasted with English schoolboys—School and marriage—Advantage of personal contact—Uses of a swimming-tank—An unpromising scholar—Unwelcome discipline—A ward of court—Morning prayers—An Afghan University—A cricket-match—An exciting finish—A sad sequel—An officer's funeral—A contrast—Just in time.

THERE are four attitudes towards educational work: that of the people at large, who desire learning, not usually for learning's sake, but because that is the portal of Government preferment and commercial success; that of the priests and religious-conservative element, who oppose it tooth and nail as subversive of the old religious ideas and priestly power; that of the missionary, who finds therein his vantage-ground for familiarizing the intelligent and influential section of the people with the doctrines and ideals of the Christian religion; and that of the Government, which, indifferent alike to the motives of the missionary and the opposition of the Mullahs, requires educated young men for administrative posts, and believes that education eclipses fanaticism.

"Any parent sending his son to the mission school will be excommunicated" was the *fatwa* of the Mullahs at Bannu when the mission school was inaugurated; the delinquent would be unable to get priestly assistance for marriage, for burial, or for the other rites so essential to a Muhammadan's religious safety. But parents and boys alike were desirous of availing themselves of the advantages of the school, so the Mullahs relented, and said: "Let the boys go to school, but beware lest they learn English, for English is the language of infidelity, and will certainly destroy their souls." But without English all the best Government appointments were unattainable, and their boys would have to be content with inferior posts and inferior pay; so pressure was again brought to bear on the Mullahs, and the fiat went forth: "Let the boys read English, so long as they do not read the Christian Scriptures, for the Christians have tampered with those books, and it is no longer lawful for true Muhammadans to read them."

Again a little patience and a little gaining of confidence, and the Mullahs tacitly retracted this restriction too, and now many of the most prominent Mullahs themselves send their sons to the mission school. The Muhammadan lads compete zealously with the others for the Scripture prizes, and in 1907 two Muhammadan officials gave prizes to be awarded to the boys who were most proficient in Scripture in the matriculation class. *Sic tempora mutantur!*

A significant occurrence was the visit of His Majesty the Amir of Afghanistan to the Islamic College at Lahore, when he made a speech, in which he reiterated the advice: "Acquire knowledge! acquire knowledge! acquire knowledge!" and went on to say that if they had been previously well grounded in their religion they need not fear lest the study of Western science might overthrow their beliefs or undermine their faith.

Thus most of the Muhammadan boys in our school have already studied the Quran in a mosque, and many continue to receive religious teaching from their Mullah while studying in school. Thus they enter school at an older age than the Hindu students, who, except in family life, take little count of their religion, and slight their priests. The danger is obvious: faith in the old order is lost, and there is nothing but a conceited and bumptious materialism to take its place.

Here it is that the mission school holds the advantage of the Government institution. The latter, in the endeavour to be impartial, excludes all religious teaching, and therewith loses the most valuable means of moral training. The mission school, on the other hand, gives special prominence to religious and moral training, which go hand-in-hand. "I prefer sending my son to the mission school," said a Muhammadan father to me once, "because he will be taught the religious incentives to moral conduct there, and I shall not be afraid of his character losing its moral balance." And this was said by a man thoroughly orthodox and zealous in his own religion. There can be no doubt that a far smaller proportion of the students in mission schools and colleges lose the religious instinct of their forefathers, and it is often the loss of this which results in moral instability and ruin.

"I never took an interest in studying my own religion till I was taught Scripture in the mission school," said a pupil to me; and, of course, we encourage the boys not only to perform the religious duties inculcated by their own religion, but to study it thoughtfully, and see how far it satisfies the aspirations of their souls. A visitor to our school hostel of an early morning would find the Muhammadans saying their prayers and the Hindus their devotions, and we encourage this, and give facilities for it by setting apart places for its performance, because it is a terrible thing to take away a boy's faith, even though it be a faith in a mistaken creed, and I think the man who has argued or bantered a young fellow out of his faith without bringing him to a higher faith has incurred a grave responsibility. The real enemy of the Christian faith is not so much Islam or Hinduism, but infidelity and a gross materialism.

It is not education that is to blame for the unrest, sedition, and materialism which threatens to engulf India, but the

Government system of education has undoubtedly much to answer for. God is ignored in Government schools, prayer is proscribed, and the teachings of English socialistic and materialistic philosophers are poured into the capacious but untrained minds of the students. The result is mental intoxication and libertinism. India has always been religious to the core, and learning and religion have gone hand-in-hand. The result of their divorce is destructive to moral stability, and the Nemesis of the policy will pursue the country for years, even if, as is to be hoped, the policy itself be discontinued.

When I first went to India I had a prejudice against mission schools, and protested against a medical missionary having to superintend one; but I have become convinced that the hope of India is in her mission colleges and schools, for it is in their *alumni* that we find young men who have been able to acquire Western knowledge without losing the religious spirit, learning without moral atrophy, mental nobility without a conceited mien and disrespect for their parents, and breadth of view without disloyalty and sedition. I should like to see the Government close all their schools and colleges except those for primary and technical education, and devote the money saved to the encouragement of private effort on lines more germane to the spirit of the country.

The Indian student is an attractive personality and well worth sympathetic study, for he is the future of the country in embryo. The schoolboy has not yet lost the ancient Indian respect, even love, of the pupil to the master, and is therefore much more readily subjected to discipline than his English counterpart. His chief failing is his incorrigible propensity to what is known in English schools as "sneaking"; schoolboy honour and *esprit de corps* are being developed in mission schools, but have very little basis on which to build. "Please, sir, Mahtab Din has been pinching me." "Shuja'at 'Ali has stolen my book." "Ram Chand has spilt the ink on my copy-book." If the master is willing to listen to tales of this kind, he will get a continuous supply of them all day long.

There are few boys who are not ready, by fair means or foul, to use a master for paying off a grudge against a fellow-student, and as the schemes are often deeply laid and the schemers very plausible, the master has to be very much "all there," or, on the plea of maintaining discipline, he will be merely a tool in a personal quarrel. Once two or three of the senior students came to bring to me serious charges against the moral character of one of the junior masters. They were *prima facie* well substantiated by witnesses, but on further investigation it turned out that the whole affair had been engineered merely because the master had broken up an undesirable clique of theirs. Such habits have, of course, to be sternly repressed.

There is much greater diversity in the social status of the boys in an Indian school than in English schools. In the Bannu Mission School every class of the community is represented—from the son of the rich landowner to that of the labourer, from the Brahmin to the outcast—and not only do they get on well together, without the poor boy having to feel by taunt or treatment that he is unwelcome or despised, but I have often come across genuine acts of charity which have been done quite naturally and without any ostentation; in fact, they tried to keep it secret in more cases than one. Thus, a poor boy, unable to buy his books, has had them supplied to him by the richer boys in the class. In one case a poor boy was left quite destitute by the death of his father, and some of the boys arranged a small subscription month by month to enable him to remain at school.

The Bannu school course commences in the infant class, where little toddles of five summers sit on grass-mats and learn their alphabet, to the big lads of eighteen in the fifth form, who are preparing for the matriculation of the

Punjab University. Visitors are sometimes surprised to be told that many of the boys in this class are married and have children, but such is unfortunately still the case. At one time even much younger boys married, but a school law was passed that any pupil marrying under the age of sixteen would be expelled. Since then some twenty or more boys have had to leave because their parents, usually much against the boys' will, insisted on getting them married below this age. But many marriages have been postponed, and there is a healthier public feeling against early marriage, and we hope that before long there will be no married boys in the school at all.

I place great importance on the influence of the school hostels. These are the boarding-houses where those students whose homes are in the remoter parts of the district reside, and the contrast between our raw material, the uncouth, prejudiced village lad, and the finished product, the gentlemanly, affectionate student who is about to leave us, is an object-lesson in itself. The boarders, though comparatively few in number, are really the nucleus of the school, and take a prominent part in matches and in school life in general quite out of proportion to their numbers. The missionary is constantly in contact with them, and they come to him at all seasons, till the relationship is more like that of a father to his family than of a master to his students. Such students leave the hostel with friendly feelings towards Christians and Englishmen, which show themselves in after-years in the hospitable and hearty reception which they accord not only to the missionary, but to others who may be visiting their village.

There is a swimming-tank attached to the hostel, and the boys bathe every morning except in the coldest winter months, when they bathe at the well, where the water is several degrees warmer. Woe betide the boy who is found asleep after sunrise! for should the manager come round and find him so, he is hauled out by two of the monitors, who, seizing him by hands and feet, toss him far into the swimming-tank before he quite knows whether he is dreaming or awake. A similar punishment is inflicted on a boy using foul language, who is thrown in, clothes and all, for purification from its stain. At one time visitors often got opportunities of seeing the punishment inflicted, but it is getting rarer now as the standard rises.

A strange fragment of frontier boyhood was Amal Khan. He was brought down to us from Afghanistan by a friendly *Sardar*, who had taken an interest in him. He was only about eleven years old, but his father and most of his family had been killed in vendettas, and his ruling passion was to grow big and strong, buy a rifle, and go in quest of the murderers or their relatives. His gentle little face and winsome manner seemed so out of keeping with the cold bloodthirstiness of the remarks he used to make with the greatest *naïveté* that he was looked on as a kind of curiosity. Later on, when he had made some acquaintance with Scripture, he used to like to hear the Gospel stories of the gentleness of Jesus—the Good Shepherd, the miracles of compassion, the parable of the Good Samaritan, and such like; but even then the passion for revenge seemed to dominate his little breast, and he finally went back to his village across the Afghan border in order to apply himself more seriously to the object of his fate.

Once a well-to-do Afghan brought down his three sons to place them in our hostel, and told me I might use any means I liked to discipline them, short of shooting them. He had evidently found them too much of a handful himself. They had been accustomed to run wild in a wild country, and any idea of sitting still in a classroom to learn lessons seemed to have never entered their heads. They seemed so accustomed to the use of knife and revolver that the other boys, Afghans though they were, came to ask me to take precautions for their safety. Finally, when I had to "discipline" them, and that was not before very long, they all three disappeared, and I never saw them till, some years later, I visited their village.

Once a Government civilian wrote asking me to take a young ward of court into my hostel. The account of him was not promising, as, though only sixteen, he had been turned out of two schools for misconduct. His family was of noble Afghan descent, but had been bereft of most of its male members owing to the wretched blood-feuds, and this boy was now the head of the family. Hoping to be able yet to save him and to make him a power for good instead of for evil, as he must by his position become one or other, I consented, and a day was appointed for his admission. The day passed, but the boy did not appear. I then got a letter from the officer responsible for him, saying that as he had just murdered his younger brother, the hope of his schooling must be abandoned.

Some of the masters of the little Government primary schools in the more remote parts lead very unenviable lives, especially if they happen to be Hindus. Their pupils often defy their authority, and they are afraid to chastise them. I have myself seen a boy allowed to sit in class with a loaded revolver in his belt. The unwillingness of the master to enforce his authority is excusable, yet, had he complained, he would merely have lost his place and his pittance. On another occasion I came upon a poor Hindu schoolmaster in a certain village who was about to send in his resignation. He had punished a boy for playing truant, and the father had just been round with a loaded rifle and dared him to touch his son again.

In the mission school the work of the day commences with roll-call, at which a portion of Scripture is read by the head-master, and the Lord's Prayer repeated. During the latter the boys have to stand. They do not object to this, but I remember once a Hindu boy being accused of having become a Christian because he had shut his eyes and folded his hands during the prayer. He told me that many of the boys really joined in the prayer, and certainly they have got to value and appreciate prayer. On a Sunday evening the boarders come to my house to sing hymns from "Sacred Songs and Solos" and vernacular collections, and if I omit to offer the usual prayer at the close, they remind me of the omission; they do not wish to go away without it.

Once, at a cricket-match with a rival school, when the issue of the game was hanging in the balance, and depended on the last man, who had just gone in, making four runs, a Muhammadan Afghan, one of the eleven, retired to a corner of the field and repeated the Lord's Prayer, closing it with a petition for the victory of the school, and returned to find the winning run just made! At meetings of the schoolboys among themselves it is not uncommon for prayer to be offered by one of the number, and at a farewell dinner given me in 1908 by some pupils a very beautiful and touching prayer was offered by an old Hindu student, now reading in the Lahore Medical College, and all the other Muhammadans, Hindus, and Christians stood up for it.

Missionaries were the first to open schools on modern lines, but at the present time Muhammadans, Hindus, and Sikhs are endowing their own schools and colleges on the most lavish scale, and teaching their own religions therein, just as the mission schools teach Christianity. This certainly has many advantages over the Government system, where religion is ignored. His Majesty the Amir of Afghanistan is alive to the necessity of keeping up with the times, and is founding a college on modern lines at Kabul, which will be the first step towards the foundation of an Afghan University. During his recent visit to India he selected a number of trained Muhammadan graduates from Lahore and elsewhere, who are to inaugurate the new scheme. He will, no doubt, encounter the opposition of some of the more fanatical Mullahs, who already look upon him as having been contaminated with many Western and heretical ideas; but the ultimate result will be good, and the attempt shows that even for Afghanistan a new era is approaching. Perhaps it may not be long before a mission school at Kabul will receive the royal sanction.

The following episode I relate in this place because it shows the striking contrast between the uneducated *ghazi* fanatic of the hills and young men of the same race and antecedents who have passed through the humanizing and civilizing influences of a mission school.

It is a lovely autumn afternoon in the little frontier town of Bannu. The trees round the recreation-ground between the city and cantonments are becoming sere and showing variegated tints of yellow and brown. There is an unusual crowd round the greensward which forms the station cricket-pitch, and as it is Friday, the Bannu market-day, a number of Wazirs and other hillmen who are coming to and from market stop for a few minutes to gaze on the scene that lies before them, and probably to wonder in their minds what mysterious ultimate object the *Feringis* have in the evolutions they are watching enacted, or whether it is some preliminary to military operations on their own hill fastnesses.

Turning to the recreation-ground itself, we find that it is a cricket-match between the garrison officers and the Mission High School students. The boys have been stealing a number of runs, and their score is beginning to draw on towards a century, when the officers put on a new slow bowler, and a succession of unwary batsmen fall victims to his wiles, and soon the innings is over with a score of eighty-eight. The officers begin to bat, and the score rises rapidly; then some good catches send several players back to the pavilion (here represented by some shady shisham-trees). The score reaches eighty-eight, and the last player goes in, a young fair-haired boy, the son of the slow bowler; the winning run is made, and the boy caught at point next ball, and the innings is over.

Just one week has passed. Again it is market-day, but no tribesmen can be seen anywhere near the recreation-ground; instead we see long lines of khaki-dressed native infantry, while sentries and patrols guard all the roads leading thereto, and all is silent as the grave. Then we see a long procession slowly, silently moving out of the fort, long ranks of native infantry—Sikh, Pathan, and Punjabi Mussulmans—with slow, measured tread and arms reversed; then a gun-carriage surmounted by a coffin covered with the Union Jack and wreaths, the masterless steed, the mourners; a group of sunburnt officers of the Frontier Force and some more troops bring up the rear. It is the funeral of a distinguished frontier officer, and the slow bowler of last Friday, now borne to his last resting-place, the victim of a dastardly *ghazi* outrage the day before.

Just facing the cricket-ground is a shady and flowery patch of ground, enclosed by a simple brick wall and containing a number of white tombstones. Here lie many gallant officers, military and civil—some killed in action; others, like the present Captain Donaldson, killed by religious fanatics in Bannu and the neighbourhood while in the execution of their duties; others, again, carried off by pestilence and disease. Here, too, in lowlier grass-grown graves, lie a number of the native Christian community. East and West, high and low, all gathered in one small plot, covered with the same Mother Earth to await their common resurrection—so glorious in its expectations for some, so dread in its possibilities for others.

Here, just facing the now deserted cricket-ground, the long procession halts; the chaplain, just arrived after a hasty drive of ninety miles from Dera Ismaïl Khan, begins to recite the solemn verses of the Burial Service, and the booted and spurred officers do their last brotherly service and shoulder their comrade's coffin from the gun-carriage to the grave. The strains of the "Last Post" sound forth—a shrill call to the sombre mountains round as the last rays of the setting sun fall slanting through the foliage on the faces of the mourners; some sharp words of command ring forth from a native officer; the troops wheel about, and all is solitude and silence.

Only the day before a new regiment was to arrive in Bannu, and, as the custom is, the station regiments were marching out with their band to welcome them in. At the head of the regiment a group of officers were riding, including the officer commanding the district, Colonel Aylmer, V.C., and his Brigade-Major, Captain Donaldson. Just beyond the fort the road narrows a little to pass over a culvert, and the officer on the outside of Captain Donaldson fell back a little to make room for him.

Behind that culvert a Mahsud Wazir was in hiding, determined to kill an infidel and gain a martyrdom in the most sensational manner possible, so that for many an evening in years to come the tribal bards might sing his praises round the camp-fires and in the village *chauks*. Just as Captain Donaldson, now on the outside rank, came abreast of him, he sprang out; a pistol shot rang through the air, and the officer fell mortally wounded. There was, of course, no escape for the Mahsud; bullet and bayonet at once disabled him, though he lived long enough to be hanged that afternoon. Our first feelings are those of horror at the enormity of the act—killing a stranger who has never seen or injured him — but who is worthy of our severer judgment, this young and ignorant soldier (for he had recently served in the Border Militia), thirsting for religious fame by a deed of daring, or the Muhammadan priest who had assiduously taught him that all *Feringis* were *kafirs*, and that to kill one of them, in no matter how dastardly a manner, was a sure passport to Paradise, and that eternal joys were awaiting him as the reward of the valour and righteousness of his deed? Here, at any rate, we see the two extremes—the gentlemanly Afghan from the mission school, entering with zest and sport into the game of cricket with the officers, and, so far from feeling any resentment towards them, ready, if need be, to fight with them shoulder to shoulder in the common cause of humanity, under the same flag, and defend them with their own blood from the fanaticism of their fellow-countrymen; on the other hand, the fanatical tool of the Mullah, who quails before his *ex-cathedrâ* denunciations, but is ready at his suggestion to meet a bloody death as a martyr in the cause of his religion.

As an example of the former, I might mention Muzaffar Khan, an old student of the Bannu Mission School, who risked his life to save that of the Political Officer of the Tochi Valley, with whom he was on tour. While that officer was viewing a Muhammadan shrine a fanatic rushed out and ran a dagger into his body; but, quick as thought, Muzaffar Khan threw himself on the would-be murderer and dragged him back before he had been able to inflict a fatal wound. The *ghazi* was secured and hanged soon after, while the officer recovered, the stab having just missed a vital part, although it had pierced right through his body.

Yet, but for the mission school, Muzaffar Khan might have been the *ghazi* himself. Race and religion were the same, but their environments had been different.

CHAPTER XII

AN AFGHAN FOOTBALL TEAM

Native sport—Tent-pegging—A novel game—A football tournament—A victory for Bannu—Increasing popularity of English games—A tour through India—Football under difficulties—Welcome at Hyderabad—An unexpected defeat—Matches at Bombay and Karachi—Riots in Calcutta—An unprovoked assault—The Calcutta police-court—Reparation—Home again.

The reader must imagine himself on a flat open piece of ground covered by the hard alluvial earth known in the Panjab as *pat*. This kind of earth is somewhat saline, and has a universally smooth surface, unbroken by grass or shrub, which is utilized by the villagers for their games and fairs, and by the British for the evolutions of their troops. Around are a number of Bannu villages, but the men and children have all collected round this piece of ground in their gala-day attire, for it is the Day of the Feast, "'Id-el-fitr," or the Breaking of the Fast, following the month of Ramazan, and is to be celebrated as usual by sports and merry-making. All the men who own or can borrow a horse are mounted upon steeds of all descriptions, more or less richly caparisoned, according to the ability of the owner. Saddles are of the high-backed pattern universally used in Afghanistan, with a long wooden croup, which helps the rider to retain his seat. They are all carrying the long bamboo iron-tipped lance for their national sport of tent-pegging, or *nezabazi*, as the Afghans call it. Some of the boys who are there as spectators are mounted two or even three on a horse, and others, mounted on riding camels, are able to get a good view of the games over the heads of the others.

The pegs, cut out of the wood of the date-palm, are fixed in the ground, three or four abreast, so that an equal number of horsemen may be able to compete simultaneously. The competitors, with their embroidered turbans and gay, many-coloured coats and shawls, form a brave show at one end of the course, as they pass the intervening time in showing off feats of horsemanship on their prancing chargers. Then, at a given word, three or four strike their heels into the horses' sides—for they wear no spurs—and as often as not rousing their own excitement and that of their horses by shouting out the Muhammadan *Kalimah* ("La ilaha illa 'llahu, Muhammadun rasulu 'llah"), career wildly down on the pegs, and, if successful, gallop on triumphantly, waving the peg at the end of their lances.

This goes on till men and horses are weary, and then a new game commences. This is known as *tod* or *kari*. The people form a large circle; then some young athlete, stripped except for his loin-cloth, tied tightly round, or secured by a leather waistband, jumps lightly out into the arena, his muscular frame showing to advantage as he contracts his muscles under his glossy, well-oiled skin. Two other athletes, similar in attire and appearance, answer his challenge from the party on the opposite side. The endeavour of the challenger is to avoid capture, while yet allowing the pursuers to come near enough for him to give them at least three slaps with the open hand; while the pursuers in their turn try to seize him and throw him on to the ground, in which case they are adjudged the winners, and a fresh challenger comes forth. Both sides are apt to get very excited, and the throws are often so violent that bones are broken, or other injuries received; and if that side believes this to be due to malice prepense, the game not unfrequently terminates in a free fight.

A FOOTBALL MATCH AT BANNU

THE BANNU FOOTBALL TEAM
Five of whom were nearly killed in Bombay.

These amusements and games go on until nightfall, when they may be followed by some fireworks, and competitors and spectators, both equally wearied, go home to their feast of *pulao* and *halwa*. Such scenes have no doubt been common in Afghanistan for centuries past, but the reader must now come with me to a different scene, and he will see how Western influences are changing even the sports of the people.

This time we are in a large grassy sward between Bannu city and the cantonments. There is a crowd, as before, of some thousands of spectators, but the football goal-posts and flags show that the game is something different. It is the day of the provincial tournament of all the schools of the province, and teams of the various frontier schools from Peshawur, Kohat, Dera Ismaïl Khan, as well as those of Bannu, have collected here to pit their skill and prowess against one another in games and athletics. The referee, an English officer from the garrison, has blown his whistle, and the youthful champions come out, amid the cheers of their supporters, from the opposite sides of the ground. The Bannu team are somewhat smaller in stature, and are wearing a uniform of the school colours—pink "shorts" and light blue shirts. The Peshawur team are heavier in build, and are wearing their blue-and-black uniform. The referee blows his whistle again, and both sides are exerting all their powers to reach their adversaries' goal.

As the ball travels up and down, and the chances of one or other side appear in the ascendant, the cheers from their supporters redouble, and as goals are attempted and gained or lost the excitement of all the spectators is not less than may be witnessed at a similar match in England. The captain of the Bannu side is a native Christian, whose father is a convert from Muhammadanism; but the other Muhammadans and Hindus in his team are loyal to him to the backbone, and carry out his every order with that alacrity which displays the new *esprit de corps* which has developed in our mission schools.

On his outside left is a young Hindu, who carries the ball past the opposing half-backs and backs right up to the corner, from which he centres with great skill to the captain. The captain is, however, being marked by the other opposing back, so he passes to a Muhammadan lad on his inside right, and then the whole line of forwards—Muhammadan, Hindu, and Christian — rush the ball through the goal, amid the triumphant cheers of their side.

The game is restarted, and Peshawur makes a number of desperate rallies and skilful rushes, which, however, are all foiled by the vigilance of the Bannu backs and the agility of the goal-keeper, a tall Muhammadan lad, whose weight and height both tell in his favour. Once one of the Peshawur forwards brought the ball right up to the mouth of the goal. The Bannu custodian seized it, but the Peshawari was upon him. The goal-keeper held the ball securely, awaited the charge of the Peshawari, who bounded back off him as from a wall, and then cleared the ball with his fist far up the field to the Bannu left half. The whistle for "time" is sounded, and the Bannu boys rush into the field and carry off their victorious school-fellows shoulder high, amid great clapping and cheering.

The next day the final cricket-match is held. In this the Dera Ismaïl Khan boys are pitted against one of the Peshawur teams. Peshawur has already defeated Bannu and Kohat, and the Dera Ismaïl Khan boys have disposed of the other Peshawur team. All the technicalities of the game are observed with as much punctiliousness as in England, and their white flannels show off well under the bright Indian sun, and but for their dark faces and bare feet one might imagine that he was watching a public school match in England. To-day the laurels rest with Dera Ismaïl Khan, and they triumphantly bear off a belt with silver shields awarded annually to the winning team.

The old order changes and gives place to the new. Tent-pegging will always retain its charm, with its brave show and splendid opportunities for the display of manly courage and dextrous horsemanship, so dear to a militant nation like the Afghans, and will always remain their favourite pastime. But the simpler native games are gradually giving place to the superior attractions of cricket and football, and the tournaments which of recent years have been organized between the various native regiments and between the different tribes inhabiting each district and between the schools of the provinces are doing much to create a spirit of friendly rivalry, and to develop among these frontier people a fascination for those sports which have done so much to make England what she is. Some tribes among the Afghans, such as the Marwats, are very stay-at-home, and soon become homesick if they enlist in a regiment or undertake a journey. Others, like the Povindahs, are perhaps the greatest overland merchants of the East. They travel down from their mountains in Khorasan, through the passes in the North-West Frontier, and traverse with their merchandise the length and breadth of India, and numbers of them engaged in the trade in camels cross over the seas to Australia and take service there.

With the idea of developing the *esprit de corps* of the school, and gratifying their love of travel, while at the same time conferring on them the benefits of a well-planned educational tour through the chief cities of India, I arranged in the summer of 1906 to take the football team of the Mission High School at Bannu on a tour through a great part of Northern India. A number of colleges and schools from Calcutta to Karachi not only accepted our challenge for football matches, but offered us hospitality for such time as we should be in their town. Our team represented all classes—Muhammadans, Hindus, native Christians, and Sikhs. The captain of the team was an Afghan lad of the Khattak tribe, Shah Jahan Khan by name, while the vice-captain was a native Christian, James Benjamin. Various difficulties presented themselves, but all were eventually successfully surmounted. Stress of work and school duties compelled us to make the tour in the slacker time of the year—viz., in July, August, and September. This was also the hottest time in most of the places we visited, and some of the matches were played in a temperature bordering on 100° F., while the spectators were sitting under punkahs.

At this time of year the River Indus is in full flood, and presents a remarkable sight as, bursting forth from its rocky defile at Kalabagh, it spreads out over the flat alluvial plain of the Western Panjab. In the winter it may be confined to one, two, or three channels, each about one to four hundred yards wide; but in the early summer, swollen by the melting snows of the Himalayas, it overflows its banks, and not infrequently forms a wide expanse of water ten miles broad from bank to bank. At such a time the villages, which are built on the more raised areas of its bed, appear as little islands scattered here and there, the people of which get to and from the mainland in their boats. It is then that the *tonga*, or cart, has often to be dragged over miles of submerged road, with water from one to three feet deep, before it reaches the place where it is able to transfer its passengers and burden to the ferry-boats, which are waiting to carry them across the deeper portions of the river, and it may be that several changes from boat to cart and cart to boat have to be made before the traveller attains the farther shore, where is the railway-station and the train waiting to carry him down to Karachi or up to Lahore.

In our case, after getting across the main stream in the ferry-boat, we put our luggage into two carts, and, removing our superfluous clothing, started to trudge through the inundated country to the station of Darya Khan, on the eastern bank. Sometimes there was a quarter of a mile or

THE INDUS IN FLOOD TIME

At this time the water covers the land for many miles to a depth of several feet.

THE FERRY-BOAT FOR THE MAIL ON THE INDUS RIVER NEAR DERA ISMAIL KHAN

so of fields not yet submerged; sometimes the water was up to our knees or hips for miles together, and in one place there was a deep channel about one hundred yards wide, where a ferry-boat was in readiness for the luggage, but we enjoyed having a swim across. Two of the team, who were less practised swimmers, and had miscalculated the strength of the current, found themselves being carried rapidly down the stream; but just as some of those who had already gained the opposite bank were about to return to the rescue, they found their feet on a sandbank, and were able to struggle across. The thirteen miles across the swollen river took us from nine in the morning till four in the afternoon, though it must be admitted we loitered several times to enjoy a swim in the cool waters of the deeper channels.

We found, too, that the football season differs in various places. While Calcutta plays football in July and August, Karachi plays from December to March, and Bombay in the spring. However, even those colleges which were not in their actual football season sportingly agreed to get up matches during our visit. In no place did we find greater enthusiasm among the colleges and schools for football and a more open-handed hospitality than in Hyderabad, the capital of the Nizam's Government, and here our team experienced their first defeat in this tour.

We had had thirty hours' travelling from Ahmadnagar, in the North, and the stations on this line were so ill supplied with refreshments that we had been unable to get anything except some biscuits and sweets, and, arriving at Hyderabad at midday, we found the match had been fixed for 4 p.m., so that the team had only time for a hastily-prepared meal before the match. The college of the Nizam put a strong team against us, and for the first time in the tour the Bannu boys were distinctly outmatched. It was, however, nice to see what good feeling was evinced by both teams in this and nearly all the matches of the tour, both sides fraternizing with the greatest bonhomie both before and after the matches, and friendships were made which continued long after our team got back to Bannu.

Tours such as this undoubtedly tend to promote that feeling of friendship and union between the races of various parts of India which has hitherto been so little in evidence. It also tends to widen sympathies and to lessen religious prejudices. Not only did the members of our team sink the prejudices which might have arisen from diversity of religious opinion, but our hosts, too, represented all classes and faiths. Thus, in Hyderabad the organizer of hospitality was a Christian missionary, the Rev. Canon Goldsmith. A house was lent us for residence by a Parsi gentleman, and dinners were given us by the Muhammadans of the place.

Further south the Hindus were more in evidence, and entertained us royally at Bezwada and Masulipatam. In the latter place we were the guests of the staff of the Noble College, belonging to the Church Missionary Society, and here an amusing incident took place. The boys in these parts are accustomed to play football with bare feet, and are light, lithe, and wiry, while our Northerners were heavy, big-boned, and wore the usual football boots; so it came about that when they saw our team arrive, their hearts melted within them for fear, and they refused to play unless our boys consented to play barefooted; and this they refused to do, as they had had no practice in playing like that. It seemed as though we should have to go away without a match, but a missionary there had a boarding-house of Christian lads of the district, and these sportingly declared that they were ready to play. Both teams appeared at the appointed time amid a great concourse of spectators. The Bannu boys, with their football boots, looked much the heavier team; but the Telegu boys proved themselves much the more nimble, and outran and ran round our boys time after time, and as the Bannu boys played very cleanly and were careful not to hack, they did not suffer from want of boots; but, on the other hand, several of our boys took off theirs at half-time, hoping thereby to become as nimble as their antagonists. They, however, lost by one goal to love, amid the greatest excitement. The teams which had refused to play were now most importunate in begging us to stop for other matches, but as we were engaged for a match next day at Guntur it could not be done.

With one exception, our Afghans had never seen the sea, and they were all greatly desirous of making its acquaintance. I accordingly arranged for the journey from Karachi to Bombay to be on one of the British India steamers which ply between those two ports. It was the height of the July monsoon, and they had not realized what their request entailed. There was a strong wind on our beam the whole of our forty hours' journey, and the little steamer *Kassara* rolled continuously the whole time, the billows sometimes breaking over her fore-deck. All but three of them suffered the terrors of *mal-de-mer* in its worst form, and earnestly wished that they had never been so rash as to dare the terrors of the ocean at such a time. We arrived at Bombay amid a torrential rain—a bedraggled, dispirited, and staggering crew. It was pitch dark, and it was only with some difficulty that we found our way to the Money School of the Church Missionary Society, where we were to receive hospitality. The shops were closed and the watchman asleep, but after some delay we aroused him, got some tea at a belated coffee-shop, and lay down on the boards to wish for the morrow. It rained almost continuously during our stay at Bombay, but we managed one match with the City Club, of which the following account appeared in the *Bombay Gazette*:

"MATCH BETWEEN THE BANNU FOOTBALL TEAM AND THE CITY CLUB.

"The visitors opened the attack last evening from the southern end of the Oval, and although the City Club at times were pressed, the game was more or less of an even nature. The Bannu combination was the first to score, and soon after followed up with their second goal. Pulling themselves together, the City Club then made several good rushes, and eventually succeeded in scoring. Soon after they annexed their second goal, and equalized matters. In the second half the game was intensely exciting, as either side tried to get the winning goal. The visitors had a warm time of it, but eventually succeeded in getting their third goal. A minute before the close of time, however, the City men equalized by a well-judged shot, and the match thus ended in a draw of three goals each."

One of the best matches of the tour was with the Y.M.C.A. of Karachi, which was thus described by the *Sindh Gazette:*

"An interesting football match was played on Tuesday evening last on the Howard Institute ground, between the team of the Y.M.C.A. and Dr. Pennell's team of Pathan boys from the C.M.S. High School, Bannu. The first goal was scored soon after the match began, by a soft drive, and was in favour of Bannu. Almost immediately the Y.M.C.A. equalized by Bannu heading into their own goal during a mêlée from a corner kick. Soon afterwards the Y.M.C.A. took the lead through a clever run up by Wolfe, who passed neatly to Morton, who netted with a neat shot. On the whole play was very even till half-time, when the Y.M.C.A. led by two goals to one. At half-time the Y.M.C.A. lost the services of their outside right, who retired on account of a weak knee. Bannu generally took the lead in attacking, and scored twice again, the last time from a stinging shot well up the field. The Bannu team played consistently, and altogether without roughness. We are glad to have seen them in Karachi, and wish them all success in the remainder of their tour."

From Guntur we travelled north to Calcutta, where a series of matches had been arranged, after which we had arranged a number of matches with the schools and colleges of the United Provinces of Agra and Oudh, and those of the Panjab; but an unforeseen and unaccountable misadventure brought our tour to a premature conclusion a few hours before the time fixed for our departure from Calcutta. It was the outcome of one of those waves of unrest which followed the outburst of the storm with which the Bengalis exhibited their resentment at the partition of Bengal. The Bengalis had organized a boycott of European goods, and in the fervour of their campaign had placed a number of boy sentinels at the doors of the shops of those merchants who dealt in articles of Western manufacture. These were largely Marwari merchants from the Bombay Presidency, and they thought to relieve themselves of this wasp-like horde of boy sentinels by circulating the rumour that a number of Panjabis and Afghans had come down from the North to kidnap boys and children whom they could lay hands on. This rumour was widely believed by the credulous mob of Calcutta, and, all unknown to us, who were ignorant even of the existence of the rumours, our team had been pointed out as some of the probable kidnappers.

We had returned on the morning of August 23, 1906, from playing a number of matches in Krishnagar, and were to leave Calcutta the same afternoon to play a match the following day at Bhagalpur. The team had broken up into two parties to get their breakfast in one of those eating shops which abound in the Calcutta Bazaar, and I had gone along to Howrah Station to purchase the tickets. It was a hot day, and on my return I stopped at a refreshment shop in the Harrison Road, near the Church Mission

Boarding-House, where we were stopping, to get a glass of lemonade.

I was sitting quietly drinking it in the shop front, when I noticed the whole bazaar was in an uproar. The crowd was rushing to and fro, and the shopkeepers were hurriedly putting up their shutters. All ignorant of the fact that it was my own boys who were being attacked, I quietly finished my glass and strolled back to our hostel, thinking there was no reason why I should trouble myself about affairs of Calcutta which did not concern me. No sooner had I entered the gates of the compound when I saw one of our team—Rahim Bakhsh—his face covered with blood, and another one injured. "Do you not know," cried one, "that our boys have been murderously assaulted, and perhaps killed?" "Where are they?" I hurriedly asked. "They are probably in the hospital by this time." A cab was passing at the moment, and I jumped in, and drove off to the hospital. Running up into the casualty room, I was horrified to find six of the team lying about with their clothes all torn and covered with blood and mud. Their heads had been shaved by the casualty dressers, and were so cut and swollen that I could not recognize them all until I had spoken to them, and then for the first time I learnt what had happened.

A party of nine had gone in a refreshment room, and were having their breakfast. Meanwhile they noticed that a crowd of many hundreds had collected outside. Scarcely realizing that *they* were the cause of the crowd, after finishing their meal, they came out to return to the Mission Boarding-House, but were met by cries on all sides: "These are the kidnappers! Kill them! kill them!" Even now they did not understand the cause of the excitement, but when they asked what it was all about, and what was wanted from them, they were only answered by derisive shouts and a shower of stones and brickbats. Before they had time

A MODERN "BLACK HOLE"

During a visit of the Bannu football team to Calcutta, several of the players were murderously attacked by a crowd excited by the report that a company of Afghans had come to steal away their children. Five of the boys were left for dead in this alley, down which their blood ran into the gutter.

to organize any resistance they were separated one from another, in the midst of a raging mob, who belaboured them with stones and sticks until they fell senseless in the street. Two only managed to escape—Rahim Bakhsh, whom I had met in the hostel, and one other, who had managed to get into a passing carriage.

Five of them, having been reduced to a state of insensibility, were taken by the mob and thrown into a back alley, where the blood from their wounds continued to flow and trickly down in a red stream into the street gutter. One of them—Ganpat Rai—was rescued by a friendly Bengal gentleman, who bundled him into his house and attended to his wounds, and afterwards sent him under escort to the hospital. Another—Gurmukh Das—was being belaboured by some ruffians while lying in the middle of the road, when an English gentleman passed in his carriage. Naturally indignant at what he saw, he jumped down and asked them what they thought themselves to be, beating a senseless man in that way; and if he had committed a crime, why did they not take him to the police-station? Someone in the crowd called out, "This Englishman is their officer: let us kill him!" and, leaving the boy, they all set on him. He defended himself for some time, when some ruffian, coming up behind, turned a basket over his head, and it would have gone hard with him had not some friendly natives pulled him into the Ripon College, which was close at hand.

We would fain have got away from Calcutta as soon as the condition of the wounded enabled us to travel, for the unaccustomed diet and climate was affecting the health of all of us; but we found ourselves prisoners to the will of the Government, who required us to remain in Calcutta as witnesses in the prosecution which the Government was instituting, and we had to spend day after day of weary waiting, hanging about the police-courts of Bow Street Bazaar. The police had secured a number of men who had been shown to have taken part in the riot, and most of these had secured barristers and pleaders for their defence; consequently, there was a formidable array of advocates on the side of the defence, each one of whom thought it his duty to cross-examine each member of the team at tedious length, and regardless of some of the questions having been asked us time after time by his brothers of the law.

The brow-beating and cross-examining which we had to undergo could not have been worse had we been the aggressors instead of the victims, while the irrelevancy of the questions and the needless waste of time, entailing constant postponement from day to day, was exceedingly trying to us in our wounded and feeble condition, only anxious to get back to our homes on the frontier. The barristers and pleaders of the defence professed notwithstanding to be very sympathetic with us in our troubles, and one and another would come up and say something like this: "We people of Calcutta are most sorry for this very unfortunate occurrence. No doubt most of the men in the dock are guilty, and should be punished for so unwarranted an attack on innocent travellers, but there is one man who has been arrested by some mistake of the police. He had nothing to do with it, and should be released, because he is quite innocent." As in each case the man "arrested by mistake" proved to be the one for which the barrister was holding a brief, their protestations lost something of their force.

A more pleasant feature was the genuine sympathy shown by a certain section of the Bengalis, a sympathy which was voiced by the Hon. Surendra Nath Bannerji, who convened a public meeting, in which he expressed the regrets of the Calcutta citizens in an address which was presented to us in a silver casket.

At last the court, taking pity on our uncomfortable condition, consented to take our examination and cross-examination previous to that of the hundred and more witnesses which the defence were going to bring, and which would have entailed some months' stay in Calcutta, had we been kept back to the end of the trial.

When we reached Bannu we were honoured with a civic reception, which went far to make up to the members of the team for the discomforts that they had undergone. The Civil Officer of the district, the Municipal Commissioners, and a great number of the citizens, met us with a band some few miles before reaching Bannu, and we were escorted in amid great rejoicings.

CHAPTER XIII

'ALAM GUL'S CHOICE

A farmer and his two sons—Learning the Quran—A village school—At work and at play—The visit of the Inspector—Pros and cons of the mission school from a native standpoint—Admission to Bannu School—New associations—In danger of losing heaven—First night in the boarding-house—A boy's dilemma.

PIR BADSHAH was a well-to-do farmer of the Bangash tribe, not far from Kohat, and he had married a woman of the Afridi tribe from over the border, called Margilarri, or "the Pearl."

He had not to pay for her, because it was arranged that his sister was to marry her brother, and in cases where an exchange like this is made nothing further is required.

They had two sons, 'Alam Gul and Abdul Majid. The father intended that the elder should be educated, and one day he hoped would become a great man, perhaps *Tahsildar* (meaning Revenue Officer) of the British Government, so he was going to give him the best education he could afford; while Abdul Majid was to look after the lands and become a farmer, for which it is not supposed that any education is necessary.

Pir Badshah was very orthodox and punctilious in all the observances of his religion, so the two boys were not to learn anything else until they had sat at the feet of the village Mullah, and learnt to read the Quran.

The mosque was a little building on the hillside. It was built of stones cemented together with mud, aud in the centre was a little niche towards the setting sun, where the Mullah, with his face towards Mecca, led the congregation in their prayers. There was a wooden verandah, the corners of which were ornamented with the horns of the markhor, or mountain goat. Beyond this was the open court, in which prayers were said when the weather was fine, and either in this verandah or the courtyard 'Alam Gul and his brother used to sit at the feet of the old Mullah, reciting verses from the Quran in a drawling monotone, and swaying their bodies backwards and forwards in the way that all Easterns learn to do from the cradle when reciting or singing.

When they had finished the Quran and learnt the prayers and other essentials of the Muhammadan religion, 'Alam Gul was sent to the village school, while Abdul Majid began to make himself useful on the farm.

He used to go out with his father's buffaloes to take them to pasture, and sometimes he used to take his brother out for a ride on one of these ungainly animals. Then, when the harvest was ripening, a bed was fastened up at the top of four high poles, and he had to sit all day on this to protect the crops from the birds. For this purpose cords are fastened across the field up to the bed, and oil-cans or other pieces of tin are fastened to them here and there, so that as Abdul Majid had all the ends of the cords in his hands, he could make a din in any part of the field where he wished to frighten away the birds, and sometimes was able to take half a dozen home for the evening meal.

'Alam Gul, on the other hand, was being initiated into the mysteries of the Hindustani language and of arithmetic.

The school was a little mud building in the centre of the village, and the schoolmaster was a Muhammadan from the Panjab, who found himself rather uncomfortable in the midst of these frontier Pathans, whose language seemed to him so uncouth and their habits so barbarous. His meagre salary of ten rupees (13s. 4d.) a month was somewhat augmented by his holding the additional post of village postmaster; but it had this disadvantage—that when one of the villagers came in to buy an envelope, and get the postmaster to address it, as probably he did not know how to write himself, teaching had to be dropped for a season: for it must be remembered that for a Pathan villager to send off a letter is quite an event, and he may well afford to spend a quarter of an hour or so, and give the postmaster a few annas extra to get it properly addressed and despatched to his satisfaction. Meantime, 'Alam Gul and his companions would take the opportunity of drawing figures on the sand of the floor, or of playing with a tame bullfinch or a quail, which they were fond of bringing into the school.

To make up for these little interruptions, the schoolmaster used to sit from morning to night, and expect his pupils to be there almost as long, only giving them an interval of about an hour or so in the middle of the day to go home and get their morning meal. Friday used to be a whole holiday, for it was on that day that all the men of the village had to assemble in the mosque for the morning prayers, and when these were over 'Alam Gul used to go out with some of the elder village boys to catch quails in the fields. This they did by means of a long net spread across about thirty or forty feet of the field. The quails were driven up into this, and the meshes of it were of such a size that, though they could get their heads through, their wings became hopelessly entangled, and they fell an easy prey to the fowlers. The male quails were then kept in little string or wicker baskets for the great quail fights, which were one of the chief excitements and pastimes of the village. This pastime is one of the most universal in Afghanistan, and even well-to-do men think there is no shame in spending a great part of the day toying with their favourite quails, and backing the more redoubtable ones against some quail belonging to a friend, while all the men of the neighbourhood will be collected round to see the two champions fight.

'Alam Gul had to spend five years in this school. At the end of this time the Government Inspector came round to examine the pupils for the Government primary examination. This was an eventful day for the schoolmaster, for on the report of the Inspector his promotion to some more congenial sphere and the increase of his salary would depend. The boys, too, were all excitement, for if they passed this examination, they would be allowed to go to the big school at Hangu or Kohat.

The schoolmaster would spend days drilling them how they were to answer the questions of the Inspector; how they were to salaam him; how they were to bring him a hookah if he required one, bring him tea, or do him any other service which it might be supposed would put him in a better mood for making a good report of the school.

The Inspector was a Peshawuri Pathan of portly presence (it is commonly believed that among the upper ranks of native Government officials a man's salary may be gauged by the girth of his body) and of supercilious manners, as though his chief aim in life were to criticize everyone and everything.

All the boys had put on their best clothes for the occasion, and 'Alam Gul had borrowed the turban which his father was accustomed to wear on feast days.

On the arrival of the Inspector, the boys hurriedly got into line. The schoolmaster called out: "Right-hand salute!" for though not a boy in the school knew a word of English, it is the custom to give all the class orders in that language. Then one boy was hurried off to hold his horse, another to go and get it some hay, a third to get a chair for the great man, while the schoolmaster himself was obsequious in obeying his every sign.

The boys were examined in Urdu, writing and reading, arithmetic, geography, and Persian. There were five boys altogether in the top class, and of these, to the delight of the schoolmaster, the Inspector declared four to have passed, among them being 'Alam Gul.

His father wanted to send 'Alam Gul to the Government school at Kohat, but 'Alam Gul had a friend who had been reading in the Bannu Mission School, and the tales that he had heard from him had given him a great desire to be allowed to go there to study. His father, however, was opposed to the idea, because the Mullah told him that people who went to mission schools must become infidels, because they were taught by *Feringis*, who were all infidels, and that if he sent his son there he would excommunicate him.

There would have been no hope of 'Alam Gul attaining his wish had it not been that just at that time the *Subadar* (native officer), an uncle of 'Alam Gul's, came to the village on leave from his regiment, which was stationed at Bannu, and it so happened that he had made the acquaintance of the missionary in charge of the Bannu School, and had been very favourably impressed with what he had seen of the institution, and he offered to take 'Alam Gul back with him to the regiment, and let him live with him.

The father had now to propitiate the Mullah, so he killed a sheep, and made some luscious dishes with the meat, and some *halwa*, or sweet pudding, which is supposed to be a delicacy to which the Mullahs are very partial, and called his reverence in to partake of the feast; and when his heart was merry, he propounded the scheme to him.

After he had heard the arguments of the *Subadar*, the Mullah relented, and said that he knew how to make a charm which, if it were always worn round the boy's neck, would effectually prevent him from being contaminated by any heretical teaching which he might have in the school;

and if 'Alam Gul were admonished to be careful always to wear this charm, he might safely be allowed to go with his uncle. So when the leave of the latter expired, 'Alam Gul was put into his charge, and went off with great excitement, filled with hopes of what he would do in the great school of which he had heard so much.

The day after his arrival in Bannu the *Subadar* sent 'Alam Gul down to the school in charge of a soldier of his regiment.

The soldier and 'Alam Gul came into the mission compound, and, seeing some boys standing about, told them their errand. One of the boys offered to take them to the head-master. They were taken to the school office, and here they found the head-master. He was an old gentleman with a grey beard and a kindly face, Mr. Benjamin by name. When a young man he had himself been converted from Muhammadanism to Christianity, so that he was able to sympathize with the religious difficulties of the boys under his charge, and he had been for thirty years head-master in this school, and was looked up to by the boys as their father.

'Alam Gul's certificates were examined, and he was told what books he must obtain, and that if he came the next morning he would be enrolled as a scholar of the Bannu Mission School.

This being an Anglo-vernacular school, where English is taught in all but the very lowest classes, boys who come from the village schools have to spend one whole year in learning English, in order that the following year they may be able to take their place with the other boys in the class to which they are entitled; so 'Alam Gul was enrolled in this, which is called the "Special Class."

The next day the soldier again brought him, and left him alone in the school. Here he was surrounded by a greater number of boys than he had ever seen before in his life—boys of all ages, all sorts, all sizes, and all religions.

There were some Muhammadans from his district, but none from his village, or that he knew, so he felt very nervous, and wished himself back again in the little village school on the mountain-side among his old playmates.

Then the letters of the English language seemed so uncouth and different from the euphonious sounds of the Arabic and Persian alphabet, to which he had been accustomed.

"A, B, C," said the master, and "A, B, C," repeated the other boys in the class; but he found he could not shape his mouth to these unfamiliar sounds, and tears began to flow at the apparent hopelessness of the task which he had undertaken with so much enthusiasm. However, day by day the work grew easier, and new friends and acquaintances began to be made among his class-mates. Every day there was some fresh astonishment for him.

In the village school he had played what they called *Balli-ball*, a village imitation of cricket, played with rough imitations of bats and wickets; but here he found that every class had its own cricket team, which played with real polished bats and balls brought all the way from Lahore. And above all was the School Eleven, composed of boys who were looked up to by young hopefuls of the lower classes, much as we might regard a County Eleven in England—boys who played in real *wilayiti* flannels, and had matches with the English officers of the garrison, and saw that the other boys in the school treated them with the respect due to their position.

'Alam Gul wondered if ever the day would come when he would find himself numbered among this favoured throng. It was not long before the captain of his class told him that he must come and practise, to see if they could make him one of their class cricket team. He would have accepted with alacrity had it not been for one circumstance, which gave his unformed religious ideas a rude shock. The captain of the party was a Hindu! It seemed to him ignominious, if not subversive of his religion, that he should subject himself to the orders of a Hindu class-fellow, and he would have refused had not a Muhammadan from his district, reading in the class above him, to whom he confided his scruples, laughed at him, and said: "You silly fellow! we do not trouble about that here; everyone has his religion ordained by Fate. What does it matter, be he Muhammadan, Hindu, or Christian, if he play cricket well?" When his fears had been thus allayed, 'Alam Gul joined his party, and soon became as enthusiastic a member of it as any.

A year passed, and he was promoted to the first middle class, where he took up the full curriculum of subjects, learning not only English, but arithmetic, Urdu, Persian, Arabic, geography, Indian history, and elementary science.

Before he had been many months in this class he was attacked by malarial fever, which is so virulent in the Bannu Valley in the autumn months. His uncle sent a soldier to say that he had sent him back to his village in charge of a man of his regiment, and that he would come back after recovering; so his name was entered on the roll of those absent for sick-leave.

About three weeks later his father himself appeared at the school one day, and requested to interview the head-master.

After the usual salutations were over, the father began:

"Sir, I have a request to make."

"What is it?"

"I wish you to strike the name of my son off the roll-call of your school."

"Why so? What has happened?"

"He is ill—very ill."

"But I have given him sick-leave. He can stop at home as long as he is ill, and then come back to school. His name can remain on the register, and he return when he is quite well."

"Certainly, he will come back if he recovers; but, then, he is very ill. Supposing he were to die?"

"If he were to die, then what matter whether his name be on our register or not?"

"Sir, the Mullah tells me that if he die with his name still on the register of the mission school, he could never go to heaven."

Arguments were useless, and the head-master had perforce to satisfy the father by giving the boy a leaving certificate.

Ultimately, however, 'Alam Gul recovered, and was allowed to go back to the mission school; but a few months later the regiment, in which his uncle the *Subadar* was, was transferred to another station, and the uncle wished to take his nephew with him there. But the boy had by this time formed a great attachment to the school, and begged to be allowed to remain, so it was arranged that he should be entered in the school boarding-house.

This hostel accommodated a number of those pupils whose homes were too far from Bannu for them to attend as day scholars, and who had no relations in the town with whom they might lodge. Each boy is provided with a bedstead and a mat, and he brings his own bedding, books and utensils.

The first night 'Alam Gul felt very strange. Instead of the small crowded room of his house was a large airy dormitory, shared by some twenty of his schoolfellows. At one end of the dormitory was the room of the Superintendent, so that he could supervise the boys both by day and night. The Superintendent was a Hindu, but 'Alam Gul had got used by this time to respect his masters, even though they were not Muhammadan, and had overcome some of his old prejudice. As the Superintendent treated him kindly, and there was a Muhammadan friend of his in the next bed, he was soon very happy there.

Attached to the hostel was a pond of water supplied daily

from the Kurram River, in which it was the duty of every boarder to bathe regularly. This tank served other purposes too, as 'Alam Gul found to his cost. It was the rule that all boarders were to be up and have their bedding tidily folded by sunrise. The Principal of the school every now and again paid surprise visits to the boarding-house about that time, and woe betide the luckless boy who was found still asleep in bed! Two of the monitors were told to take him by the head and heels and swing him far into the middle of the tank.

'Alam Gul had not been many weeks in the boarding-house before one morning he overslept himself, and before he had time to rub his eyes or change his clothes he found himself plunged in the water, which at that time—the early spring—was cold enough to become a real incentive to early rising.

Schoolboys freshly joined were often found to have the bad habit of freely abusing each other, and using foul language. The swimming-tank formed an excellent corrective for this too, because the boy found guilty was treated in the same way, being pitched in with all his clothes on, and allowed to creep out and dry himself at leisure.

Once, indeed, 'Alam Gul felt very much like leaving the school altogether. Every day in each class a period is set apart for the Scripture lesson. At first 'Alam Gul did not wish to be present at this, but when he found that all the other boys attended it without demur, and remembered the power of the charm which the Mullah had given him, he thought it did not, after all, matter; he need not pay attention to what was taught, and so he went. But this day a verse came to his turn to read in which were the words, "Jesus Christ, the Son of God." He remained silent. The catechist who was teaching him said:

"Why do you not read?"

"I cannot read that."

"Why, what is wrong? Read it."

"That is blasphemy. God had no son. I cannot read that."

"It is written in the Book, and you must read it."

"I will not read it!"

The catechist was not willing, however, to grant him exemption, and gave him some punishment.

'Alam Gul had a fit of Pathan temper then, and there was a serious breach of discipline, which could not be overlooked. Before, however, he had time to arrange with his father for leaving the school, he had cooled down sufficiently to take a less prejudiced view of the case, and decided to undergo the discipline, and stay on with us.

CHAPTER XIV

'ALAM GUL'S CHOICE (*continued*)

The cricket captain—A conscientious schoolboy—The Scripture lesson —First awakenings—The Mullah's wrath—The crisis—Standing fire —Schoolboy justice—"Blessed are ye when men shall persecute you for My Name's sake"—Escape from poisoning—Escape from home—Baptism—Disinherited—New friends.

About this time three circumstances occurred which brought about a change in 'Alam Gul's ideas.

The first happened in this way. The captain of the cricket eleven chanced to be a Christian boy, and as two or three of the members of the cricket eleven had left, he was in need of some fresh talent to fill their places; so a match had been arranged with a number of the boys of the school who were aspirants to places in the coveted eleven.

'Alam Gul by this time had developed into a very steady player, who could be relied upon to keep his wicket up at times when his side was going to pieces; and on this particular occasion he was one of those selected for trial, and it so happened that he made one of the best scores of the match. This was the commencement of the friendship with the cricket captain, which went a long way to mould his ideas. Hitherto he had rather fought shy of making friends with the Christian boys, for fear anything should be said repellent to his religious ideas; but as his friendship with the cricket captain increased, they had many a chat—not only on cricket and school matters, but on deeper things that concerned the faith in their hearts.

The second circumstance arose in this wise: On the occasion of a paper-chase the track had led through an orchard, and some of the boys were not proof against the temptation of helping themselves to the fruit, and the next day the owner of the garden came in high dudgeon to the Principal of the school to complain that some of the fruit had been stolen.

"You call yourself a mission school, and here are your boys coming into my orchard and taking my fruit!"

The next day the Principal had a roll-call of the school, and made a short speech to them, saying that he much regretted that some of the boys had brought a bad name on the school by stealing plums. He then ordered that the boys who had taken any should fall out and stand in a row in front. After much exchange of glances and hesitation, twenty or so of the boys fell out. These were ranged up in line, facing the rest of the school, while the Principal told them that he intended to make an example of them as a warning to others not to sully the fair name of the school.

One of the printers from the mission press was then called, with his printing-roller well inked, and this was rolled three times down the face of each boy, leaving one long black streak down the forehead and nose and one down each cheek, which they were not allowed to wash off for the rest of the day.

'Alam Gul was rather surprised to see that one of these boys was a member of the cricket eleven, who evidently felt the indignity very acutely. 'Alam Gul had been by his side during the paper-chase, and he had noticed that he had passed by the fruit without taking any; so he went up afterwards to console him, and ask him why he had fallen out with those who had taken the fruit. He told him that when he saw the other boys plucking the plums, he had himself taken one; but then he thought how they had been told in the Scripture lessons that that was a wrong thing to do, and so he had thrown the plum away.

'Alam Gul had hitherto never looked on the Scripture lesson as a time for moral improvement, but rather as a time when fidelity to his religion required him to shut his ears; so when he found his schoolmate with a conscience that had become so tender through listening to the Scripture teaching that he even thought it necessary to confess to having plucked a single plum which he had not eaten, his mind was filled with an inrush of new conflicting ideas.

The third influence came to him through the Scripture lesson itself. The Indian pastor was teaching them from that chapter of the greatest pathos in all history—the Crucifixion of our Lord. When it came to his turn he read the verse: "Father, forgive them, for they know not what they do." Not very long before he would have resented even having to read a verse addressing the Almighty as "Father," but now his heart was full of new emotions. "How could the Prophet Christ pray for the forgiveness of enemies?" He remembered how an uncle of his, on his death-bed, in making his last testament to his sons, had enumerated his enemies and what evil they had done him, and impressed upon them that revenge for those wrongs was the heirloom which he had bequeathed to them, and which they must regard as their bounden duty to perform. He remembered, too, how many of his own family had been killed in blood-feuds, and even now his uncle, the *Subadar* in the regiment, took precautions against somebody whom he suspected of being his enemy. If Christ was able to die in this way and His teaching had still such moral power, how was it that Muhammad, who professed that his teaching had superseded that of Christ, had not been able to give his followers an equal power? Why were there Muhammadan tribes always torn with discord and feud and bloodshed on every side, and by those who professed to do such deeds in his name?

'Alam Gul now began to study the Gospels for himself, and an interest was awakened in his heart which surprised him;

and instead of trying to shirk the Scripture lessons, he began always to look forward to them, and asked many questions which showed the greater insight that he was gaining into their meaning. The next vacation, when he went home, he took an early opportunity of visiting the old Mullah who had given him the charm when first he joined the school five years before, and asked him about some of his difficulties. He wanted to know why the Muhammadans always spoke of the Book of the Law and of the Gospels with respect, and yet would not allow people to read them, and why the Gospels spoke of Christ as the Son of God, which he had been taught to consider blasphemy.

The Mullah, however, did not deign to try to solve his difficulties, but became very angry, and abused him roundly, and that evening went to his father to tell him to take his son away before he became utterly corrupted.

'Alam Gul got a great beating that night, and ran away to the house of a relation, and did not come back for three days, and asked no further questions.

His father, no doubt, thought that the beating had had its effect, and, when the time arrived for rejoining school, allowed him to go back.

The crisis came on the day of a school picnic. It was a May morning, and the masters and boys were going to a shady spot on the banks of the Kurram River, where the day would be spent in aquatic sports and merry-making. 'Alam Gul sought counsel of the missionary in a quiet spot under the trees, where he might unburden his heart without being disturbed.

"Does Christ demand that I should confess Him openly? Should I not wait till my parents are dead?—because it will be a great trouble to them when they hear that I have become a Christian, and they will never want to see me again. Cannot I be a secret follower, and continue to live as a Muhammadan, and attend the prayers in the mosque?"

"Whoever shall be ashamed of Me and My words, of him also shall the Son of man be ashamed." "He that loveth father or mother more than Me is not worthy of Me."

How pulsating with the deepest verities of life these sayings seem, when we put them forward to such an inquirer in answer to such questions! How charged with the magnetism which draws the seeking soul almost in spite of itself—a two-edged sword dividing asunder the bones and the marrow!

"No; you must go home and tell your father what your intention is. Persecution must come, sooner or later, and unless you are willing to bear it for Christ's sake now, how can you be received into the company of His soldiers? You have a duty to your parents, from which you cannot absolve yourself, and no blessing of God will rest on your actions when you are deceiving them, and till you are of full age you are bound to obey them."

'Alam Gul was awake a long time that night after the lights were out and all the other boys in the dormitory were fast asleep under their quilts. At last he got up, and, with his pocket-knife, cut the cord that still bound the charm that the old Mullah had made for him, and stuffed it away among his books. He then knelt down by his bedside for a few minutes, and when he got into bed again he had made his choice, and his mind was made up; but there were to be many vicissitudes before the goal was reached.

'Alam Gul was in the matriculation class now, and a member of the coveted cricket eleven. He still performed his Muhammadan prayers, and kept the fast of Ramazan; but the moments which gave him most satisfaction in the day were those in which he took his little English Testament into a quiet corner on the roof of the school-house, and read the words of our Lord, calling the weary and sin-laden to Himself, and, after set portions of the Muhammadan prayers were over, in the part reserved for the *munajat*, or private petitions, he would pray earnestly in the name of Christ that God would make the way clear to him to become His disciple, and to incline the hearts of his relations thereto as well. He had to stand fire, too, among his school-fellows, now that it had become known that he was an inquirer; but his position in the school, and the fact that he was nearly the best bat in the cricket team, and therefore of value to the honour of the school in the inter-school tournaments, prevented them from carrying the persecution very far, and it was more banter and sneers than anything worse. A few irreconcilables, however, tried to injure his reputation by spreading lying rumours about him, even going to the head-master with some concocted evidence against his moral character, which, had that official been less conversant with the wiles of the backbiters, might have resulted in his expulsion from school, but actually resulted in their utter discomfiture.

One Muhammadan youth, who professed great zeal for his religion, was always starting some recriminating religious discussion, till the other boarders passed a resolution that any of their number starting such a discussion was to be fined one rupee.

Before the lapse of many days there were the two at it again, hammer and tongs, in the middle of the dinner-hour. A schoolboy court was appointed to name the culprit responsible for starting the discussion, and it is a pleasing tribute to the schoolboys' love of fair play that, though the judges chosen were one Muhammadan and one Hindu, they both decided that the Muhammadan was guilty, and should be fined. The latter declared that he was going to pay no fine! They then held a fresh council, to settle how they were to bring the pressure required for the carrying out of their law. At last one boy said: "I have it. Till he pays the fine, not one of us is to speak to him or have anything to do with him, on the pain of a fine of one anna." This bright idea was passed unanimously, and, after a few anna fines had been levied, the recalcitrant member gave in. Sweets were bought with the proceeds, there was a general merry-making, and no more disturbances of the peace on 'Alam Gul's account, who was tacitly allowed to have what opinions and fads he liked without further interference.

He had not so easy a time, however, when the vacation came round and he went home, and in much fear and trembling made his longings known to his father.

First they resorted to blandishments, reminded him of his good family and noble ancestors, and of the bright future which lay before so clever and well educated a boy. His brother was about to be married; even then they were preparing for the wedding-guests. This would have to be all stopped, for the family of the bride would refuse to give her into a family disgraced, and then his brother would die of shame, and no one would be able to wipe the stain away for ever.

When these tactics failed, the old Mullah was called. He was too wroth to argue when he found that 'Alam Gul no longer wore the charm, and abused him with all the epithets that he could think of, and left the house threatening to excommunicate the whole family. Later on he came back in a calmer mood with two older Mullahs from a neighbouring village, who were much revered for their learning and sanctity, and these surrounded 'Alam Gul, and argued for hours to show him the error of his ways and the corruption of the Christian Scriptures. 'Alam Gul had one argument, to which they had no answer to give:

"If you say these Scriptures are corrupted by the Christians, then where have you genuine copies by comparison with which we can see the proof of it? Had the Muhammadans themselves no copies of the Scriptures which they were able to preserve from those wicked people who wanted to corrupt them?"

Finding their arguments of no avail, they formally cursed

him with all the anathemas of the Quran, both for this life and the next.

The next trial was to be the most heart-searching and trying of all, and 'Alam Gul felt he would ten times rather have had the anathemas of the Mullahs or the beatings of his enemies. It was when he went into the zenana. His mother was there with other women, and as soon as they saw him they began weeping and loudly lamenting. His mother came with her hair dishevelled, and, falling down before him, beat her breast, and bewailed with loud cries and frantic gesticulations that she had borne a son who was going to disgrace the family and bring down her grey hairs with sorrow to the grave.

'Alam Gul burst into tears, and besought his mother to be comforted; saying that she had been misinformed as to what he was going to do, and who the Christians were. He was not going to forsake her, but would serve her to the day of his death.

"I adjure thee," she said, "swear to me that you will never go near those Christians again or read their books."

"No, mother, I cannot do that; for their book is the *Kalam Ullah* [the Word of God], and God is with them of very truth."

The women were still weeping, and 'Alam Gul persuading, when his father came in, and, seizing 'Alam Gul, pulled him outside, and, getting a thick stick, beat him till he was black and blue all over, and then left him with a kick and a curse.

That night 'Alam Gul found that all his clothes had been taken away, and he was left with only a loin-cloth. This had been done lest he should run away and escape, they thinking that in a few days, finding the hopelessness of his position, he would relent and submit.

Six days he remained thus, being given nothing more than a bit of stale bread once a day and a little water. Still he remained firm, and refused to go to the mosque or repeat the *Kalimah*; and when he found himself alone for a time, he knelt down and prayed for help and deliverance.

On the seventh morning an uncle came, and sat down by his side, and began to commiserate him and profess his sympathy for the hardships he was undergoing. He then untied the corner of his shawl, and got out some sweetmeats and gave them to 'Alam Gul, as some amends for the privations he had been undergoing. Something, however, in his demeanour made 'Alam Gul suspicious, and he excused himself for not eating the sweetmeats at once, and put them in a handkerchief by his side.

When his uncle had departed, he gave some of the sweetmeats to one of the dogs in the house. Very shortly afterwards the dog began to vomit and show signs of pain. He was now sure that the plan had been to poison him in such a way that his death might be reported as due to some ordinary sickness, and he made up his mind to escape at all costs.

It was midday, and nearly everyone was enjoying a sleep during the oppressive noon of a summer day. Searching about, he found a shirt and an old turban, and, donning these, he slipped out, and was soon through the deserted village street out in the fields beyond. He dared not take the direct route to Bannu, for he knew that pursuit would be made, and the pursuers would probably take that direction; so he turned northwards towards Kohat, and came to the village of a schoolmate, who gave him shelter and food for that night in his house and a pair of shoes for his feet, which had become blistered on the hot rocks over which he had been travelling.

The next night he slept in a mosque, and then reached the highroad from Kohat to Bannu, and got a lift on a bullock-waggon travelling to the salt-mines of Bahadur Khel. On the fifth day after leaving his village, very footsore, tired, and ragged, he appeared in the mission compound at Bannu.

He was now nineteen years of age, so nothing stood in the way of his being admitted as a catechumen, of which he was greatly desirous, and the following Easter he was baptized into the Christian Church.

He had, of course, been publicly disowned and disinherited by his family, who now regarded him as one dead; but he was supremely happy in his faith, and was always seeking opportunities of leading, not only his schoolmates, but also Mullahs and others whom he encountered in the bazaar or elsewhere, into conversation concerning the claims of Jesus Christ.

His original acquaintance with the Quran and Islam had been deepened and extended by the study of books of controversy and his knowledge of Christianity by daily Bible study, so that even the Mullahs found they had to deal with one who could not be silenced by the threadbare arguments and trite sophisms which were all that most of them knew how to use.

There was a great crowd of students and others both inside and outside the native church on the day when, arrayed in clean white clothes, he came to receive the rite of baptism, and the deepest silence was upon all when he answered a clear, unfaltering "I do" to each of the questions of the native clergyman who was officiating. His reception afterwards by his Muhammadan acquaintances was not altogether a hostile one. Students form a remarkable contrast to the ignorant portion of the population in the comparative absence of religious fanaticism and their ability to recognize and honour sincerity of motive, even in those who are to them apostates, and many of his Muhammadan schoolmates maintained their friendship with him, and others who at first had joined in the opposition and abuse of the crowd came round before long and resumed their old relations as though nothing had happened.

Judging by other cases, even his own relations will probably resume friendly relations after the lapse of time has enabled them to do so without incurring a fresh stigma among the villagers, and they will be all the more ready to do this if he has won for himself a good position in Government service, and is able to help them to meet the dunnings of the money-lender in a bad season.

When 'Alam Gul had to find some way of earning his own living, he found many avenues closed to him. The Muhammadans would not give him work, and even in Government offices, if his immediate superior was at all a bigoted Muhammadan, he would find it impossible to stop there without getting involved in traps that had been laid for him almost every day, and which would ultimately and inevitably result in his dismissal in disgrace.

Finally he obtained a post in the Government Telegraph Office, and, by his industry and punctuality, rapidly made progress and attained a position which was a universal silencer to the common taunt, "He has only become a Christian for the sake of bread," with which young converts are assailed, even when the charge is palpably untrue.

CHAPTER XV

AFGHAN WOMEN

Their inferior position—Hard labour—On the march—Suffering in silence—A heartless husband—Buying a wife—Punishment for immorality—Patching up an injured wife—A streaky nose—Evils of divorce—A domestic tragedy—Ignorance and superstition—"Beautiful Pearl"—A tragic case—A crying need—Lady doctors—The mother's influence.

In all Muhammadan countries women hold a very inferior, almost humiliating, position, being regarded as very distinctly existing for the requirements of the stronger sex. In Afghanistan they labour under this additional hardship, that the men are nearly all cruel and jealous to a degree in their disposition, and among the lower sections of the community the severe conditions of life compel the women to labour very hard and continuously—labour which the men think it beneath their dignity to lighten or share.

The wife has to grind the corn, fetch the water, cook the food, tend the children, keep the house clean—in fact, do everything except shopping, from which she is strictly debarred. The husband will not only buy the articles of food required for the daily household consumption, but he will buy her dresses too—or, at least, the material for them—and the lady must be content with his selection, and make up her dresses at home with what her lord is pleased to bring her. How would their sisters in England approve of that?

The fetching of the water is often no sinecure. If the well is in the village precincts it may be pleasant enough, as it no doubt affords excellent opportunity for retailing all the village gossip; but in some places, as, for instance, during summer in Marwat, the nearest water is six or seven, or even ten, miles away, and the journey there and back has to be made at least every other day. In Marwat the women saddle up their asses with the leathern bottles made from goatskins long before daybreak, and the nocturnal traveller sometimes meets long strings of these animals going to or returning from the watering-place under the care of a number of the village women and girls. The animals in these cases have to be satisfied with what they drink while at the source of the water-supply.

When the women get back to their houses it will be still scarcely dawn, but they have a busy time before them, which will occupy them till midday. First the grain has to be ground in the hand-mills; then yesterday's milk churned; then the cows and goats milked; then the food cooked, the house cleaned, and a hundred and one other duties attended to which only a woman could describe.

When on the march the women are heavily loaded. They can often be seen not only carrying the children and household utensils, but driving the pack animals too, while the lordly men are content to carry only their rifle, or at most give a lift to one of the children. Yet it is not because the men are callous, but because it is the custom. Their fathers and forefathers did the same, and the women would be the first to rebuke a young wife who ventured to complain or object.

Some of the women of the Povindah tribe are splendid specimens of robust womanhood. These people travel hundreds of miles from Khorasan to India, carrying their families and household goods with them, and the women can load and manage the camels almost as well as the men, and carry burdens better. The outdoor, vigorous, active life has made them healthy, muscular, and strong, and buxom and good-looking withal, though their good looks do not last so long as they would were their life less rough. But when a baby is born, then comes the suffering. The caravan cannot halt, and there is seldom a camel or ox available for the woman to ride. She usually has to march on the next day, with the baby in her arms or slung over her shoulder, as though nothing had happened. Then it is that they endure sufferings which bring them to our hospital, often injured for life. If there is no hospital, well, they just suffer in silence, or—they die.

The Afghan noblemen maintain the strictest *parda*, or seclusion, of their women, who pass their days monotonously behind the curtains and lattices of their palace prison-houses, with little to do except criticize their clothes and jewels and retail slander; and Afghan boys of good family suffer much moral injury from being brought up in the effeminate and voluptuous surroundings of these zenanas. The poorer classes cannot afford to seclude their women, so they try to safeguard their virtue by the most barbarous punishments, not only for actual immorality, but for any fancied breach of decorum. A certain trans-frontier chief that I know, on coming to his house unexpectedly one day, saw his wife speaking to a neighbour over the wall of his compound. Drawing his sword in a fit of jealousy, he struck off her head and threw it over the wall, and said to the man: "There! you are so enamoured of her, you can have her." The man concerned discreetly moved house to a neighbouring village.

The recognized punishment in such a case of undue familiarity would have been to have cut off the nose of the woman and, if possible, of the man too. This chief, in his anger, exceeded his right, and if he had been a lesser man and the woman had had powerful relations, he might have been brought to regret it. But as a rule a woman has no redress; she is the man's property, and a man can do what he likes with his own. This is the general feeling, and no one would take the trouble or run the risk of interfering in another man's domestic arrangements. A man practically buys his wife, bargaining with her father, or, if he is dead, with her brother; and so she becomes his property, and the father has little power of interfering for her protection afterwards, seeing he has received her price.

The chief exception is marriage by exchange. Suppose in each of two families there is an unmarried son and an unmarried daughter; then they frequently arrange a mutual double marriage without any payments. In such cases the condition of the wives is a little, but only a little, better than in the marriage by purchase. If a man and a woman are detected in immorality, then the husband is at liberty to kill both; but if he lets the man escape, he is not allowed to kill him subsequently in cold blood. If he does, then a blood-feud will be started, and the relations of the murdered man legitimately retaliate, or he must pay up the difference in the price between that of a man's life and that of a woman's honour. In practice, one often finds that a man has been murdered where, by tribal custom, he should only have had his nose cut off; as it is obviously easier for the aggrieved husband to ambush and shoot him unawares than to overpower him sufficiently to cut off his nose.

Every year in the mission hospital we get a number of cases, many more women than men, where the sufferer has had the nose cut off by a clean cut with a knife, which sometimes cuts away a portion of the upper lip as well. This being a very old mutilation in India, the people centuries ago elaborated an operation for the removal of the deformity, whereby a portion of skin is brought down from the forehead and stitched on the raw surface where the nose had been cut off, and we still use this operation, with certain modifications, for the cases that come to us. Two years ago a forbidding-looking Afghan brought down his wife to the Bannu Mission Hospital. In a fit of jealousy he had cut off her nose, but when he reflected in a cooler moment that he had paid a good sum for her, and had only injured his own property and his domestic happiness, he was sorry for it, and brought her for us to restore to her as far as possible her pristine beauty. She had a low forehead, unsuitable for the usual operation, so I said to the husband that I did not think the result of the operation would be very satisfactory; but if he would pay the price I would purchase him an artificial nose from England, which, if it did not make her as handsome as before, would at any rate conceal the deformity.

"How much will it cost?" said the Afghan.

"About thirty rupees."

There was a silence: he was evidently racked by conflicting sentiments.

"Well, my man, what are you thinking about? Will you have it or no?"

"I was thinking this, sir," he replied "you say it costs thirty rupees, and I could get a new wife for eighty rupees."

And this was said before the poor woman herself, without anything to show that he felt he had said anything out of the common! I am glad to say, however, that he ultimately decided to have the original wife patched up, paid the money, and I procured him the article from England, which gave, I believe, entire satisfaction, and the last time I heard of them they were living happily together. Perhaps he is able to hold out the threat of locking up her nose should she annoy him, and knows he can remove it as often as he likes now without having to pay up another thirty rupees.

In a case where I procured a false nose for a man, the shop in England sent out a pale flesh-coloured nose, while his skin was dark olive! Obviously this had to be remedied, so I procured some walnut stain, and gave him something not very different from the colour of the rest of his face. Unfortunately, he started off home before it was dry, and was caught in a rainstorm. He was annoyed to find himself the centre of merriment on his arrival at his village, and came back to me to complain. The nose was all streaky!

The fine physique and good health of the hill Afghans and nomadic tribes is largely due to the fact that their girls do not marry till full grown, not usually till over twenty, and till then they lead healthy, vigorous, outdoor lives. They form a great contrast to the puny Hindu weaklings, the offspring of the marriage of couples scarcely in their "teens."

The two greatest social evils from which the Afghan women suffer are the purchase of wives and the facility of divorce. I might add a third—namely, plurality of wives; but though admittedly an evil where it exists, it is not universally prevalent, like the other two—in fact, only men who are well-to-do can afford to have more than one wife. The Muhammadans themselves are beginning to stem the evil and explain away the verses in the Quran which permit it, by saying that there is the proviso that a man may only marry a plurality of wives if he can be quite impartial to all of them; and as that is not possible, monogamy must be considered the law for ordinary mortals.

The following, which was enacted under my eyes, shows the evil that results from divorce and polygamy. There were three brothers, whom we will call Abraham, Sandullah, and Fath, all happily married to one wife each. Abraham, the eldest brother, died. The second brother was now entitled to marry the widow; but she did not like him, while she had a decided liking for the youngest brother, Fath. She had, however, a hatred for Fath's wife, and was determined not to be junior wife to her. Fath, carried away by the charms and cajolings of the widow, consented to divorce his own wife on condition of the widow marrying him. She agreed, vowing she would never marry Sandullah, and then Fath divorced his wife. But meanwhile Sandullah insisted on his rights, and forced the widow to marry him. She perforce submitted, but I think he got some lively times at home, and the woman took opportunities of meeting Fath. Then what does the insatiable and foolish Sandullah do but marry the divorced wife of his younger brother. The widow was now furious: she had refused to marry the man she fancied unless he divorced that woman, and now she is married to the man she did not want, and has got the hated woman as co-wife into the bargain.

There was a man of desperate character in the village who had been captivated by the widow's charms. She had so far refused his advances, but now, to have her way, she told him that if he desired to gain his end he must first dispose of her present husband. That was no obstacle to the lover, and, with the collusion of the woman, he enticed the man out into his cornfield one day, and there strangled him. The murder eventually was brought home to the unscrupulous lover, and he got penal servitude, while the foul enchantress was left free to marry the youngest brother, Fath, whom she originally desired.

Very few of the Afghan women can read the Quran; for the rest they are absolutely ignorant of all learning, and often when we are trying to explain some directions for treatment in the hospital, they excuse their denseness by saying: "We are only cattle: how can we understand?"

They know very little of their own religion beyond the prayers and a variety of charms and superstitions.

Some time ago we had a strange case in the women's (Holtby) ward. She was a feeble old Hindu woman who felt she had not long to live, and who had such a horror of her body being burnt to ashes after death, as is the custom with Hindus, that to escape from her relatives she came into the hospital, saying, she wished to become a Muhammadan, so that she might be buried. We began to explain to her the Gospel of Christ, but she appeared too old to take in something so novel, and finding we were not the Muhammadans she took us for, she sent word to a Muhammadan *anjuman*

Women Carrying Water-pots

to have her taken away. We assured her that we would nurse and care for her, and not burn her body; but no! perhaps we might only be some kind of Hindus in disguise! So she went off with her Muhammadan friends, and in due time was buried.

Unlike this old lady, some of the cases that come into our women's ward are tragic beyond words. Let me give one story as told us by the poor sufferer herself, and she is only one of many who are suffering, unknown and uncared for, in Afghanistan at the present time. For, indeed—for the women especially—it is a country full of the habitations of cruelty. Her name was Dur Jamala, or "Beautiful Pearl." She and her husband were both suffering from cataract, and lived near Kabul. They were trying to resign themselves to lives of blindness and beggary when someone visited their village who told them of a doctor in Bannu who cured all kinds of eye diseases. So, getting together all they could, which only came to about eighteen rupees, they started out on foot on their long and weary journey to Bannu—one hundred and fifty miles of rough road, with two mountain passes to cross on the way! They took with them their only child, a girl of about ten, and travelled slowly, stage by stage, towards Bannu. But before they had got far on their way, in a lonely part of the road, some cruel brigands robbed them of all their savings, beat her husband to death before her eyes, and tore away the weeping child, whom they would sell for a good price into some harim.

Poor Dur Jamala was left alone and helpless, crushed with grief. From that time it took her just ten months to get to Bannu, having been helped first by one and then by another on the way. She reached Bannu very worn and weary, and in rags, and was very grateful indeed to us for a comfortable bed and a good meal. The operation was successful, and resulted in her obtaining good sight in that eye. But meanwhile someone had frightened her, telling her that hell would be her punishment for listening to our teaching. She wept very much, and refused to allow us to operate on the other eye or listen to any more of our "wicked religion." We saw no more of her for about four months, when she appeared one day in our out-patient department in great pain from suppuration of the second eye. She had been to some charlatan, who, in operating on it, had completely destroyed the vision of that eye, and she had suffered so much that she was only too glad to put herself again under our treatment. The second eye had to be removed, but she is able to work, as the sight of the first is good, and she often comes to us now and listens to the teaching, although she still says: "Your medicine is very good, but your religion is wicked." Yet in listening to the Gospel story she finds some solace in the great sorrow which has so clouded the life of poor "Beautiful Pearl."

If some of our medical ladies and nurses in England saw how their poor Afghan sisters suffered, often in silence and hopelessness, would not some of them come out to do the work of Christ and bear His name among them? "I was sick, and ye visited me." Though till now we have only had a man doctor in Bannu, yet forty or fifty women attend the out-patients' department nearly every day, and many of these have undertaken long and wearisome journeys to reach us.

There are the Hindu women from Bannu city collected together in one corner of the verandah, lest they should be polluted by contact with the Muhammadan women from the villages. For the women are much greater sticklers for the observance of all the niceties of Hindu ceremonial than their more Westernized husbands, and would have to undergo the trouble of a complete bath on returning home if they had been in contact with anything ceremonially impure. One can recognize the Hindu women at once by their clothes. They wear the same three garments winter and summer—a skirt reaching down to their ankles; a curious upper garment,

WOMEN GOING FOR WATER AT SHIMVAH

WATER-CARRYING AT SHIMVAH

Women bring the water, frequently from a great distance, in skins slung on either side of donkeys.

like a waistcoat with no back to it; and a veil, which falls over and covers their otherwise bare back, and which they hurriedly pull over their faces when they see a man.

The Muhammadan women have indeed the veil, but the other garments are quite different. The upper garment is a full dress, coming down at least to the knees, and full of pleats and puckers, and ornamented by rows of silver and brass coins across the breast, while the nether garment is a pair of loose, baggy pyjamas of some dark-coloured material, usually blue or red, with very remarkable funnel-like extremities below the knees. At this point the baggy portion is succeeded by a tightly-fitting trouser, the piece about twice the length of the leg, and which is, therefore, crowded up above the ankle into a number of folds, which accumulate the dust and dirt, if nothing worse. The Povindah women—strong, robust, and rosy from the bracing highlands of Khorasan—are dressed almost entirely in black, the Marwat women in blue veils and red-and-blue pyjamas, the Bannuchi women in black veils and red pyjamas, and the women of other tribes each in their own characteristic dress.

Even the style in which the hair is plaited and worn is sufficient not only to indicate what tribe the woman belongs to, but also whether she is married or unmarried. The Povindah women are very fond of blue tattoo marks over their foreheads, while all alike are proud of the row of silver coins which is worn hanging over the forehead. The Hindu women plaster the hair of the forehead and temples with a vermilion paste, not merely for cosmetic reasons, but because it is sacred to their god Vishnu. Then, the sturdy, sunburnt faces of the Wazir women tell tales of the hard, rough outdoor life they perforce lead, and contrast with the more delicate and gentler faces of the Hindus. Notwithstanding the careful way in which all except the hill women veil their faces from masculine gaze, they are very sensitive as to what is being thought of them, and sometimes an impudent man meets a woman who at once closely veils herself, and remarks to his companion: "Ah! her nose has been cut off!" This imputation, not only on her looks, but on her character, is usually too much for her, and she indignantly unveils her face, to cover it up again at once in shame when she finds it was only a ruse!

The hill women rarely, if ever, wash either their bodies or their clothes, and suffer much in the hot weather from skin troubles as a result. The Hindu women, on the other hand, who appear to aim at doing in everything the exact opposite to their Muhammadan sisters, bathe on the slightest pretext, summer and winter, and often women who carefully veil their faces when passing down the street bathe in the river and streams in a state of nudity, regardless of passers-by.

Most of the women have a great aversion to telling their own name, because it is considered a very indelicate thing for a married woman to mention her own name. It would be very difficult to make the necessary entries in the register were it not that there is usually some other woman with her, and etiquette does not prevent her friend telling what her name is. Otherwise she will usually mention the name of her eldest son, who may be a baby in arms, or may be a grown man—never, of course, of a daughter: she must only be mentioned in a whisper, and with an apology, if at all—saying: "I am the mother of Paira Lal," or "I am the mother of Muhammad Ismaïl."

Notwithstanding the state of servitude in which the women are kept and their crass ignorance and superstition, they have great power in their home circles, and mould the characters of the rising generations more even than the fathers.

This fact was brought home very forcibly to me one day in school. A subject had to be fixed on for the next meeting of the school debating society. Various subjects had been proposed and negatived. I suggested · "Who has most influence in moulding our characters—our fathers or our mothers?" "How could we have so one-sided a debate?" responded half a dozen boys at once. "Who could be found to argue for the fathers? Of course, our mothers have all the influence." How important, then, for the future of the nation that something should be done to raise, and elevate, and purify the mothers of the nation!

CHAPTER XVI

THE STORY OF A CONVERT

A trans-frontier merchant—Left an orphan—Takes service—First contact with Christians—Interest aroused in an unexpected way—Assaulted—Baptism—A dangerous journey—Taken for a spy—A mother's love—Falls among thieves—Choosing a wife—An Afghan becomes a foreign missionary—A responsible post—Saved by a grateful patient.

In the highlands between Kabul and Jelalabad is a secluded valley, girt with pine-clad hills, and down which a tributary of the Kabul River flows, fertilizing the rice crops which rise terrace above terrace on the slopes of the hills, and meandering in sparkling rivulets through the villages which lie nestling among orchards of peaches and apples, interspersed with fine walnut and plane trees. This is the Valley of Laghman, and, like the Kabulis, the men are great merchants, and travel about between Central Asia and Hindustan. One of these merchants took his young son, Jahan Khan, down with him to India on one of his journeys, in order that he might serve his apprenticeship in the trade of his father and see something of the wealthy cities and beautiful buildings of India, the fame of which had so often roused the boyish imaginations of the youth of Laghman, and made it the desire of their lives to travel down once to India and see for themselves its glories and its wealth.

Father and son travelled about for two years, buying and selling and taking contracts for road-making, at which the Afghans are great adepts, till one summer the father was stricken down with dysentery. The boy took him to a mission hospital, where for the first time he heard the story of the Gospel; but he had been always taught to look upon the English as infidels, and he used to stop his ears, lest any of the words spoken by the mission doctor might defile his faith. The disease grew worse, and the father paid some men to carry him to the shrine of a noted saint in the neighbourhood, called Sakhi Sarwar, which was renowned for its power in healing diseases. He made a votive offering, but still the malady grew worse, and at last one morning Jahan Khan found himself an orphan hundreds of miles away from home and relations, with no friends and no money to help him home. It is the great desire of an Afghan who dies away from his country to have his body embalmed and carried back, it may be, hundreds of miles on a camel, to be interred in his ancestral graveyard; but how could the poor boy, without money or friends, perform this duty? He had to be content with burying his father near the tomb of the famous saint, whose benign influence might be expected to serve him in good stead on the Day of the Resurrection.

Jahan Khan then took service with some Muhammadans of the country, and it was in this way that I first met him. Soon after my arrival in India I wanted a body-servant who knew no language but Pashtu, in order that I might the more easily gain proficiency in that language. The Muhammadan gentleman to whom I applied recommended me Jahan Khan; but Jahan Khan himself resented the idea of becoming servant to a *Feringi* and an infidel, which he thought would jeopardize his faith and his salvation. His Muhammadan patron laughed at his scruples, and quoted the Pashtu proverb, "The *Feringis* in their religion, and we in ours," saying: "So long as you say your prayers regularly, and read the Quran, and keep the fast, and do not eat their food, lest by any chance there should be swine's flesh in it, you have no reason to fear."

For some time Jahan Khan served me well, but was

evidently chary of too dangerous an intimacy. I had at that time an educated Afghan who was teaching me Pashtu, and he sometimes twitted Jahan Khan with his inability to read. This made the boy desirous of learning, and he persuaded the *munshi* to give him a lesson every day. When the alphabet had been mastered, the *munshi* was looking about for some simple book for reading-lessons, and he happened to take up a Pashtu Gospel which had been given him and laid aside, and from this Jahan Khan got his first reading-lessons. Before long the teaching of the book he was reading riveted his attention. It was so different from the old Muhammadan ideas with which he had been brought up. Instead of the law of "Eye for eye and tooth for tooth," was the almost incredible command to forgive your enemies. His reading-lesson became the event of the day for him, not merely on account of the advance in learning, but because of the new ideas which were stirring in his mind. When the *munshi* observed that a change had come over him, he became alarmed, and told Jahan Khan that he must have no more reading-lessons at all, and that he had better give up all idea of learning to read. The seed was, however, already sown, and despite the adjurations of the *munshi*, Jahan Khan astonished me one day by coming to ask that I should continue the reading-lessons with him.

It was a delight to notice week by week the growth of the Spirit in the boy's heart, but with all that there were many storms to brave and many seasons of darkness and unbelief, which threatened to crush the young seedling before it was yet able to weather the storm. The Afghan nature is hot-tempered and reckless, and he found it difficult to curb his spirit under the taunts of those around him. One afternoon, as I was sitting in my room, I heard shouts from outside—"O Daktar Sahib! O Daktar Sahib!"—and on running out found that two Muhammadans had seized him and were beating him, while they were trying to stifle his cries by twisting his turban round his neck. This was only the first of many times that the young convert was to bear the reproach of the Cross, and he had not yet learnt to take the vindictiveness of his Muhammadan compatriots with the forbearance which was a later growth of the Spirit. This assault, however, resulted in a parting of the ways, and from that time Jahan Khan publicly avowed himself a Christian. He had many a battle yet to fight—not so much with outward enemies as with his own Pathan nature—but the Spirit was to conquer.

Some time after his baptism Jahan Khan conceived a burning desire to revisit his childhood's home. His widowed mother was still living there with his brothers and cousins, and he wanted to tell them of his new-found faith. We pointed out to him the great dangers that attended his enterprise. In that country, to become a pervert from Muhammadanism was a capital offence, and even the nearest relation could not be depended on to incur the odium and danger of protecting a relative who had brought disgrace on Islam. Jahan Khan could not, however, be dissuaded, and at last the preparations were made. Some copies of the Gospels in the Persian and Pashtu languages were sewn inside his trousers, a baggy Afghan garment, lending itself appropriately to this kind of secretion.

On reaching Jelalabad, some of the Afghan police arrested him on suspicion of being a spy of the ex-Amir, Y'akub Khan, and he was in imminent danger of discovery. A few rupees in the hands of the not too conscientious officials saved the situation, and after sundry other vicissitudes he reached his home. His mother and brothers received him with every token of delight, and for some days there were great rejoicings. Then came the time when he had to make known his change of faith. At first, when the villagers missed him from the public prayers in the mosque, they thought it was merely the weariness of the journey; but as the days passed by, and he still did not appear, it became necessary to give explanations. No sooner was it known that he was a Christian than the villagers clamoured for his life. An uncle of his, however, who was himself a Mullah, managed to appease them on condition that he should leave the country at once; and that night there were great weepings in his house, for his mother felt that she was not only going to lose her newly returned son, but that he had sold his soul to the devil and disgraced her whole family. Still, however, mother's love conquered, and she prepared him his food for the journey, and parted with many embraces. "O that you should have become a *Feringi!* Woe is me, but still you are my son!" He left the books with some Mullahs there, who, though they would have been afraid to accept them openly, or let it be known that they were in the possession of such heretical literature, were nevertheless actuated by curiosity to hide the books away, that they might see, at some quiet opportunity, what the teaching of the book of the Christians was.

Jahan Khan's dangers were not yet, however, over. Travellers from Kabul to India could not venture through the passes in small parties, but joined one of those enormous caravans which pass twice weekly through the Khaiber Pass. In these caravans, besides the honest trader and *bona-fide* traveller, there are usually some unscrupulous robbers, who try by trickery or by force to get the property of their fellow-travellers. A common method with them is some evening, after the day's journey is over, to propose a convivial party. "We have just slain a kid," they will say to the unsuspecting traveller, "and we have cooked the most delicious soup. Will you come and share it?" But in the soup they have mixed a quantity of a poisonous herb, which causes insensibility, or it may be madness, in those who partake of it. Whether they knew of Jahan Khan's secret, or whether they thought that he might be carrying money with him, I cannot say; but he, all unsuspectingly, joined in one of these evening feasts, and remembered nothing more until, some days later, the caravan entered Peshawur. With a great effort he struggled up to the mission bungalow, but it was some days before he was able to undertake the journey to Bannu, and still longer before he regained his previous health.

His visit to his home had not been without fruit, and about a year later a brother and two cousins journeyed down from Laghman to Bannu, and while there one at least was brought to ask for Christian baptism, and is to this day working in one of our frontier medical missions. The others placed themselves under instruction, but they could not stand the heat of the Indian summer, and became so homesick for their mountain village that they returned there.

Among the thousand and one duties that fall to the lot of a frontier missionary is that of becoming a matchmaker to some of the converts. It may be that in one station a number of young men are brought into the Christian fold where there is no corresponding women's work, whereby they might be enabled to set up house for themselves, while it would be courting many dangers to expect them to live for an indefinite period in a state of single blessedness. Thus it came about that I undertook a journey with Jahan Khan down to India, and in one of the zenana missions there we found a girl who was to become his helpmeet through life. She came of one of those Afghan families which had long been domiciled in British India, and had been brought to the Christian faith through the devoted efforts of some lady missionary. She had also received the training of a compounder and midwife from the lady doctor where she had been converted, and so was able to be, not only a light to his home, but also an efficient helper in the work of the mission.

Some time after the happy pair had made their home in Bannu, and after on three successive occasions the arrival of a young Afghan had brought still more happiness into their married life, a letter came from a devoted missionary working in a difficult outpost in the Persian Gulf. The letter set forth how the missionary had been left almost without a helper in one of the most difficult and fanatical fields of missionary effort among Muhammadans, and ended by an appeal for some native worker to come out and help. It was difficult to resist such an appeal, and though loth to lose the services of Jahan Khan even for a time, one felt that one had no worker more eminently suited for stepping into the breach. The Afghan makes an excellent pioneer. His pride of race and self-reliance enable him to work in an isolated and difficult field, where a convert from the plains of India would quickly lose heart. So it came about, in a few weeks' time, that we had a farewell meeting in Bannu for bidding God-speed to Jahan Khan and family in their new sphere of missionary labour; and we felt what a privilege it was, for not only had we seen the first-fruits of the harvest of Afghanistan, but had also seen an Afghan convert going out as a missionary to what was as much a foreign country for him as India is for us. For some time he shared with the devoted American missionaries the vicissitudes of work among the fanatical Arabs of Bahrain, and here his eldest daughter was taken from him and laid to rest in the little Christian cemetery. When some time later he could be spared to return to Bannu, we put him to work in the mission hospital, where he was not only able to influence the numerous Afghans who every week came from over the border as patients, but was able also to acquire great proficiency in medical and surgical practice.

Some years after this we had occasion to open fresh work in a village—Karak—in the midst of the Pathan population of the Kohat district, and when we were in need of a thoroughly reliable man to place in this isolated outpost, we found no one better suited than Jahan Khan. Karak is a chief salt mart in the Kohat district, and in the centre of a

NEAR SHINKIARI, HAZARA DISTRICT

Rice fields and irrigation, with cattle feeding.

fertile valley, which, from the amount of grain it produces, has been called the "Granary of the Khattaks." Hard by are salt-quarries, which employ a good number of labourers, and attract merchants with their caravans from distant parts. I first visited this town in 1895, in company with Jahan Khan, and found a rough and fanatical population, who refused to listen to our message, and even rejected our medical aid. As years passed by many of them had occasion to become patients in the Bannu Mission Hospital, and they carried back good accounts to their fellow-townsmen of the benefits they had received and the sympathy that had been displayed towards them, with the result that before long our visits were welcomed, we were able to preach in their bazaars, and eventually they asked us to open permanent work there, gave us a suitable site close to the town, and raised subscriptions to help in the building.

When first Jahan Khan and his devoted wife started work at Karak, they had a great deal of prejudice and antagonism to overcome, owing to their being converts from Muhammadanism; but, by patience and consistency of life, by uniform kindness to all the sick and needy who came for their aid, they gradually lived it down. I have now no greater pleasure in my work than to visit Karak, and to see these two faithful workers in their hospital, surrounded by the sick and needy, telling them of the precious sacrifice of Christ—the very Muhammadans who were once, in their fanaticism, thirsting for his blood, now quietly sitting round and listening attentively while he recounts, day by day, the story of the Cross. I will give an instance to show how a consistent Christian life can influence even such wild, ferocious Pathans as those of Karak. Some fanatical Muhammadans, irritated at the preaching of the Gospel in their town, hired a professional assassin to come to shoot Jahan Khan; but the man happened to be one who had been indebted to the young doctor for recovery from a severe illness, in which he had, by his unremitting attention, been the means of saving his life. When he found who it was he was required to kill, he returned the money and informed Jahan Khan, that he might be on his guard. Jahan Khan called for the men who had hired the assassin, expostulated with them for their ingratitude for the benefits they had received in the hospital, and, when they expressed their contrition, freely forgave them, and now they are his staunch partisans.

CHAPTER XVII

THE HINDU ASCETICS

The Hindu Sadhus more than two thousand years ago much as to-day—Muhammadan faqirs much more recent—The Indian ideal—This presents a difficulty to the missionary—Becoming a Sadhu—An Afghan disciple—Initiation and equipment—Hardwar the Holy—A religious settlement—Natural beauties of the locality—Only man is vile—Individualism *versus* altruism—The Water God—Wanton monkeys—Tendency to make anything unusual an object of worship—A Brahman fellow-traveller—A night in a temple—Waking the gods—A Hindu sacrament—A religious Bedlam—A ward for imbeciles—Religious delusions—"All humbugs"—*Yogis* and hypnotism—Voluntary maniacs—The daily meal—Feeding, flesh, fish, and fowl.

ALL the travellers and tourists who have recorded their experiences of India mention the strange, fantastic, ochre-habited ascetics who are met with in town and village, by the roadside and at fairs—nay, even in the modern railway-station, where they seem strangely out of place. But few have cared to cultivate their more intimate acquaintance; they have little in them that is attractive to the Western eye, and often appear absolutely repulsive. Yet, to a missionary at least, there is a fascination about them. They embody the religious ideals of the East, and carry one back to the hoary past, long before Alexander marched into India, when the same enigmas of life were puzzling the mystical mind of the East, and the same Sadhus were seeking their solution in her trackless jungles and beside her mighty rivers. Sadhus, I say, because then there were no faqirs. Faqirs are of comparatively recent origin, dating from the time of the Muhammadan invasions, about the tenth century of our era. Now the distinction is often lost sight of. The word "faqir" is an Arabic one, and denotes a Muhammadan ascetic; while the word "Sadhu" is Sanskrit, and is best retained for the Hindu ascetic.

The Muhammadan faqir is altogether different from the Hindu Sadhu in his motives, his ideals, his habits, his dress —in fact, in nearly everything; yet contact with the Hindu Sadhus has had a profound effect upon him, and their philosophies have coloured his religious ideas. The Hindus have, on their part too, not been unaffected by the influx of Muhammadans, bringing their new monotheistic ideas, and some of the Hindu orders appear to be attempts to graft the Muslim monotheism on to the mystical Hindu pantheism. This is seen most developed in the Kabir Panthis and the various orders originating from Guru Nanak. A desire to propitiate and attract their Muhammadan conquerors was probably not wanting in the moulding of these new orders; indeed, Kabir and Guru Nanak seem to have had visions of elaborating a creed in which Muhammadan and Hindu could unite together.

The Indian religious ideal has always been ascetic and despondent: ascetic, perhaps, because life seemed sad and hopeless. On the other hand, the Western ideal is an altruistic and optimistic one.

The young missionary, who very likely appeared to his sympathetic friends in England to be making great sacrifices in order to go "to preach the Gospel to the heathen," sometimes ignorantly imagines that the people round him in India will recognize what he has denied himself in order to come among them, and will respect him in due proportion. Poor deluded man! The modern Christian in England has not even learnt the alphabet of austerities and self-denials practised in the name of religion, of which the Indians are past masters. He appears to them as one of the ruling race, surrounded by the comforts and luxuries of a house, many servants, books, flowers, photographs, pictures, and the various little creations of civilization, which custom has made the Western no longer to look on as superfluous articles of luxury! Their ideal has been nearer that of the Swami, who had so overcome the bonds of the flesh that he required neither clothes nor viands, but sat nude and impassive, maintaining his vitality on an occasional banana or mango!

Should the missionary try to accommodate himself to the Eastern ideal, and forego many things that are lawful to him in order to gain more influence with the people for his message? Every Indian missionary has probably asked himself this question at some period of his career. At one time such questionings forced themselves on me with great importunity. There seemed such a gulf between myself, in my comfortable house, surrounded by so many conveniences, and the poor people around me. The multitudinous administrative duties of the missionary in charge of a station seemed to leave so little time for spiritual dealings with inquirers, and at the end of a long day weariness made it difficult to maintain that very essential equipment of every missionary—"a heart at leisure from itself to soothe and sympathize."

Then I had a desire to learn more about these men, who might be supposed to represent the embodiment of the religious ideals of the East. The best way seemed to be to adopt their dress and habits, and travel about among them for a time. A young Afghan, who was a pupil of mine and a Muhammadan student in the school, begged to be allowed to accompany me as a *chela*, or disciple. As the time at my disposal was limited, it would not have been possible to visit many of the places where Sadhus most do congregate had we confined ourselves to the more orthodox method of progression on foot, so we decided to ride our bicycles. This did not seem to affect the reception we met with from the fraternity—in fact, it is not at all uncommon to see Sadhus riding; often pious Hindus seek to gain merit for themselves by providing them with the means for doing so.

When we left Bannu, we took no money with us; but we seldom were in want, as we received ungrudging hospitality from Hindus, Muhammadans, and Christians alike. The ochre-coloured garments are sufficient passport all over India, and people give alms and offer hospitality without requiring further evidence of the genuineness of the claims of the applicant on their charity. In fact, unless the Sadhu is of known bad character, the Hindu would gain his end—that of acquiring merit by almsgiving—as much by giving to one as another; and he would be very unhappy were he not afforded these opportunities of keeping up the credit side of his account, all the more if his gains are ill-gotten, or he is conscious of some underhand dealings which require corresponding acts of merit to balance them.

One of the most interesting places we visited was Hardwar, the holy bathing-place on the Ganges, which is visited by tens of thousands of Hindu pilgrims from every part of India every year, and the neighbouring Sadhu colony of Rishikes. The latter is a village inhabited only by the Sanzasis and other Sadhus, who have built themselves grass huts in a very picturesque spot, where the Ganges River emerges from the Himalaya Mountains, and commences its long course through the densely-populated plains of India. It is at Hardwar that the great Ganges Canal, one of the great engineering feats of the British rule, has been taken from the river to vivify thousands of acres of good land in the United Provinces to the south, and supply their teeming populations with bread. A little above the town of Rurki a massive aqueduct carries the whole volume of the canal high above a river flowing beneath, and yet higher up two river-beds are conducted over the canal, which passes beneath them. The uniqueness of this piece of engineering is dependent on two other factors—the crystalline limpidity of the blue water and the glorious scenery which forms a setting to all.

I no longer needed to inquire why the common consent of countless generations of Hindus had made this neighbourhood their Holy Land; the appropriateness of it flashed on my mind the moment the glorious vista opened before me. There beyond me were the majestic Himalayas, the higher ranges clothed in the purest dazzling white, emblem of the Great Eternal Purity, looking down impassive on all the vicissitudes of puny man, enacting his drama of life with a selfish meanness so sordid in contrast with that spotless purity; and yet not unmoved, for is there not a stream of life-giving water ever issuing from those silent solitudes, without which the very springs of man's existence would dry up and wither? And then, in the nearer distance, the lower ranges clothed in the richest verdure of the primeval forest, vast tracts not yet subdued by the plough of man, where the religious devotee can strive to rise from Nature to Nature's God, amid those solitudes and recesses where no handiwork of man distracts the soul from the contemplation of the illimitable and mysterious First Cause.

While looking down from the elevation of the canal, there was spread out at our feet a bucolic scene of peace and plenty, where villages and hamlets, surrounded by green fields and cultivation, lay scattered among sylvan glades, drinking in vivifying streams which had journeyed down by chasm and defile, through valley and meadow, from those distant solitudes.

How natural it seemed that in those early Vedic ages, when the reverence for the forces of Nature was still unsullied by the man-worship engendered by the development of his inventive genius, this vast cathedral of God's own architecture should have been made the chosen place of worship of the race, where the more devout spirits strove not only to worship and adore, but to shake off the trammels of a mere mundane corporal existence, till the spirit was as free as the birds in the air around, as clear from earthly dross as the limpid waters below, and as integral a part of the great eternal whole as Nature around, so diverse in its manifestations, yet knitted together in one congruous whole by a pervading and uniform natural law. But *facilis descensus Averni!* How often the most glorious inspirations are dragged down and down till they subserve the basest instincts of man! So here a little farther on—at Hardwar—we were to have the spiritual elation engendered by the natural scene cruelly shattered by a sight of the vileness and sordidness of the most repulsive aspects of humanity, and by realizing how the most Divine conceptions can be dragged down and abased to pander to all that is brutal and evil in man. Not, of course, that all the Sadhus at Hardwar and Rishikes have debased their holy profession. Many among them, as I shall shortly describe, are as earnest seekers after Divine illumination as could be met with in any country; but, by one of those strange paradoxes so common in the East, they live side by side with the basest charlatans and the most immoral caricatures of their own ideals without evincing any consciousness of the impropriety of it, or resentment at their profession being thus debased before the public eye.

The individualistic idea eclipses that of the public weal, and each is so intent on perfecting his own salvation, and drawing himself nearer, step by step, to his goal of absorption in the Eternal Spirit, that he has come to forget that man has a duty to those around him from which he cannot absolve himself. St. Paul tells us, "No man liveth to himself, and no man dieth to himself." The Sadhu says each unit is only concerned in building up its own *karma*, or balance of good and evil actions, whereby it must work out its own destiny regardless of the weal and woe of those around. The Hindu idea connects the soul with those other souls before and behind it in a long concatenation of births; the Christian idea connects the soul with the other souls around it, contemporaneous with its own corporeal existence, and linked with it by the good and evil vibrations of its own vitality. Thus the vista of the Sadhu is always introspective, even to a vesting of the natural vital functions of the body with spiritual significations, which require the most laborious practisings and purifications to make them all subserve his great ideal of absolute subjection of the body to the spirit. The vista of the Christian missionary and philanthropist is extrospective, seeking to make his own life a means for elevating spiritually and materially the lives of those around him, and disciplining his own body and soul rather, that he may thereby more effectually further this end. "For their sakes I sanctify myself, that they also may be sanctified."

A constant stream of pilgrims is ever passing through the bazaar of Hardwar to and from that particular part of the river, the water of which is supposed to possess a superlative sanctity. Here they bring the calcined bones and ashes of their dead relations, and there is ever a stream of pious Hindus bringing these doleful relics for consignment to the sacred stream. As I looked down into the crystal waters I could see the fragments of white bones lying about on the pebbles beneath, with the fish playing in and out among them. Strange commingling of life and death! And this has been going on at this spot for three thousand years, for woe to the Hindu who has no son to perform his funeral rites, no relative to bring his ashes to the cleansing waters of the mighty Ganges! His soul will wander about restlessly, and the sequence of its reincarnations leading to its ultimate absorption in the Eternal Spirit, will be hampered and retarded! There they fill the glass bottles of all sizes, which they have brought for the purpose, and then place them in wicker baskets on the two ends of a bamboo pole, which is balanced over the shoulder, and with which they will often travel hundreds of miles on foot till they reach their destination. If the Hindu for whom the water is being obtained is well-to-do, he will have the water fetched with great pomp and ceremony, ringing of bells, playing of instruments, and chanting of *mantras*, while the baskets containing the water are gorgeously decorated, and a servant is deputed to fan the aqueous god as he is borne along. Probably the Hindu would grudge a tenth part of the cost to purify or amplify the water-supply of his own village!

Naturally the town drives a thriving trade in the bamboo rods, baskets, bottles, and all appurtenances of the mighty pilgrimage. The bazaar is crowded with monkeys, the feeding of which affords boundless opportunities to pious Hindus for accumulating merit. These favours the monkeys repay by surreptitiously snatching sweetmeats and fruits from the open shop-fronts and darting off with the booty to the roofs of the shops opposite, where they devour them in quiet with sly winks and leers at the luckless shopkeeper. Though inwardly wrathful, he cannot retaliate on the sacred animals, lest he be dubbed a heretic and his trade depart. Here, too, we see everywhere exemplified the irrepressible faculty of the Hindu for worshipping anything which can possibly be made into an object of veneration.

Probably all the world through, no race is to be found so bent on turning all the events and circumstances of life into religious acts of worship. If anything or anyone is pre-eminently good or pre-eminently bad, or has any particular quality, good or evil, developed to excess, or is a monstrosity in any way, then he or it is sure to become an object of worship. A Hindu addicted to wine-bibbing will sometimes turn his drinking orgy into an act of religious worship, in which the wine-bottle is set up on a pedestal and duly garlanded, apostrophized, and adored. A Sadhu may be a notoriously bad man, but if his vices have given him a pre-eminence over his fellow-men, he will find multitudes of Hindus, men and women, who will regard them only as so many proofs of his divinity, and worship him accordingly. It is not that the Hindu does not recognize or reprobate vice—he does both; but, then, he holds the idea that spirit is eternally pure and good, and matter eternally gross and evil, and that if a Sadhu attains the stage where spirit has triumphed over body, his actions become divorced from ethics, and are no longer to be judged as though his spirit was capable of contamination from the acts of its earthly tabernacle.

Hence it is that the stories of the Hindu divinities, which seem to us distinctly immoral, do not strike the pantheistic Hindu mind as such, for ethics have ceased to be a concern to one whose austerities have won for him union with the Divine Essence. Here in Hardwar was a weird collection of bovine monstrosities—cows with three horns, one eye, or a hideous tumour; calves with two heads or two bodies. These were paraded forth by their fortunate possessors, who reaped a good harvest of coins from the devout visitors, who worshipped them as illustrations of the vagaries of divinity, and hoped, by offering them alms, to propitiate their destinies.

Rishikes, the city of the Sadhus, is eighteen miles higher up the river from Hardwar, and the road lies through a dense forest. The road is only a rough track, but pious Hindus have erected temples and rest-houses at short intervals, where travellers can spend the night and get refreshment. After proceeding some distance through the forest I met a Brahman journeying the same way with a heavily-laden pony. The pony was obstreperous, and the luggage kept falling off, so the Brahman gladly accepted the offer of my assistance, and after repacking the luggage in a securer manner we got along very well. The Brahman beguiled the time by telling me histories of the past glories of the Rishis of the Himalayas, and how the spread of infidelity and cow-killing was undermining the fabric of Hinduism. False Sadhus and Sanyasis from the lower non-Brahman castes were crowding into their ranks for the sake of an easier living, till it was almost impossible to distinguish the true from the false, and a bad name was brought upon all.

Any Hindu of the three upper castes may become a Sadhu, and should, according to Manu's code, become a Sanyasi in his later years. But he does not thereby attain to the sanctity of a Brahman, and the Brahmans have many stories to relate to show how many have undergone extreme austerities and bodily afflictions in order to obtain spiritual power, and have thereby gained great gifts from the gods, but without attaining the coveted sanctity of the born Brahman.

The sun had already set, and the forest path was becoming difficult to follow in the gathering gloom when we reached a clearing with a temple and a few cottages built round it, so we decided to spend the night there. Through the kind offices of the Brahman, I was given a small room adjoining the temple, on the stone floor of which I spread my blanket, and prepared to make myself comfortable for the night. I had consumed my supper of bread and pulse, and given the remnants to the temple cow, and settled myself to sleep, when I was roused by a fearful din. The temple in which I had found refuge was dedicated to Vishnu and Lakshmi, and their full-size images, dressed up in gaudy tinsel, were within. The time for their evening meal had arrived, but the gods were asleep, and the violent tomtoming and clashing of cymbals which awoke me so suddenly was really intended to make the drowsy gods bestir themselves to partake of the supper which their worshippers had reverently brought them.

When the gods were thoroughly roused, and the dainty food had been set before them, the priest proceeded to fan them with some peacocks' feathers while the meal might be imagined to be in course of consumption, and meanwhile the worshippers bowed themselves on the floor before them, prostrating themselves with arms and legs extended on the stones and foreheads in the dust, the more zealous continuing their prostrations as long as the meal lasted. In these prostrations eight parts of the body have to touch the ground—the forehead, breast, hands, knees, and insteps—and I have seen pilgrims travelling towards a holy place some hundreds of miles distant by continuous prostrations of this kind, the feet being brought up to where the hands were, and the prostration repeated, and thus the whole distance measured out by interminable prostrations. This formidable austerity may take years, but will gain the performer great sanctity and power with the gods whose shrine he thus visits.

The meal over, the worshippers knelt reverently in line, and received a few drops each of the water left over, and a few grains of corn that had been sanctified by being part of the meal of the gods, taking them from the priest in their open palm, and drinking the water and eating the corn with raptures of pleasure and renewed prostrations. One could not but be forcibly reminded of a somewhat ceremonious celebration of the Christian Eucharist. This over, the worshippers departed, the gods were gently fanned to sleep, the priest and the most substantial part of the dinner were left alone, and I became oblivious.

The next morning the Brahman and I were up betimes, and girded ourselves for the accomplishment of the nine miles of forest which still lay between us and our destination, before reaching which we had to ford several small rivers. However, the rays of the sun had scarcely become pleasantly warm when we found ourselves elbowing our way through the Sadhus and pilgrims who were crowding the small but striking bazaar of Rishikes. This place has so little in common with the world in general, is so diverse from all one's preconceived notions and ideas, its mental atmosphere departs so far from the ordinary human standard, that it is hard to know whether to describe it in the ordinary terms of human experience, or whether to look on it as a weird dream of the bygone ages of another world. As for myself, I had not been wandering among its ochre-habited devotees for a quarter of an hour before my mind involuntarily reverted to a time, many years past, when I was a student of mental disease in Bethlem Hospital, and to a dream I had had at that time, when I imagined I found myself an inmate, no longer as a psychological student, but with the indescribably uncanny feeling, "I am one of them myself. Now these madmen around me are only counterparts of myself." So now, as some of these forms of voluntary self-torture and eccentricity, nudity, or ash-besmeared bodies, aroused feelings of abhorrence, I had to check myself with the thought: "But you yourself are one of them too: these weird Sadhus are your accepted brothers in uniform." And so the illusion continued so long as I moved among them, and when finally I left Rishikes behind me, it was like waking from some nightmare.

Accompany me round the imaginary wards, and we will first visit that for imbeciles. We find most of them sitting out in the jungle under trees or mats, avoiding the proximity of their fellow-creatures, recoiling from any intrusion on their privacy, preserving a vacuous expression and an unbroken silence, resenting any effort to draw them into conversation or to break into the impassivity of their abstraction. They do not look up as you approach; they offer you no sign of recognition; whether you seat yourself or remain standing, they show no consciousness of your presence. Flies may alight on their faces, but still their eyes remain fixed on the tip of their noses, and their hands remain clasping their crossed legs. They have sought to obtain fusion with the Eternal Spirit by cultivating an ecstatic vacuity of mind, and have fallen into the error of imagining that the material part of their nature can be etherealized by merely ignoring it, until the process of atrophy from disuse often proceeds so far that there is no mind left to be etherealized at all, and there is little left to distinguish them from one of those demented unfortunates who have been deprived by disease of that highest ornament of humanity.

Leaving these, let us proceed to the ward set apart for delusional insanity. The first Sadhu tells you that he is possessed by a spirit which forbids him to eat except every third day. Another avers that he is in reality a cow in human form, and therefore must eat nothing but grass and roots. A third I found sitting in nudity and arrogance on his grass mat, and repeating sententiously time after time: "I am God, I am God!" I remember a patient at Bethlem whose delusion was that he was himself the superintendent of the asylum, the one sane man among all the mad, and he went round the ward pointing out to me each patient with the remark: "He is mad—quite mad. He, too, he also is mad," and so on. But I was much surprised to meet the same gentleman here. He was in the form of a Bengali Babu, a B.A. of the Calcutta University, and had held high posts under Government; but now, in later life, in dissatisfaction with the world at large, had thrown it all up and sought in the garb of a Sanyasi recluse at Rishikes for that peace which an office and Babudom can never afford.

Recognizing me as a novice, he took me by the arm, saying in English (which in itself seemed strange and out of place amid these surroundings): "Come along; I explain to you jolly well all the show." We strolled in and out among the various groups of Sadhus, and at each new form of Sadhuism he would deliver himself after this manner. "See this man—he is a humbug, pure humbug. See that man lying on all the sharp stones—he is a humbug. Look at these here—humbugs! There, that man, reciting the *mantras*—he pure humbug. All these humbugs!" and so on.

Here is the section for the study and practice of hypnotism. These *yogis* maintain that by a knowledge of the spiritual states engendered by various *samadhs* or contorted positions of the body and legs, and by elaborate breathing exercises, they are able to subdue the unruly and material currents of the bodily senses and the brain, and tap that inner source of spiritual knowledge and divinity which makes them *ipso facto* masters of all knowledge, able to commune at will with the Deity Himself.

The contortions into which they are able to thrust their limbs, and the length of time that they are able to sit impassive and imperturbable in what appear to be the most painfully constrained postures, show that years of practice, commenced when the joints and sinews are supple, must be required for the attainment of this ecstatic state. There can be no doubt, I think, that masters do exercise the power of hypnotism on their *chelas*, and are thereby able to perform painful operations on them (such as piercing various parts of their anatomy with iron skewers) without their wincing or showing visible signs of pain. Other practices which these *yogis* have been carrying on for centuries in their haunts in the Himalayas remind one forcibly of the *modus operandi* of the Western hypnotist, and no doubt both attain success through a knowledge, empirical though it may be, of the same psycho-physiological laws.

Leaving these, let us examine some of the cases of mania—a few of them acute, others more or less chronic, or passing on into a drivelling dementia. Here is a man quite naked, except for the white ashes rubbed over his dusky body, who, with long dishevelled locks and wild expression, hurries up and down the bazaar barking like a dog, and making it his boast never to use intelligible language. Another, after painting his naked body partly white and partly black, has tied all the little bits of rag he has picked up in the road to various parts of his person. A third has adorned his filthy, mud-covered body with wild-flowers, whose varying beauty, now withering in the noonday sun, seems a picture of how his mind and conscience, once the glory of his manhood, have now faded into a shadow. Another is lying by choice in the mud by the roadside, to be fouled by the dust of the passers-by, and almost trampled on by the cows, hoping by this abject affectation of humility to be thought the greater saint. For, by a curious paradox, it is often those who make the greatest display of humility and subjection of the passions who show the greatest sensitiveness to public opinion of their sanctity, and quite fail in concealing their jealousy when some other Sadhu outdoes them, and gains the greater meed of public admiration.

There is another man to be seen wandering aimlessly about and picking up bits of filth and ordure, and putting them in his mouth and chewing them. But to give a further account of these caricatures of humanity would be loathsome to the reader, as their contemplation became to me—the more so as the thought kept recurring to my mind, "And you are one of them, too, now"; and who knows to what point the imitative faculty of man, that contagion of the mind, may not raise or lower him?

By this time, however, the long fast and the fresh, keen air from the Ganges made me begin to wonder how I was going to satisfy a call from within. It was now close on midday, and I saw the Sadhus collecting round certain houses with bowls, gourds, and other receptacles. These were the kitchens established by pious Hindus of various parts of India with the object of acquiring sufficient merit to counterpoise their demerits—the bribery, chicanery, and lying of their offices, or the more covert sins of their private life. A rich Hindu may establish a kitchen in his own name alone, but more often a number unite together to form a guild to keep the kitchen going, and the merit is portioned out like the dividends of a joint-stock company to its shareholders. There were some twenty or more of such kitchens here, in each of which three chapattis and a modicum of dal, potatoes, greens, or some other vegetable were given; and there was nothing to debar a Sadhu from going to as many kitchens as he desired—in fact, he knew he was conferring a benefit on the shareholders by consuming their victuals and supplying them thereby with merit.

The gnawing pangs of hunger made me mingle with the shoving, jostling throng, and hurry from kitchen to kitchen till I had accumulated nine chapattis, and vegetables in proportion. Modesty then made me withdraw, but not so most of my companions. One of these who rejoined me a little later had been to eight kitchens, and brought a supply of twenty-four chapattis, and a large bowl of dal, potatoes, and other vegetables. The custom of the place then required me to descend to the margin of the Ganges, and, squatting on a stone which was lapped by its pellucid waters, to consume my portion with draughts of the holy water. But not without a preliminary ceremony, for while the Sadhus had been collecting round the kitchens, the cows and bulls had been collecting on the banks of the river, and it was *de rigueur* first to set aside three portions, and give one to these holy animals, a second portion to the birds in the air, and a third to the fish in the river, after which the remainder, whether one chapatti or twenty, might be consumed with an easy conscience and a courageous digestion.

CHAPTER XVIII

SADHUS AND FAQIRS

Buried gold—Power of sympathy—A neglected field—A Sadhu converted to Christianity—His experiences—Causes of the development of the ascetic idea in India—More unworthy motives common at the present time—The Prime Minister of a State becomes a recluse—A cavalry officer Sadhu—Dedicated from birth—Experiences of a young Sadhu—An unpleasant bed-fellow—Honest toil—Orders of Muhammadan ascetics—Their characteristics—A faqir's curse—Women and faqirs—Muhammadan faqirs usually unorthodox—Sufistic tendencies—Habits of inebriation—The sanctity and powers of a faqir's grave.

There were, however, some bright spots even in Rishikes, gems among the rubble, lumps of gold concealed among the mass of baser metals—minds earnestly seeking a higher spiritual life, losing themselves, wearying themselves in the quest after truth, intensely conscious of the vanity of this world and its pursuits and pleasures, and striving to obtain in a contemplation of the One only Pure, the only Unchangeable, the only True, that peace of mind which they instinctively felt and experimentally found was not to be realized in the pursuit of material objects. The painful mistake which made their quest so hopeless was the endeavour to divest themselves of the bonds of their bodily material tabernacle, which, if subjugated to the spirit, forms the basis on which that spirit can work healthily and naturally to its divinest development, but which, if altogether ignored and contemned, reduces that same spirit to a morbid fantasy.

With regard to the learning of many of the Sanyasis

there is not a shadow of doubt. There are men there fit to be Sanskrit professors in the Universities, and who are deep in the lore of the ancient and voluminous literature of Hinduism. Yet who benefits by all their learning? They may transmit it to a few disciples, or it may live and die with them; they make no attempt to methodize it, to draw conclusions, to contrast the old order with the new, to summarize or to classify, but cultivate it purely as a mental exercise or religious duty, without apparently even the desire to benefit the world at large thereby. This self-centred individualism, each mind self-satisfied, self-contained, with the springs of sympathy and altruism hard frozen, ever revolving on itself, and evolving a maze of mysticism, at length becomes so entangled in its own introspection that other minds and the world outside cease to have any practical existence for it. This is at once the most salient and the saddest feature of the learned and meditative Sadhu.

But there they are—men who might have shone academically, who might have enriched the world with thought, research, and criticism, but who have chosen to live for and within themselves, careless whether others live or die, are instructed or remain ignorant. Though they have categorically rejected altruism, and denied that they have a duty towards their neighbour, and done their best to shut up the doors of sympathy, yet even with them human nature refuses to be utterly crushed, and will assert itself. One can often discern a suppressed, yet insuppressible, hunger after sympathy, and one has no doubt but that the sympathy which finds its highest expression in the love of Christ, whether acted or recounted, will penetrate their hearts, and find a response. Unused, any organ will atrophy, and so their capacity for sympathy may be latent and not easily roused. Let someone, however, go to them as a fellow-creature, full of love and sympathy—not to despise and to fault-find, but to take hand in hand and bring soul to soul—and he will find that the Sadhus of Rishikes are human, very human, with the same spiritual hungerings and thirstings, and able to realize and rejoice in the same salvation.

It is a pity that more missionaries have not devoted themselves to working among these people. They would need to be men of great devotion and self-abnegation, but there have been many such in other spheres. They would be repelled and disappointed by the callousness and fraud of the majority, but there are the gems to be sought out, and how much hard granite is the miner willing laboriously to crush when he is sure of finding nuggets of gold here and there! And among these Sadhus are men who, converted to Christianity, would be apostolic in their zeal and devotion, and might, by travelling up and down India, not now in the vain accumulation of merit, but as heralds of the Gospel of goodwill, become the Wesleys and Whitefields of a mighty mass movement of the people towards Christ.

As an example of such a one and the way in which he was converted from the life of a Sadhu to that of a Christian preacher, I will quote here the account that Rev. B. B. Roy gives of his conversion. It shows how strong a hold the ascetic Sadhu idea has on a religiously-minded Hindu, and how spontaneously his heart seeks in austerity and retirement for the peace which a growing sense of sin and of the evil of the world has taken away. At the same time it shows that, as in the case of Buddha, asceticism fails to afford any lasting comfort or peace to the weary storm-tossed soul. He says: "Constant starvation and exposure to all sorts of weather reduced my body to a living skeleton.

"After a few months' travel I came to Hardwar, and then proceeded to a place called Rishikes, celebrated for its Sadhus and Sanyasis. My intention was to stay there and practise *yoga* [a kind of meditative asceticism], to attain to fina. beatitude; but a strange event took place, which entirely changed my purpose. The rainy season had already set in; the jungle path was muddy, and at places full of water, so when I reached Rishikes I was almost covered with mud. Leaving my things in a *dharmsala*, I was going to bring water from the Ganges when I smelt a very bad odour. As I turned round I saw a dead body in the street, rotting in the mud. Around the corpse were the huts of the Sanyasis, who were performing *tap-jap* almost the whole day; but none of them had even enough of compassion to dispose of the body of the poor man who had died helpless on the street. I thought that if this was religion, then what was irreligion? My spirit revolted against these Sadhus.

"I perceived in my heart of hearts that *yog-sadhan* cannot create that love in man which makes a man feel for a fellow-man. Where there is no such love there can be no religion from God."

And then he goes on to relate how, leaving Rishikes, he fell in with a Christian preacher, and eventually found in Christ that peace which all his voluntary hardship had failed to afford, and how he had been led on and on in his pilgrim walk, till he had now the blessed and responsible work of teaching others of his fellow-countrymen how best to bring the good news of the eternal love to all the hungry and thirsty souls around. (He was then Principal of a theological seminary.)

There have already been many such cases of Sadhus and faqirs converted to Christianity, and these men and women have, as might be expected, exerted an immense influence on their fellow-countrymen. They have presented them with a Christianity in an Eastern dress which they can recognize as congenial to the sentiments of their country, and exemplified in their own self-denying lives, full of the spirit of that austerity which the Indian has long believed to be inseparable from religious zeal.

Devotion, austerity, and asceticism in the cause of religion have been characteristic of India as far back as history records. Life has always been precarious for the majority of the population in the East, and plagues, famines and wars have familiarized them with the tragic spectacles of multitudes of young and old being suddenly carried off in the midst of business or enjoyment. Consequently, their sages dwelt much on the uncertainty of life, and developed the doctrine that the world and its gay shows were only an illusion of the senses, and the goal of the spirit was to divest itself of this illusion and rise superior to the limitations of matter. By the practice of austerities, the grossness of the flesh, the demands of the body, and the storms of the passions, would be subdued, and the spirit gain freedom from the endless round of reincarnation, and ultimately join the illimitable sea whence it came, as the drop on the lotus-leaf falls back into the water and is lost therein.

Then, it is universally believed that by these austerities the ascetic gains power with the gods, and can bring down blessings from above for himself and his votaries. He can, in fact, extort favours from the unwilling gods if he only carry his self-torture and privations to the requisite extreme.

We find much the same idea in the ascetic saints of the early Christian era. Thus Tennyson, in his poem "St. Simeon Stylites," puts the following words into the mouth of the saint. He is addressing a crowd of people who have come to worship him, and who believe that, owing to his great austerities, he has the power of granting their requests.

> "Speak! is there any of you halt or maim'd?
> I think you know I have some power with Heaven
> From my long penance; let him speak his wish."

The idea of merit is ever present to the Hindu. By practising austerity himself, or by paying another to practise it for him, he can accumulate merit, which will render each succeeding birth more propitious, and bring him nearer his ideal of bliss, when his soul will be finally freed from the endless chain of reincarnations. It must, sad to say, be admitted that with the great majority of the Sadhus of the present day the motives which actuate them are much more mundane and sordid than what I have described above. Lazy good-for-nothings, too indolent to work, find that in the garb of a Sadhu they can be assured of a living which, though it may not be a luxurious one, is yet one free from anxiety and toil. Fraudulent scamps enrich themselves on the credulity of the people by counterfeiting austerities and miraculous powers, which successfully deceive the simple-minded, who, without even a desire to examine their claims and reputed performances too critically, freely bestow gifts of money and kind on them, in the hopes of gaining their favour for the attainment of some benefit or cure, or other object.

Then, there are the political faqirs, who use their position to disseminate political propaganda, usually of a seditious nature. From their habit of travelling all over the country they have special opportunities of becoming the channels for the transmission of news, and before the days of telegraph and post-office the people would get most of their news of the rest of the country through these pilgrims and ascetics ; and even at the present day they are able to disseminate secret intelligence and transmit the orders of the organizing authorities in such a way as to be very difficult of detection. When I travelled as a faqir I was frequently shadowed by the police, and sometimes a talkative and inquisitive companion would join me who eventually proved to be a detective in his disguise.

As examples of the superior Sadhu—the man who from high aspirations has voluntarily given up position, honour, and wealth in the world for the life of a recluse—I will give the two following instances.

I met a man at Rishikes who had been the Prime Minister

of a Native State. While in that capacity he had to deal with bands of robbers who infested the highways, and had committed some cold-blooded murders for the sake of the money and goods of the travellers. When a number of these men had been caught and participation in murders proved against them, he found it his duty to condemn them to death by hanging. The sentence was duly executed, but from that day he got no rest at nights. Visions of the culprits would rise before him as soon as he lay down on his couch, and they would appear to be pointing their fingers at him as the cause of their death. This so unnerved him that he could not get a night's rest, and dreaded going to sleep. Want of rest and nervous perturbation prevented him from duly carrying on the work of the State, and he asked for leave, nominally to attend the funeral of his mother, but really to expiate his sin, and gain repose of mind by a pilgrimage to a noted holy place. But he failed to get ease of mind there, and had it impressed on him that only by leaving the world and spending the rest of his days in seclusion, meditating on God, would he find rest from the blood-guiltiness that was tormenting him. He forthwith resigned his position in the State, divided his property amongst his family, put on the garb of a Sanyasi, and was spending the rest of his days in contemplation and religious exercises

The other case I met in a village on the Pir Panjal Range, where he had built himself a cottage with a garden, in which he spent his days in religious studies and contemplation, and receiving the many people who used to come to him for advice, or to derive advantage from contact with his superior sanctity and wisdom. He had been Risaldar-Major in one of the regiments of Bengal Cavalry, and had fought under the British flag in several campaigns, and won wounds and medals. On retirement he forsook his home and relations and all worldly pursuits, and spent his time in the contemplation of the Deity and such works of charity as came in his way.

Both these men were truly devout, unostentatious spirits, who had found that the delights of Divine communion exceeded the pleasures of this transitory world.

Some Sadhus are set aside from birth for this life by their parents, and as a good example of such a one I will tell the story of a man who joined company with me on the road near Ludhiana. I will relate it in his own words:

"My father is a small Hindu farmer in the State of Patiala, and when three sons had been born to him, he made a vow that he would consecrate the fourth to the service of God. When I was born he allowed me to stop with my mother only till I was four years old, and then he took me to a certain large city, where there is a famous shrine, and a very holy man who is renowned for his piety and deep learning. At first I wept much at being taken away from my brothers and sisters, but the Swami treated me kindly and gave me sweetmeats, and I used to fetch his mat and books and put oil in his lamp and do other little services for him. Then, as I got older, he taught me to read, first in Bhasha and then in Sanskrit, and he taught me all the laws of worship and guides to *bhagti* (devotion). When I became a lusty young man, he told me to make pilgrimages to various sacred places and to visit other sages and holy men, and I went forth on my first journey, taking with me only a staff, a gourd for drinking-water, a blanket, and a couple of *shasters* (holy books).

"I had never been out in the world before, and at first I was very timid of asking people for food in new places that I had never hitherto seen; but people were nearly always kind to me and gave me food to eat and shelter at night, and so I got bolder, and I would recite to them verses out of the holy books in return for their kindness, for I had no money or anything else to give them. In this way I have travelled many hundreds of miles on foot, and seen many sacred places and holy men. After each journey I return to my preceptor, and tell him my experiences, receive fresh counsel and instruction from him, and now I am just starting on a fresh journey to Dwarka."

Looking down at my bicycle, I felt quite a luxurious traveller compared with this brave fellow, starting off with no hesitation and no misgivings on a journey of hundreds of miles, with not a pice in his wallet, and a kit even more slender than my own.

He had little idea as to where Dwarka was, but was content to ask his way day by day, and trust to God and the hospitality of his co-religionists on the way for sustenance.

"Yes," he said, "sometimes I do want to see my family. My brothers are all *gryasthas* (married householders) now, and I sometimes take a few days' leave from my master to visit them and my parents. I am quite happy in this life, and do not desire money or service or children; for when my heart is lonely I read in my copy of the Bhagvad Gita and get consolation, and I like that better than any other book because it makes my heart glad. No, I have never met anyone who has spoken to me of Christ, and I do not know anything about Him; but I am quite happy because I am sure that if I continue a life of penury and celibacy and pilgrimage I shall attain salvation."

To resume my own experiences at Rishikes. When night came on I was given shelter in one of the monasteries, and though the floor was stone, and a chill wind blew through the cloisters, I should have slept soundly had not my next bed-fellow—or rather floor-fellow, for there were no beds—thought it incumbent on him to spend the night shouting out in varying cadence, "Ram, Ram, Jai Sita Ram, Ram, Ram!" I suggested that keeping a weary fellow-pilgrim awake all night would detract from the merit he was acquiring, but only received the consolation that if he kept me awake I was thereby sharing, though in a minor degree, in that merit; so it perforce went on till, in the early morning hours, my ears grew duller to the "Ram, Ram," and my mind gradually shaped itself into an uneasy dream of ash-covered faqirs, chapattis, cows, and squatting Sadhus. Next day, in the forest road near Rishikes, I came across a string of hillmen bowed down under heavy loads of firewood, which they had been cutting in the hills near to sell for a few pice in the bazaar. This was their daily lot, earning just sufficient by continuous hard labour to find for themselves and their families sufficient coarse food for a meagre sustenance. The question rose in my mind, Who approached nearer the ideal?—the idle Sadhu, who makes religion an excuse for living in greasy plenty on the hard-won earnings of others, while doing next to nothing himself, or these woodmen of the forest, and all the dusty toilers in the ranks of honest labour? And an answer came, clear and sure:

"Honest toil is holy service; faithful work is praise and prayer.
They who tread the path of labour follow where My feet have trod;
They that work without complaining do the holy will of God.
Where the many toil together, there am I among My own;
Where the tired labourer sleepeth, there am I with him alone."

The ascetics of Afghanistan are almost all Muhammadans, and I shall therefore speak of them as faqirs, that being the counterpart of the Hindu Sadhu. These faqirs have started from an entirely different religious standpoint, and travelled along a very different experimental road to those of their Hindu brethren; but the ultimate result is strikingly similar in many salient features, and Hindu asceticism and pantheistic thought have deeply coloured their ideas and habits.

There are endless different orders of Muhammadan faqirs, most of which had their origin in Central Asia, Bukhara and Baghdad having contributed perhaps the largest share. Each of these orders has its own method of initiation, its own habit of dress, set phrases and formulæ, and other characteristics.

Except in a few cases in India, none of these orders of faqirs or dervishes adopt the ochre garments of the Sadhus. The most characteristic garment of the faqir is known as the *dilaq*, which is a patchwork, particoloured cloak. The owner goes on adding patches of pieces of coloured cloth which take his fancy, but I have never seen him washing it, and as it gets old he stitches and patches it till very little of the original is left. The older and more patched it is, the greater is the pride he takes in it, and he would not part with it for love or money.

The order which is most commonly seen in Afghanistan is that known as *Malang*, or wandering dervish. These men have a *dilaq*, a staff, and a begging-bowl, and travel all about the country begging. They are nearly all illiterate, and their knowledge of their own religion does not usually extend beyond certain chapters from the Quran and stock formulæ. But they have a wonderful vocabulary of words of abuse and curses, and the people are in great fear of being visited by some calamity if they offend one of them and incur his wrath, as they believe in their being able to blast the life of a child or the offspring of a pregnant woman, or to bring other calamities down from heaven on the heads of those with whom they are wroth. Once while I was stopping in a village on the border one of these gentlemen came to say his prayers in the mosque, and had left his shoes at the entrance, as is the custom. After he had said his prayers with great sanctimoniousness he went to resume his foot-gear, but found, to his dismay, that some thief had gone off with them. Then followed a torrent of curses on whoever the thief might be, in which all imaginable calamities and diseases were invoked on him and his relations, accompanied by every epithet of abuse in the Pashtu vocabulary, and that is pretty rich in them! The very volubility and eloquence of his anathemas would have dismayed any ordinary thief had he been within earshot, but whether he ever got back his shoes or not I cannot say.

Women who are childless will visit various faqirs, whose prayers have a reputation for being efficacious for the removal of sterility. They write charms, and dictate elaborate instructions for the behaviour of the woman till her wish be fulfilled, and they take the gifts which the suppliant has brought with her. Were this nothing more than a fraud dictated by avarice, it would be reprehensible, but worse things happen; and when a child is born after due time, the husband of the woman cannot always claim paternity. It is a strange thing that in a country where husbands so jealously guard their women from strangers they allow them so much freedom in their dealings with faqirs, whom they know to be morally corrupt. It recalls the Hindu Sadhu and divinity, who is popularly supposed to have attained an elevation where ethics are no longer taken account of.

In a religion such as Islam it is scarcely possible for an order of dervishes to be orthodox, and, as a matter of fact, most of them are extremely unorthodox, and there is often considerable disputing between them and the priesthood on this account. But the faqirs have such a hold over the people at large, and in many ways are so useful to the propagation of Islam, that the Mullahs find it more politic to overlook their heresies and use them in the promotion of religious zeal and fanaticism.

It will be found that the underlying current of religious thought in nearly all these orders is that of Sufism, and Sufism is the product of the aspiration of the Mussalman soul, wearied with the endless repetition of forms and ceremonies, after something more spiritual; and in its search after this spirituality it has drawn most on the pantheistic philosophies of Hinduism.

Pantheism is, of course, the antithesis of the Judaic theocracy of Islam, and we read of a faqir who went about calling out, "Ana hu, ana el haqq" ("I am He, I am the Truth"), being put to death for blasphemy; but all the same, these Muhammadans, who feel most the aspirations of the soul for Divine communion, find it in a greater or less assimilation of pantheistic doctrine.

Most of the faqirs one meets with in Afghanistan are lazy fellows, who abhor hard work, and find they can make an easy living by begging, and acquire at the same time, what is so dear to many natures, the homage and respect of the credulous and superstitious. When one does meet with one who is willing and able to converse on spiritual topics, one usually finds that he is a disciple of Hafiz, the great Sufi poet of the Persians. Like the Hindu Sadhus, they are much addicted to the use of intoxicants (though rarely alcohol), and *charras* and *bhang* (Indian hemp) are constantly smoked with tobacco in their *chilams*. When thus intoxicated they are known as *mast*, and are believed by the populace to be possessed by divinity, and to have miraculous powers of gaining favours from heaven for those who propitiate them.

When such a faqir dies he is buried in some prominent place, often at the crossing of roads, and his tomb has even greater efficacy than he himself had when living; and those who wish to obtain his intercession with the Almighty for themselves bring little earthen cups full of oil, with little cotton wicks, which they burn at his grave, as a Roman Catholic burns candles at the shrine of a saint. The most propitious time for doing this is on Thursday night, and at such times one can see the tombs of most renowned sanctity a veritable illumination with the numbers of little lamps burning far into the night. At the same time offerings are given to the custodian of the shrine, who is himself a faqir, by preference a disciple of the one whose grave he tends.

In one such shrine that I visited there were the remains of

what must once have been a fine sycamore-tree, but which was then, with the exception of one branch, a mere withered shell, which had to be propped up to prevent its falling to the ground. The one green branch was said to be miraculously kept alive by the shadow of the tomb falling on it; and if any childless pilgrim would take home a few leaves and give a decoction of them to his wife, he would assuredly before long be the happy father of a son; while for the relief of the other ills to which flesh is heir there was a masonry tank outside, in which the sick, the halt, and the blind bathed, and were said to receive the healing they came for. Many of our hospital patients have already been to this and similar faith-healing establishments, so they are not always efficacious.

CHAPTER XIX

MY LIFE AS A MENDICANT

Dependent on the charitable—An incident on the bridge over the Jhelum River—A rebuff on the feast-day—An Indian railway-station—A churlish Muhammadan—Helped by a soldier—A partner in the concern—A friendly native Christian—The prophet of Qadian—A new Muhammadan development—Crossing the Beas River—Reception in a Sikh village—Recognized by His Highness Yakub Khan, late Amir—Allahabad—Encounter with a Brahman at Bombay—Landing at Karachi—Value of native dress—Relation to natives—Need of sympathy—The effect of clothes—Disabilities in railway travelling—English manners—Reception of visitors.

In this chapter I shall recount a few of the more interesting incidents that befell me and my disciple when on our pilgrimage as Sadhus. As we were travelling without money, we were dependent on the offerings of the charitable not only for our daily food, but for such little items as the toll required for crossing the bridges over the five great rivers of the Panjab. The first river we came to was the Indus, and there being no bridge over that part of the river, it is crossed in ferry-boats. We had no difficulty here, for we were known, and one of my pupils was on duty at the ferry and assisted us over. It was not so easy, however, at the Jhelum River When we reached the western end of the bridge, the toll-keeper stopped us for payment. I told him that I was a Christian Sadhu journeying to Hindustan, and that we had no money of any kind with us. He may have believed us, he may not; but from the way he eyed the bicycles, probably he did not. Anyway, he told us plainly—no pice, no path; and no setting forth of the peculiar privileges of a Sadhu could make him budge from the practical financial view of the question, so we had nothing for it but to sit quietly down by the roadside and await events.

Shortly afterwards a party of Hindus, on their way to their morning ablutions in the river, sauntered up, and stopped to gaze at the novel combination of bicycles and Sadhus. This soon led to conversation, in the course of which we told them the object of our journey and the cause of our detention. They then tried with no little earnestness to get us to relinquish the preaching of the Gospel for the promulgation of the Vedas, and even offered to pay the two annas required for our toll if we would accede to their plan. This gave me an opportunity for pointing out the attraction of Christ, which made it impossible for one who had once tasted the sweets of following in His footsteps to desert Him for another master.

They clothed their contempt for the message of the Cross in their compassion for our hopeless predicament, as they considered it; "for," they said, "there are no Christians here to help you over, and it is not likely that Hindus or Mussulmans would help you on such a mission." I replied that I was content to wait by the roadside till help came, and that I felt sure we should not have long to wait. "Go back into the town—there are Christian missionaries there who will help you; but no one will be coming this way if you wait all day." I replied that if it was the will of Allah that we should cross, He could send to us there the means requisite, as much as in the city. I had scarcely spoken when we saw an officer, attended by a *sowar*, riding up in the direction of the bridge. When he reached us we recognized an officer from the frontier, who had, as we learnt, just then been sent down to Jhelum on special duty. He recognized me, and appeared amused and surprised at meeting me under such peculiar circumstances. When he learnt what was the cause of our detention, naturally the toll-keeper had not long to wait for his two annas, and I was able to point out to my Hindu friends that it had not taken long for God to send us help from even so far as Peshawur, and we went on with light and thankful hearts. Truly, two annas is worth much more in some circumstances than one hundred rupees in others!

We then wheeled comfortably along the interesting Grand Trunk Road, now to the north and now to the south of the railway-line. The crisp morning air of a Panjab winter has an exhilarating effect on the appetite, and we were only exceptional in that we had the appetite but no wherewithal in our wallets to satisfy the same. To tantalize us the more, it was the feast-day succeeding the great Muhammadan fast, and in all the villages the men were feasting, and the children, gaily dressed in their gala clothes, were amusing themselves on numerous swings, hung up on the trees round the villages, or in playing about on the roads. My Afghan companion, who had been having the fast without the feast, finally went up to a party of merrymakers, and, after saluting them with the customary "Salaam alaikum," said that he was very hungry, and would be glad of a share of the '*Id* cakes. The man addressed surveyed us in a leisurely fashion from head to foot, and said: "You! you call yourselves faqirs, ride bicycles, and beg your bread! Phew!" and turned his back on us. My companion turned to me with a very un-Sadhu-like expression on his face, saying: "We Afghans used always to say that Panjabi Muhammadans are only half Mussulmans; but now I see we were wrong: they are not a quarter. In our country we call in every stranger and traveller to share our feast." The latter part of his statement was certainly true; as to the former, I must leave those who know them best to judge.

Shortly after midday we reached Lala Musa, and, visiting the station, found the train had just come in. We mingled with the bustling crowd, and watched the native sweetmeat and refreshment vendors going from carriage to carriage, calling out: "Garm chapati! garm chapati awe dal!" (Hot rolls! hot rolls and pulse!); "Ghi ki pakorian!" (Vegetable fritters fried in butter!); "Garm dudh!" (Hot milk!), and various other delicacies; and we watched the fortunate possessors of pice selecting some tempting sweetmeat or *pancake*. Then we passed on to the refreshment-rooms, where the European passengers were taking a hurried meal, and I remembered many occasions when I had been into that same refreshment-room without being a tithe as hungry, and now, how could I venture inside? Should I not be greeted with: "Now then, out of this; no faqirs wanted here!" So I wandered back among the third-class passengers. A Sikh native officer spoke kindly to me and offered me some cardamoms, and then the whistle blew. The passengers hurried to their seats, and we were left alone.

A railway porter entered into conversation, and, finding who we were, directed us to go to the village, where there was a Christian preacher. We went to the caravanserai, where there were some Afghan traders sitting on a bed. They seemed surprised at getting a greeting in Pashtu, but returned it heartily. Then I saw a well-dressed man walking off towards the bazaar, and something in his face and a book in his hand seemed to indicate him as the Christian preacher, and, on introducing ourselves, we found we were not mistaken. He asked us into his house to rest, and informed us that he was an agent of the Scotch mission at Gujrat. After the rebuff of the morning we were loth to say that, though the sun was now declining towards the west, we were still awaiting our breakfast; so after a time I rose to go, when, to our no small satisfaction, the kind man asked us to stop till tea was ready.

It was my custom at most of the towns to preach in the bazaar, and usually, during or after the preaching, someone in the audience would offer us hospitality. When we reached Pind Dadan Khan, however, it was too late for this, darkness

DR. PENNELL TRAVELLING AS A SADHU OR MENDICANT PILGRIM

having set in; and after wandering about the bazaar for a time, and talking to a few people, none of whom offered us hospitality, we went to the public serai, or inn, known as "Victoria Ghar," where travellers can rest without payment, and spent the night there. Someone had given us two pice, and with this we bought a pice chapati and a pice of sugar-cane, and dined off this. Being thirsty, I asked a respectable Muhammadan who was dining on a bed hard by for a glass of water. He gave it; but when I raised the glass to my lips, he said: "I would like to know first what your religion is." I replied: "I am a Christian." Hearing this, the gentleman took the glass from me, saying: "I do not wish to sully my glass with your touch." This was a bigotry which I am glad to say I rarely met with, and is certainly not justified by the teaching of the Quran, which permits commensality with Christians and Jews.

After this rebuff we did not care to ask any other inhabitant of the place for water. The next day we travelled on to Khewra, and, on passing through the bazaar, saw the Government doctor, a Hindu assistant-surgeon, sitting outside the dispensary seeing patients. He knew us, and in place of water brought us milk, and then got us a breakfast. Welcome as this was, his kind greeting cheered us even more.

The next river we had to cross was the Chenab. On arriving at the bridge, I found a detachment of English soldiers on the march, and one of these gave the two annas required for our toll. About two years later, when visiting Lahore, a missionary friend there said to me: "I met a friend of yours the other day.'

"Indeed! Who was that?"

"I was travelling up to Peshawur by rail, when some English soldiers got into the carriage, and one of them, looking at me, asked me if I was a *Padre*. On my answering his question in the affirmative, he then said he was glad of that, because he took an interest in missions. I asked him why he did so. 'You see,' he said, 'some time ago we were on the march to Lahore, and at the Chenab bridge there was a missionary chap who hadn't the money for crossing the bridge, and so I paid it for him. I became a kind of partner in the concern ; that is why I take an interest in missions.' This was your friend, was it not?" I, of course, recalled the incident at the Chenab bridge, and hope my friend has continued his practical interest in mission work.

The last day of the year 1903 found us at Narowal, a village famed in the missionary annals of the Panjab. Leaving that, we soon reached the Ravi River, which lower down flows by the walls of the capital of the Panjab. Here it was running clear and cold below a sandy cliff on its western bank. It had evidently been encroaching on the lands of the farmers, and engulfing many a fertile acre, and the houses of the village, too, the ruins of the latter showing some way along the bank. The east bank was a low, wide expanse of sand, which had long been left dry by the receding stream. Seeing no other way of crossing, we were preparing to doff our clothes and ford, when a good soul of a *zamindar* came up.

"Peace be with you."

"And on you be peace."

"Whither are you going, O Sadhu-log, and what is your order and sect?"

"We are Christian Sadhus travelling from Afghanistan to India, and are seeking means to cross this river."

"Then you are my teacher," said the *zamindar*, brightening into a smile, "and I will get a boat and take you across."

Although the good fellow had been brought to the brink of ruin by the destruction of his lands and house by the rapacious river, he went and procured a boat and rowed us across, knowing that it was not in our power to give him any reward, except to pray for him that he might recover his lost land, and to give him some spiritual comfort.

After the pleasure of meeting with this brother so opportunely, we went on encouraged, and soon reached Dera Baba Nanak, the residence of the descendants of the famous Guru and the seat of a *darbar* (Sikh temple), the gilded dome of which we saw glittering in the sun. Passing over our stay here and at other intervening places, I might mention our visit to Kadian, rendered famous by being the headquarters of the Muhammadan reformer Mirza Ghulam Ahmad, who died in 1908. This man had collected round him a band of zealous followers, but, unfortunately, the good he might have done was nullified by his impious claim to be the returned Messiah, in accordance with which he professed miraculous powers, and demanded a correspondingly abject obedience.

Heavy rain-clouds were overcasting the sky when we set out, and we had scarcely covered the eleven miles of unmade road that connects Batala with Kadian when the downpour commenced, and continued throughout the day. Moulvi Muhammad Sadiq, the head-master of the Mirza's High School, received us with the greatest courtesy, and gave us one of the schoolrooms to rest in, and shortly afterwards, as the Mirza himself was indisposed and unable to see us, we were taken into the presence of his lieutenant, Moulvi Moha-ud-din. This Moulvi is very learned, probably the most learned in Kadian; he comes from the town of Bhera, in the Panjab, but has travelled a good deal. He was teaching theology to a large class of youths and men in Eastern fashion, reclining on a simple mat and cushion himself, while his pupils sat on the ground round him. Tea was brought in for us and him while he went on teaching. The Hadis from which the pupils were reading was on the subject of prayer, and the Moulvi explained the passages with great force and perspicuity as the pupils read them out turn by turn. After some dissertation on the correct intonation of prayers, he took up (probably for our benefit) a comparison of the texts of the Quran and the Bible, showing how the custom of committing the former to memory had resulted in its verbal correctness. Following the same line, Muhammad Sadiq compared with this the recent criticisms on the Bible by the Christian expositors; and the "Encyclopædia Biblica," which he seemed to have studied minutely, afforded him an inexhaustible store of argument.

After this the midday meal was brought in, and then we were sent for by a relation of the Nawab of Maler-Kotla, who had become a disciple of the Mirza, and had devoted himself and his resources to his service, and was living in the village in a simple, almost Spartan, manner. After conversation with him and others, I was shown the high school, college classes, and boarding-house. Though the buildings for the latter were second-rate, yet the management seemed good, and the inmates orderly and well trained. In particular I noticed that, though the next morning was chilly and drizzly, yet all were up at the first streak of dawn, and turned methodically out of their warm beds into the cold yard, and proceeded to the mosque, where all united in morning prayers, after which most of them devoted themselves to reading the Quran for half an hour to one hour. Many of the masters, too, seemed very earnest in their work, and had given up much higher emoluments to work for quite nominal salaries in the cause to which they had devoted themselves.

We were fairly tired out with a long day of talking and interviewing, and slept soundly. We were disappointed, too, in receiving a message that the Mirza was still too unwell to see us, but would do so in the morning. However, when morning dawned we heard with much regret that he had passed a bad night and was still unable to see anyone. As his attendants were unable to hold out any prospect of a speedy interview, and as, indeed, we felt doubtful whether the interview was desired, we prepared for an early start. We had been kindly and hospitably received, and there was something inspiriting in seeing a number of educated men thoroughly zealous and keen in the active pursuit of religion, though the strong spirit of antagonism to Christianity was saddening. Moreover, one could not but feel that, as in similar cases in England and America, here was a man of great ability who had effectually deceived himself, and had then been the means of deceiving a multitude of others into believing his false claims. As we read in Matthew xxiv. 11, "False prophets shall arise and shall deceive many."

The next river we came to was the Beas, and when approaching it from the direction of Gurdaspur, on a bright winter's morning, we were struck by the beauty of the landscape. On our left was a glorious panorama of the Himalaya Mountains, range surmounting range of glistening snow, a vision of dazzling white. All was set off by the varying greens and browns of the rich Panjab Plain to the east and south, the forests and fields of which lay mapped out before us, and the River Beas a gleaming streak of silver meandering through its fertile tracts. Reaching the river, we found that the toll-keeper was on the farther side and the river itself unfordable. Asking the boatmen whether we could cross without paying toll, as we had no means of doing so, they said the only way was for one of us to cross over and ask. We thought on our part that it would be better for both of us to cross over and ask, and as the boatmen saw no objection to this, we heaved our machines on board one of the boats and crossed over with a number of camels and bullocks. Safely arrived on the other side, we went to the toll-office and did what most Easterns do when they are in a quandary—sat down and waited to see what would turn up. The official in a leisurely way took the toll of all the passengers, quadruped and biped alike, eyed us narrowly without speaking, and then, in still more leisurely fashion, began to smoke his hookah. As time passed we both became contemplative, he on the wreathing columns of smoke from his pipe, I on the bucolic landscape around me. His patience was the first to waver, and he broke the silence with: "Now, Sadhu-ji, your pice."

"Indeed, I carry no such mundane articles."

"Then what right had you to cross the Sarkar's river in the Sarkar's boat?"

"Indeed, our purpose was to crave a favour of your worthy self."

"What do you desire of me, O Sadhu-ji?"

"Merely that, as we are on a pilgrimage to India and have no money, you would allow us to cross without paying toll; and as you were on this side and we were on that, and nobody would take our message, there was nothing for it but to come in person to ask the favour."

"Very well, Sadhu-ji, your request is granted, and may you remember me."

As an instance of the reception we got in a Hindu village, I may cite the case of one which we reached in the late afternoon in the Sirhind district. Most of the men must have been working out in the fields when we arrived, for we scarcely saw anyone as we wended our way to what seemed the principal house in the village, and, sitting down outside it, my companion began to sing a popular Indian hymn: "Zara tak soch ai ghafil kih kya dam ka thikana nai' (Think a little, O careless one, how little certainty there is of this life.) First some children and then some men collected, chief among the latter being a venerable and stately old Sikh, the owner of the house and the religious *guru* or *sodhi* of the place.

The song ended, he inquired who we were, and what were our object and destination; and when he had been satisfied on all these points, he informed us that, though he had never entertained Christian Sadhus before, yet if we were ready to be treated like other Sadhus, he would be very glad to offer us the hospitality of his house. We thankfully accepted his offer, and he prepared a room for us, and later on brought us a supper of rice and milk in his own vessels, which to us, after a long and tiring day, seemed quite a royal repast.

It was not often that I was recognized as a European, until I had declared myself, but the following occasion was a notable exception. I was sitting in the little jungle station of Raval, and a party of gentlemen in semi-Indian costume arrived from a hunting expedition. The chief was an elderly thick-set man with an iron-grey beard, dark piercing eyes and gold spectacles. He eyed me narrowly a short time, and then said to one of those with him in the Persian language: "That man is an Englishman." I replied, "I recognize you gentlemen as Afghans." He assented, and I entered into conversation with one of the Afghans with him, who told me that it was His Highness Yakub Khan, ex-Amir of Afghanistan, who had thus recognized me.

On the other hand, at Allahabad I was going on my bicycle along a road which was slippery from a recent shower of rain. In turning a corner the machine skidded and I fell, and as I was picking myself up, an English girl who was passing, called out: "O Sadhu! you must have stolen that bicycle, and that is why you do not know how to ride."

Finally we made our way to Bombay, having been helped the last part of our journey by a friend who bought us our railway-tickets. Here we desired to return homewards by taking the steamer to Karachi. We then had no money, but I was asked to give a lecture on my travels, and after the lecture several of the audience gave me sums amounting altogether to eleven rupees. When, however, we went down to the docks to take passage, we found that our steerage fare cost ten rupees, and five rupees was demanded for each of the bicycles too! We purchased our tickets and stood on the quay awaiting developments. Among the crowd was a Brahman holy man, who was sprinkling the passengers with holy water and receiving a harvest of coppers in return. He came to sprinkle us, but we declined the honour. He then asked why we were waiting instead of going aboard with the other passengers. I told him that we were waiting because we could not pay the fare of our bicycles. He retorted that unless we invoked his blessing (for a remuneration) we should assuredly never start, but that, having done so, everything would turn out well. When we still declined, he went away prophesying that all sorts of misfortunes would befall us.

The last of the passengers had gone aboard, the appointed time for starting had arrived, but no friend had appeared to help us out of the difficulty. The Brahman came back and taunted us with our position, and what it might have been had we but accepted his offer. All I could say was, "Wait and see." Just as the steamer was about to start a ship's officer called to us and said that the captain was willing to take our bicycles free of charge. With a friendly nod to the Brahman, we crossed the drawbridge and in a minute more were under way.

We had now one rupee left for food, but still we were not left in want, for when that was finished the Goanese cooks came and inquired about us and gave us a share of their own dinner. At Karachi the steamers anchor out in the harbour a considerable distance from the landing wharves, and passengers are taken ashore in native boats, a number of which crowd alongside the moment the ship is moored. But these boatmen naturally require remuneration, and we had none to give, so that it now seemed as though we should have greater difficulty in getting off the steamer than we had in getting on. Just then a launch came alongside for the mails, and a ship's officer came up and asked if we would like to go ashore on it. Of course we accepted the offer with alacrity, had our machines on board in a trice, and were safely on *terra firma* again before the native boats had got away from the steamer.

This pilgrimage gave me many opportunities for philosophizing on the rôle that a man's clothes play in gaining him a reception or a rejection. My missionary brethren took various views on the subject. Most exhibited incredulity as to the expediency of donning native garb, while showing some sympathetic interest; few were antagonistic on principle, though one missionary brother, indeed, weighed the matter a long time before admitting us into his house. He thought that the gulf between East and West was *a priori* unbridgeable; therefore no attempt should be made to bridge it, and that the relation between a missionary and his native associates should be sympathetic (patronizing?), but not familiar. To go about with an Indian brother, sharing the same plate and same lodging, seemed to him the height of unwisdom, even to shake hands being to go beyond the bounds of propriety; while as for an Englishman donning native clothes, he was dimming the glamour of the British name in India, which in his eyes was next door to undermining the British rule itself. My mind had been made up on this subject before I had been very long in India, and on no occasion did circumstances tend to weaken my own opinion that the gulf is by no means unbridgeable, and that the sooner and the more heartily we set about bridging it, the better it will be for the promotion of the kingdom of Christ in this land.

Sympathy cannot be wholly made to order: it is largely dependent on extraneous and adventitious circumstances, and I believe that the adoption of native dress increases that sympathy on both sides—on the side of the missionary, because it enables him to realize more vividly what treatment is often meted out to our native brethren and how they feel under it, and on the part of the Indians because the restraint which they usually feel—at least, in country districts—in approaching a Sahib is removed.

No doubt one reason why Indian Christians are so largely adopting Western dress is that they receive much more courtesy, conspicuously so when travelling on the railway. I had occasion to make some inquiries in Batala Station office. I might have drummed my heels on the threshold till I was tired had I not been fortunate in meeting an Indian brother wearing English dress, who walked in without diffidence, though when I attempted to follow him, I was met with a push and a "Nikal jao!" (Get out!). On another occasion, travelling by the night mail from Lahore, I was anxious to get some sleep, and I saw that the native compartment was crowded, while in the European compartment there was only a single English soldier. He barred my entrance with a "Can't you see this is only for Europeans?" I humbly suggested that I belonged to that category, but his prompt "Don't tell me any blooming lies!" made me think it better to seek my night's rest in another compartment. While at Lucknow I essayed to visit the European cemetery at the old Residency, but the custodian would not hear of admitting me, utterly discrediting my statement that I was a European. Surely this unnecessary and most offensive restriction might be removed. I can readily judge from my own feelings at the time how naturally and greatly self-respecting Indians would resent this piece of racial antipathy, which permits a common gate-keeper to subject any Indian to indignity.

One naturally associates with those who give the heartiest welcome, and when in native garb the attraction is to those for the sake of whom we have come out to this land, while, on the other hand, there is danger that, when dressed for the drawing-room or the tennis-courts, we may spend too much of our time on that side of the gulf. If we English realized how much pain we often cause our

Indian brethren, not so much by what we say or do as by the way we say or do it and the way we act towards them, a great cause of racial misunderstanding and ill-feeling would be removed.

Suppose a Sahib is seated in his study, and the bearer announces "A Sahib has come to call," the answer is given at once: "Ask him into the drawing-room." A moment after an Indian gentleman arrives, and the bearer is told to give him a chair in the verandah, or he may be even left standing in the sun, as happened to me more than once, till the Sahib had finished eating his lunch or writing his letters. At more than one bungalow, whether it belonged to a missionary or an official, the bearer would not even report my presence till he had catechized me as to who I was and what I wanted. I have had to wait as long as two hours before the Sahib found leisure to see me, being left meanwhile without a seat except God's good earth, in the wind and cold, or in the heat and sun, as the case might be. A missionary, of all people, should not have a room set apart and tacitly understood to be "for English visitors only," or make a habit of receiving the two kinds of visitors in altogether different style, or allow his menial servants to hustle and hector the already diffident and nervous native visitor.

When I was on my pilgrimage with my disciple, how our hearts opened to those true friends who received both of us alike, and did not chill us at the outset with the suggestion, "I suppose your friend would like to be taken to the house of the catechist." Why, forsooth? Many a time we were both the guests of the humblest of our Indian brothers, and perfectly happy in unrestrained communion with them; others, too, of stations high above our own received us both with an unreserved hospitality, in which nothing was allowed to show that any difference was made between English and Indian, and we honoured and loved them for it. Why, then, should others be at pains to show that they had one treatment for the Englishman and another for the Indian, or perhaps conceal that feeling so poorly that we were never able to feel at ease with them? Which, I ask, is more likely to remove racial antipathy and unrest, and to make our Indian brethren feel that the Christianity which we preach is really genuine and means what it says?

CHAPTER XX

A FRONTIER EPISODE

A merchant caravan in the Tochi Pass—Manak Khan—A sudden onslaught—First aid—Native remedies—A desperate case—A last resort—The *Feringi* doctor—Setting out on the journey—Arrival at Bannu—Refuses amputation—Returns to Afghanistan—His wife and children frightened away.

It is evening, and a party of Lohani merchants are slowly defiling with their camels through the Tochi Pass, one of the mountain gorges which connect our Indian Empire with Afghanistan, and its last beams are shining in the faces of a dozen stalwart men now returning to their homes near Ghuzni, with the proceeds of their winter's trading on the plains of India. The men and some five or six women are on foot, while their children and two or three more women are mounted on some of the camels, which would otherwise be returning unladen, their loads having been sold in Multan. The women, veiled as usual, show little more to the passer-by than one eye and a small triangular piece of cheek; while the men are either holding the nose-strings of the camels, or walking beside them with their guns over their shoulders, and a pistol and long knife or sword peeping out from their open cloak; for the weather is getting hot now with approaching summer, and they are passing through the hostile country of the Wazirs, that wild border mountain tribe who think it their ancestral right to harass and plunder the merchant caravans passing through their district as much as opportunity allows.

Among the merchants we are struck by one fine, tall,

broad-shouldered fellow, stalking along by the side of the foremost of his three camels, his gun and sword ready for use, but, in the absence of any sign of an enemy, walking at ease, humming quietly to himself a native ditty, in expectation of speedily seeing his home again, and rejoining his wife and three children, who have not accompanied him on this journey.

These three camels form his wealth and the centre of his hopes and prospects, for by means of them does he yearly take down his merchandise of skins and fruit to the markets of India, and return in early summer—it is now the month of May—with the proceeds to his home.

Manak Khan—for that is his name—has been down many a winter now with his three camels to the Derajat, or that part of India nearest Afghanistan, and has had more than one scuffle with the Wazirs, while passing through their land, in defence of his little stock-in-trade. His fellow-travellers evidently consider him one of their boldest and best men, for it requires no little knowledge of the country, and courage, too, to lead a party composed largely of women and children, and encumbered by a lot of baggage, through mountain passes, where they are daily and nightly exposed to the attacks of the mountaineers hiding behind the rocks, or crowning the heights on either side, and thirsting for their small possessions.

The sun has now disappeared behind the hill before them, and, like good Muhammadans, they make a brief halt for the evening prayers. The men cleanse their hands and feet with sand—for there is no water to be had here—and, selecting a smooth piece of ground, spread their shawl and, facing the Holy City, perform the requisite number of genuflections and calls on God.

Suddenly there is the loud report of several guns; the bullets whistle through the midst of the party, and in a moment all is confusion and uproar. The camels start up and try to escape; the women seize their children or the camel-ropes; while the men snatch their guns, which had been just now put down, and hastily take aim at some dozen men running down the mountain-side in the direction of the camels, with their long knives ready for action. But the first volley had not been without effect: Manak Khan is lying on the ground, blood flowing fast from a wound in his left leg just above the knee, and anxiously is he watching what is now a hand-to-hand conflict close by him. The Wazirs have rushed among the camels and have cut their cords, and are attempting to drive them off; while the other merchants, having discharged their matchlocks, attack them with their swords, and camels and men are mingled in one shouting, slashing mêlée.

Fortunately for the Lohanis, two of the leading Wazirs fall quickly with fatal sword wounds, and the remainder, seeing that the Lohanis have not been caught napping, and that the tide is turning against them, make off as quickly as they appeared, and the merchants have far too much to do in quieting their frightened camels to think of a pursuit. A hasty council is held. It is found that one man has his arm broken by a sword cut, and Manak Khan has his leg broken, the ball having passed through the bone and opened the knee-joint, while most of the remainder can show smaller cuts.

The women now come to the rescue. A veil is torn up and the wounds bound, some being stitched by the women pulling hairs out of their own heads, and using their ordinary sewing-needles on their husbands' skin. An immediate march is resolved upon, but then comes the difficulty about Manak Khan. Moving him causes him great pain and the blood to gush forth afresh, while to leave him is out of the question, for his throat would be cut long before morning. Whatever may be the faults of an Afghan, he is not one to forsake a friend in the hour of need, and so it proves here. A piece of cloth is half burnt, and the blackened shreds, soaked with oil, rubbed over the wound, and the leg then bound to a musket with the ample folds of a shawl, and, lastly, our hero is tied on a rough bed, and mounted high on the back of a camel.

Great were the lamentations when Manak Khan reached his village home; and instead of his strong step and hearty greeting consoling his wife for her long winter of separation, she came forth only to see the pain-marked face and helpless form carried in on a bed, and to hear the account of the night attack in the dread Tochi Pass. "Bismillah! let the will of God be done," consoles the village Mullah, while some practical friend starts off for the nearest *hakim*, or doctor. The latter shortly arrives; and the wife retires into the cottage, while the greybeards assemble in the courtyard to offer their bits of experience and advice, and vow vengeance over the Quran on the luckless Wazirs who committed the deed.

After no little ceremony and interchange of ideas, the doctor decides on a combination of two remedies, for the case is a serious one: the leg is greatly swollen from the groin to the calf, and unhealthy matter is issuing from both the apertures of entry and exit of the bullet, while the shattered bones grate on each other, and cause the man to bite convulsively the rolled-up end of his turban, on the slightest movement.

For the first remedy a fat sheep is bought and slain and immediately skinned, the reeking skin being applied at once to the bare leg, with the bloody side next the skin, from groin to heel, and the whole bound up and placed in the hollow formed by burning out the central core from the half of a three-foot length of tree-trunk.

For the second remedy a message is sent to a certain religious devotee, who has an asylum in the neighbourhood and a great reputation for charms which will cure all manner of diseases (when it is the will of God that they shall be cured). Next day he arrives, clad in simple goatskin, with the hair outside, and a cap of similar material. Many long prayers are gone through with the help of the Mullah, and at last a small piece of printed paper torn from an Arabic tract is produced, and carefully sewn up in a small piece of leather, and tied in the name of God round the man's ankle.

Then comes the last ceremony, and one not to be overlooked on any account—that of providing a feast at the sick man's expense for all parties concerned. His little store of rupees is fetched out, and returns lighter by a third to the folds of the old turban in which it was carefully hoarded, while the charm-maker is seen leading away a fine milch goat.

Day follows day, and night follows night, but still Manak Khan lies tossing feverish on a bed of pain, and still is the patient Sadura watching by his bedside, and daily bringing in fresh milk and butter and sugar, and making tempting pancakes, only to be left half tasted by the fever-stricken frame of her loved one. At last the tenth day comes, on which the sheepskin is to be removed, and the *hakim* comes, and the Mullah comes, and the greybeards come, and prayers are read, and money is given; but, to the disappointment of all, the limb is found no better, swollen as before, and bathed in evil-smelling matter, which makes his friends, all but his faithful wife, bind a fold or two of their turbans over their noses and mouths.

So week follows week. One herb is tried after another; the last of his rupees disappears among the *hakims*, for, peradventure, think they, the doctor did not heal it at once because his fee was not high enough, so a larger fee is given, and a hint that if only he will say for what price he will speedily heal it, they will go all lengths to pay him; for it must be unwillingnesss, not incapability, that prevents his doing so.

So two months passed away, but still the limb was swollen and sore, still was he unable to rise from his bed of pain.

Then they determined to send a messenger to the neighbouring town of Ghuzni, and call in a doctor of great repute from there. True, his charge was high—one of the three camels must be sold to defray it—but what hope was there for them with the breadwinner hopelessly crippled? So the messenger went and the doctor came, and his remedy was tried. Two bunches of wool were thoroughly soaked in oil and then set fire to, and fastened on the skin near the knee; the pain was great, but Manak Khan stood it bravely, tightly biting his turban-end and grasping his friend's arm in a spasmodic grip. When the burnt flesh separated after a few days the ulcers left were dressed with some leaves from a plant growing on the shrine of a noted saint, and renewed every two or three days. Still there was no improvement, though charms and amulets were bought at high prices from many a saint, and the Ghuzni doctor came again and took away his second camel.

Manak Khan and Sadura were beginning to lose all hope, when one day a traveller was passing through their village on the road to Kabul, and as he was sitting with the villagers, telling them the latest news from India, one of them asked him about a scar on his left arm.

"Ah," he said, "when I was in Dera Ismaïl Khan I had a terrible abscess; but there was an English doctor there, and he lanced it, and got it quite well in a couple of weeks; and," he went on, "numbers of people have been going to him, and I have seen some wonderful cures."

"Really!" say they; "and had you to pay him a great deal?"

"No; that is the strange part. he will not take any money from anyone, but sees all the people that go to him, be they ever so poor, for nothing."

"That cannot be; he must have a reason behind it all."

"No, not unless it be this—that you know he is a *Feringi*, and, like all other *Feringis*, an unbeliever; but, more than that, he seems to want all the people to believe on Hazrat 'Esa" (Lord Jesus) "as being the Son of God" (here the Mullah and several of the men spit on the ground and say, "Tauba, tauba"), "and to this end he has got an assistant who preaches to all the people who go to him, and tells them about Hazrat 'Esa, and how he was a *hakim* and cured people."

"Well, this is strange, but I wonder if he could cure Manak Khan."

And so all particulars are asked, and the advice of all the greybeards, while Manak Khan catches at the idea as a dying man at a straw. Sadura, however, is not so easily convinced. She did not relish the idea of her husband being separated from her once more, and moreover, said she, where the doctor of Ghuzni had failed, how was it likely that another doctor, and he a blasphemer of their Prophet, would succeed?

So the idea was waived for a time, and things went on as before, while their last camel was sold to pay their increasing debts, and gloom settled on the little circle. But as the September days were lengthening and still no hope appeared, they settled that they would try the *Feringi's* medicine. But then came the difficulty as to ways and means; their last camel had been sold, and Manak had no friends who would take him down to the plains free of expense.

At last a bright idea struck them: their little daughter, Gul Bibi, was now seven years old, and many a man would be willing to lend eighty or ninety rupees on condition of her being kept for his wife. And so it was settled: the bargain was struck, and with the proceeds a man was engaged to take him on camel-back down to the Derajat plains. The village carpenter made a kind of litter, which could be fastened on the back of a camel, and as his wife must stop for the children, his old mother volunteered to take the journey with him and tend him through it.

It was a sad farewell this time, and long did Sadura stand at the outskirts of the village watching the camel and its precious burden, with the old mother and sturdy camel-driver trudging by the side, gradually disappear round a corner of the defile.

On the seventh day they emerged from the Gomal Pass on to the Plain of Tank, and here they stayed a little to recuperate with the kind Dr. John Williams, of the Christian hospital there; then going on till the trees and mudhouses of Dera Ismaïl Khan came in sight. Here a fresh disappointment awaited them: the *Feringi* doctor had left Dera, and gone to carry on his work in Bannu, one hundred miles farther. But what cannot be cured must be endured, and so the camel's head is turned towards Bannu, and the weary march resumed one more. Five days later, as the evening was drawing on—it was now late in November—Bannu was reached, and the new *Feringi* doctor inquired for; and a few minutes later the camel, with its strange burden, came through the gates of the mission compound, and the long tedium of the three hundred miles' journey was brought to a close.

Such was the story with which Manak Khan came to me, and which he gradually unfolded to me some two months later, as confidence had increased, and I used to sit by his bedside hearing tales of his mountain home. Great was the sorrow with which I had to tell him that his case was incurable, that his leg had become thoroughly disorganized, and amputation was necessary; but, like most of his race, his aversion to the loss of a limb made him prefer the long months of a bed of sickness and the tedious and repeated operations performed in an endeavour to save the limb in a usable condition. In this way he and his mother remained with us till the middle of April, when, as the heat of the plain began to be felt, they were compelled to return to their mountain home, with little or no improvement.

Yet with one great difference, which lightened up the sadness of his departure: he had learnt to believe on Christ Jesus as his own Saviour, and to look up to Him as the One who carries us safely through sickness and trial, and is preparing a home for us at last; and very earnestly did he assure me that during the long days of patient suffering in our little mission hospital he had learnt to lift his heart in prayer to Him who hath borne our griefs and carried our sorrows, and look up to Him as his Saviour.

"And," said he, "if God spares my life, I will tell my people of Him, and come back with my family to be received into the Christian Church."

So he left us, and our prayers followed him on his long and painful journey home; and may it not be that he is a light shining in a dark place, and witnessing in that little Afghan village of how he went for bodily healing, but God saw fit to pour light into his soul instead, and make the very tedium of a protracted illness in the Bannu Mission Hospital the guiding light to heaven?

Every now and again we got news of Manak Khan. He had taken with him some books in the Pashtu language, a New Testament and some others, and these used to be read by a Mullah in his village and some other friends of his who could read. His leg, however, never got well, and was the cause of his death some three years later. When on his death-bed, he directed his wife to go to Bannu with her children and place herself under my protection, and one autumn morning she arrived, with three children. Before she had been with us many days, however, others of her tribe came and warned her that if she stopped with us she would lose her religion, sell herself to the Evil One, and be lost for ever, and they accompanied these admonitions with threats, so that ultimately she left us, and we have not seen her since. But who knows? Sometimes after the lapse of years these people return to us, and the thread of circumstance is picked up again where it had been cut, as though there had never been any breach of continuity at all! Or it may be the seed goes on growing in some distant Afghan village unknown to us, but known to and tenderly cared for by Him who will not let even a sparrow fall to the ground without His will, and who has counted among His own many a one now resting in a Muhammadan graveyard against that day when the secrets of all hearts shall be revealed.

CHAPTER XXI

FRONTIER CAMPAIGNING

The Pathan warrior—A Christian native officer—A secret mission—A victim of treachery—A soldier convert—Influence of a Christian officer—Crude ideas and strange motives of Pathan soldiers—Camaraderie in frontier regiments—Example of sympathy between students of different religions in mission school—A famous Sikh regiment—Sikh soldiers and religion—Fort Lockhart—Saraghari—The last man—A rifle thief—Caught red-handed.

SOME of the finest fighting material of the Indian Army comes from the Pathan tribes, both on the British side of the border and across it in Tirah and Waziristan, and very pleasant fellows some of these Pathan warriors are. Often when wandering about the frontier have I received the hospitality of some outpost or stayed with the native officer in some blockhouse, and listened to them recounting tales of active service or of their mountain homes. Many of these native officers are old students of the frontier mission schools, and these extend a doubly hearty welcome. Some are serious religious inquirers, and, from having travelled and mixed with all kinds of men, are able to examine the claims of Christianity with less prejudice than the priestly class.

A notable instance is that of Delawar Khan, who was a *Subadar* of the famed Corps of Guides. He was at one time a notorious robber on the Peshawur frontier, and a price had been set on his head. The Rev. R. Clark relates of this man * that once a Government officer met him in a frontier

* In a booklet published by the Church Missionary Society, entitled "Delawar Khan."

village beyond the border, and offered him service in the Guide Corps if he would lead an honest life, or the gallows the first time he was caught within our territory if he refused. The excitement of his adventurous career had a great charm for him, and the teaching of the priests had persuaded him that he was doing God's service in his lawless course. He, therefore, scornfully refused the Englishman's offer, saying he would continue his lawless life, in spite of whatever the Sahibs could do. After a time, however, he thought better of it, and as a price was set on his head, he determined to apply for it in person, thinking he might as well have it himself as anyone else, and so, taking his own head on his shoulders, he went and claimed the reward. The officer, knowing the kind of man he was, again offered him service, which he then accepted, and enlisted as a soldier in the Guide Corps, in which, by his bravery and fidelity, he rapidly rose to be a native officer. Ultimately he became convinced of the truth of the Christian doctrine which he had heard the missionaries preach in the Peshawur bazaar, and, with his characteristic bravery, did not hesitate publicly to acknowledge himself a Christian and receive Christian baptism. Through his example and under his protection some other soldiers in the same corps also became Christians.

His death is thus related by the Rev. R. Clark in his account of his life: "A few months ago he was sent by Government on a secret mission into Central Asia. He was a Christian, and Government trusted him. He passed safely through Kabul on his way to Badakhshan. As he was travelling in disguise, a man who had heard him preach in the Peshawur bazaar betrayed him to the judge, who condemned him to be blown away from a cannon as an apostate. During the trial a copy of one of Dr. Pfander's works dropped from his bosom. The judge took it and tore it in two. The King of the country, however, heard of it, and asked to see the book, and, having read a part of it, pronounced it to be a good book, and set Delawar Khan at liberty. Soon after, however, he died in the snow on the mountains, a victim to the treachery of the King of Chitral."

A native officer in the native levies of the Kurram Valley was converted through reading a Pashtu Testament which an officer gave him, and when I visited him in his home in Shlozan, in the Kurram Valley, I found that he was in the habit of reading the book to some of his neighbours who came together to listen; and although up to that time he had never met a missionary, he had made much progress in Christian experience and knowledge of the Bible.

I had a pupil in the mission school who enlisted in one of the frontier regiments. He was the son of a Mullah of the Khattak tribe. After he had been in the regiment about a year he wrote me a letter saying that he desired Christian baptism, and was looking forward to the day when he would be standing by my side preaching the Gospel to his fellow-countrymen. This was through the influence of a Christian officer in his regiment. Not that the officer tried to convert his men—far from it—but the beautiful transparency of his character and the sincerity of his religion drew his men irresistibly to him, and several desired to become Christians. A Pathan becomes very much attached to an officer whom he admires, and will bear any hardship or danger for him, and therefore it is not surprising that some have become desirous of adopting his religion. For a long time there was a sect on the frontier called the Nikal Sains, who formed a kind of schismatic Christian sect owing to their devotion to Nicholson, of Delhi fame, which amounted in their case almost to a worship of him.

On one occasion a Pathan soldier in a frontier regiment came to me, urgently begging me "to make him a Christian." He was so ignorant of what Christianity meant that I could only offer to give him instruction, but he was so much on outpost duty that this was very difficult. He knew that in order to become a Mussulman it was sufficient to repeat the *Kalimah* in a mosque, and he thought that there must be some corresponding Christian formula, and that by repeating it in our church he might become a Christian. He thought, further, to prove his sincerity to me by saying he was ready to wear a *topi* (hat) instead of a turban. His desire apparently rose merely from an admiration of his Christian regimental officers.

In the Tochi Militia there was a Wazir *Subadar*, a fine fellow, who had seen much active service, and would soon be retiring. One day he was murdered, possibly by a Sepoy whom he had been obliged to punish.

Shortly afterwards his son came to me, earnestly begging me to admit him to the Christian Church. Apparently it was to escape from the duty that devolved on him as a Muhammadan of revenging his father's death by another murder. He was not a coward by any means, but knew he would be killing an innocent person, for the real murderer was beyond his reach, and he recoiled from committing such a crime, and he knew that our teaching was against revenge, and therefore desired to become a Christian. As he was a soldier, I would not act without a reference to his commanding officer, and as he was excited and suffering from much mental tension, I thought it better to wait. Ultimately he did shoot a man, who may have been his father's murderer or not, and I believe was sentenced to penal servitude for life in consequence.

There is something peculiarly attractive, I think, about the frontier regiments. They have very hard service, constant outpost duty, few nights in bed, with ever the danger of the Pathan rifle thief and ambuscades. And yet officers and men are always cheerful, hospitable, and full of the spirit of camaraderie. Even the Sikhs and Pathans seem to lay aside their hereditary feuds, and fight and work heartily together, shoulder to shoulder. Some of the most striking tributes to the influence of the Christian rule of England are seen in this fellowship between different races and religions. In the little frontier wars one sees Pathan soldiers side by side with the stalwart Sikhs, or, it may be, the little Gurkhas with the tall Panjabi Muhammadans. Much the same is seen in the playing-fields of our mission schools, where Christians, Muhammadans, Hindus, and Sikhs are as loyal to one another as if they had never had a religious difference.

A scene I shall always remember was the funeral of a young Sikh student, who was a brilliant member of the school football eleven, and was carried off one summer recently by sudden illness. His Muhammadan, Christian, and Hindu fellow-students vied with each other in showing honour to his memory, and accompanied the body to the burning-ground on the banks of the Kurram River. For the Muhammadans at least this would have at one time been considered as most inconsonant with their religion.

The fine, tall Sikh soldiery of the frontier regiments are some of the nicest men one could have to deal with; the native officers are such perfect gentlemen, and so gentle and docile when conversing about their Sikh religion or the Christian Scriptures, that it is difficult to realize what lions they are in the fight, and how they are the heroes of so many a frontier epic. A Sikh soldier is always ready to talk on religious matters, and delights in singing the beautiful theistic hymns of Kabir and Nanak and others of his countrymen; and they will sit round untiringly, listening with unflagging interest for hours, while I talk or read to them from the Christian Scriptures. In the frontier war of 1897 no Sikh regiment covered itself with greater glory than the 36th, which was quartered at Fort Lockhart when the Afridi rising first broke out. I was in camp on the Samana Range, outside Fort Lockhart, that August just before the outbreak, and these fine soldiers used to sit round me on the rocks outside the fort while we talked of the teachings of our Lord Jesus

Christ, and of those of Guru Nanak, which present so many points of resemblance to them. A few weeks later, and many of those very men had died fighting bravely on the rugged mountains and defiles of Tirah, on which we were then looking down.

One incident will bear repetition, as possibly some of the very men to whom I was then speaking were the heroes of it. A few hundred yards from Fort Lockhart is a small fort called Saraghari, which commands one of the eminences of the Samana Range. This was occupied by a handful of these Sikhs under a native officer. Looking down westward from the Samana Range are the terraced valleys and a labyrinth of the rugged mountain ranges of the Afridis; and so suddenly did these tribes respond to the tocsin of war when Seyyid Akbar and his associate Mullahs sounded it all through Tirah that the various forts on the Samana were surrounded by the *lashkars* before it was possible to reinforce or withdraw the little garrison of Saraghari. The garrisons of Forts Lockhart and Gulistan had, in fact, their hands full with the tribesmen who had entrenched themselves in *sangars* all around, from which they kept up such a fire that no one could show himself. The Afridis saw that the post of Saraghari was the most easily won; the fort itself was smaller and less strongly built, and contained only a small garrison of their hereditary enemies, the Sikhs.

There was a signaller in the little garrison, and he signalled over their dire straits to Fort Lockhart, but from there the answer was returned to them that it was impossible to send reinforcements—they must fight to the end. For them to retreat was impossible, for the few hundred yards between the two forts was swept by the Pathan bullets, while their riflemen swarmed in the *sangars* and behind the rocks all along. Not a man could have lived to reach a distance of twenty yards from the fort. The Sikhs knew that the Pathans would give them no quarter, so they prepared to sell their lives dearly. The Afridis worked nearer and nearer, and many of the brave defenders fell. The signaller signalled to Fort Lockhart, " Five of us have fallen "—ten, twelve, and finally there was only the signaller left. The Pathans swarmed over the walls with their exulting "Allahu Akbar!" and the throat of the last wounded Sikh was cut; so the noble garrison fell at their posts to a man. The fort has never been rebuilt, but there is a monument at the place to record this gallant bit of frontier warfare, and another monument to them was erected in the centre of their holy city, Amritsar, not far from the Golden Temple, their chief place of worship. Here I made the acquaintance of the gallant officers of this regiment, who were in a few weeks to bear the brunt of the severest of the fighting and hardships of that campaign. I read service on the last Sunday before hostilities commenced, and among the officers who attended was their brave commander, Colonel Haughton, whose commanding presence and bravery made him an easy target later on for the tribesman's bullet, but not before he had covered himself and his regiment with glory.

I will here record two little episodes, which are of common enough occurrence on the frontier, but illustrate the dangers that the sentries run when on duty among such cunning and stealthy rifle thieves as the Pathans; and show also that, wily though he is, the Pathan is not infrequently caught by an equally wily native police or levy officer.

A regiment had marched into Bannu, and, there being no quarters available, were encamped on the parade ground. The night being dark and rainy, sentries had been doubled, and were much on the alert. Suddenly two of them were stabbed from behind by Pathans who had crept into the lines unnoticed, and watched their opportunity for running their long Afghan knives into the chest of the unsuspecting soldiers. The thieves got off with both rifles, and, though a hue and cry was raised, no trace of them was found.

Once I was spending a night in a levy post on the frontier, when the native officer in the command of the post got information through a spy that an Afridi was about to cross the frontier, having in his possession a number of cartridges that had been stolen from the lines of a British regiment in Peshawur. A train was just about to arrive from Kohat, and the officer went down to meet it. All the passengers seemed quite innocent; some traders returning from market, a few soldiers going on leave, and some camp followers, appeared to be all who had arrived. There was, however, a Mullah with a Quran, which he was carrying rather ostentatiously, and a wallet, which was less obvious, under the folds of his shawl. Here was his man. He went up to him. The Mullah was indignant at the supposition—he had merely been into Kohat to buy a few household trinkets. He was marched off to the levy post all the same, and, on turning out the contents of his wallet, eighty-one Lee-Metford cartridges were disclosed. That night the Mullah spent in the cells reciting passages in the Quran with a long and monotonous intonation which kept me awake a long time with its weirdness. I suppose, however, it may have been meant to procure some indulgence for his offences, or to serve as a proof of his sanctity; but it certainly did not soften the heart of his captor, the native officer, himself a Muhammadan and a Pathan; nor, I trow, did it mitigate his subsequent punishment.

I was once travelling in the garb of a Mullah from Kohat to Peshawur. I had walked through the Kohat Pass, and reached a village called Mitanni, about sixteen miles from Peshawur. I was tired, and finding here a *tumtum* about to start for Peshawur, I obtained a seat therein for one rupee. Two other Peshawuris were fellow-passengers, but were not present when I paid the driver my fare. On the road the driver stopped at a village, and his place was taken by another man. The first driver omitted to tell him that I had already paid my fare, so when we got near Peshawur he demanded it.

I told him I had already paid the other driver, but he would not believe it. Unluckily the other passengers were unable to corroborate my statement; an altercation ensued in the bazaar at Peshawur, and he wanted to keep my bedding in lieu of the fare. As a crowd was collecting, it was decided to settle the case by driving me to the police-station. The driver began volubly to tell the police inspector how "this Bannu Mullah has got into the *tumtum* at Mitanni, and now refuses to pay his fare." The inspector asked me a question or two, and took in the situation, and then told the driver to take me to my destination, and the case would be seen into, if necessary, when the other driver arrived. Before alighting I told the driver who I was, and that I was sorry he seemed to put so little faith in the word of a Mullah. "Ah, Sahib," said he, "this is an evil age, and even if the Mullah swears on the Quran, we can only believe what we see."

When travelling in native garb one often sees the reverse of the picture, and is able to see common events in new lights. Officers of the Government while on tour are often quite unconsciously a great tax on the village where their camp is pitched. Their servants take provisions from the people at merely nominal prices, or even without payment at all. Many officers, knowing how villainously some native underlings will extort when they get the opportunity, often insist on all payments being made before them according to a fixed scale. Even then the men find other ways of living in clover at the expense of the villagers. This was brought home to me one night when I was stopping at a village called Moach. The police officer of the district was in camp there, but I arrived late, and went to the house of a native, where an old patient of mine visited me, and, finding me hungry and tired, went off to get me some milk. He sent it me by the hand of a young boy, who had to pass by the camp of the police officer, where his cook was preparing his dinner. By his side was a saucepan containing several pints of milk which had been ordered for the great man's supper, each house bringing its share according to a roster kept for the purpose at the police-station. The cook saw the boy coming with the milk, and said to him :

"Come along ; pour it in here."

"But I have not brought this for the Police Sahib. I have brought it for——"

"Nonsense ! Who else here wants milk ? All the milk has been ordered for the Sahib. Pour it in, or I will send you to the lock-up."

I got no milk for *my* supper, and I do not suppose the officer had more than would go into a custard-pudding and a cup of cocoa ; but his myrmidons—they knew how to look after themselves, and enjoyed a good time.

CHAPTER XXII

CHIKKI, THE FREEBOOTER

The mountains of Tirah—Work as a miller's labourer—Joins fortune with a thief—A night raid—The value of a disguise—The thief caught—The cattle "lifter"—Murder by proxy—The price of blood—Tribal factions—Becomes chieftain of the tribe—The zenith of power—Characteristics—Precautionary measures—Journey to Chinarak—A remarkable fort—A curious congregation—Punctiliousness in prayers—Changed attitude—Refrains from hostilities—Meets his death.

Between the Khaibar Pass on the north and the Kurram Valley on the south lies a tangled mass of mountains and valleys called Tirah. Here almost inaccessible escarpments, on which the wary goatherd leads his surefooted flock, alternate with delightful little green glens, where rivulets of clear water dance down to the rice-fields, and hamlets nestle among the walnut and plane trees. In one of these villages was a poor country lad called Muhammad Sarwar. His father was too poor to own flocks, and, having no land of his own, Sarwar took work with a miller. It was one of those picturesque little mills which you see in the valleys of the Afridis, where a mountain-stream comes dashing down the side of a hill, and is then trained aside to where the simple building of stones and mud covers in the mill-stones, while two or three mulberry-trees round give such delightful shade that the mill becomes a rendezvous for the idle men and gossips of the village to wile away the hot summer noons.

But Sarwar was of a restless disposition, and the pittance of flour which, together with a kid and a new turban on the feast-days, was all he got for his labours, did not satisfy his ambition. Then there was his friend Abdul Asghar, who, though as poor as himself to start with, now had four *kanals* of land of his own and a flock of some forty sheep and goats browsing on the mountain-side. It would not do to inquire too closely how Abdul Asghar came by this wealth, but he used to be out a good deal of nights, and he was one of those who was "wanted" at the Border Military Police-station at Thal for his part in several recent cases of highway robbery with violence.

This kind of life was more to the taste of Sarwar than the drudgery of mill-grinding, and before long he and Asghar had joined hands. Once, indeed, they were fairly caught, though they escaped the penalty of their misdeeds. They were on the prowl one dark night, when they saw a shrouded figure creeping along by a farm wall. They had scarcely hid behind a bush when the unknown man turned and came directly towards them. Thinking they had been observed, Asghar called out: "Who are you? Stand, or I fire." The figure halted, and said in a low tone: "It is well; I am your own." The man then came up and suggested that they should spend that night together and share their luck. He told them, too, that there was a fine fat *dumba* in the farm-yard hard by that they might begin upon. Asghar slipped over the wall, while Sarwar and the stranger kept guard, and soon returned with the sheep across his shoulders, its head wrapped up in his *chadar* to stop its cries. They took it off into the jungle, and as the stranger said he wished to be home early that night, they decided to stay and divide it there and then.

The stranger surprised them by saying that he would be content with merely the head as his share, so the "Allahu akbar" was pronounced, the throat cut, and the head given to the stranger, who went off with their parting greeting, "May it be well before you," which he returned by saying, "In the safety of God."

Next morning they were astonished by the sudden appearance of a posse of the Border Military Police, who, before they were able to escape or offer resistance, handcuffed them and led them off, vouchsafing no more explanation than that the *Chota Sahib* had ordered it. They were much mystified, and could not think which of their enemies had got up a case against them ; but they could learn nothing from the police, who either could or would tell nothing more. When, finally, they were taken before the Sahib, and he started away with, "So, you have been after your old game again, and stole a sheep last night from the farm of Nuruddin" (the light of religion), it was with difficulty they could conceal their astonishment and compose themselves quickly enough to reply that they were honest men, had never stolen anything all their lives, and could bring witnesses to prove that last night they never stirred from the *chauk* of Fath Muhammad of Dilrogha village.

The Sahib had a twinkle in his eye as he led them on with further questions to forswear themselves still more hopelessly, and then finally turned to a Sepoy by his side and simply said, "Bring it in." The Sepoy saluted, went out, and in a moment returned bringing something wrapped up in a *chadar*, which he placed on the table before him. The Sahib unrolled it, and exposed to their astonished gaze the very sheep's head they had given to the stranger the night before. He had been none other than the Sahib himself! They could no longer hide their confusion, and could say nothing more than "La haula wala kowata illa bi 'llah" (There is no majesty or power but in God ; He only is great). They were treated to a very pointed lecture, and told that none of their movements could remain concealed from the eyes of the *Sarkar*, and that next time they were caught they would be lodged in the *hawalat* (gaol).

Though Sarwar and his friend gained hereby a wholesome dread of the ubiquity of their ruler, yet the lesson did not restrain them from carrying on their depredations. Not long after Asghar was killed in a cattle-lifting raid on a neighbouring tribe. The villagers were aroused by the barking of the village dogs, started a *chigah* in pursuit, and, though Sarwar escaped, a stray shot hit Asghar in the chest and put an end to his career. Sarwar made such progress in the art, and carried his depredations so far afield, that he became known on all the hills round by the sobriquet of "Chikki," or the "Lifter."

One day a chance circumstance gave a fresh turn to his career. Mullah Darweza, of Saman village, had a bitter grudge against a *malik* of the village because he had enticed away one of his *talibs*, a beautiful boy of thirteen, and now, instead of the boy spending his days over the Quran and Sheikh Sadi, the Persian poet, he was walking about the village with his eyebrows blackened with antimony and a gold-braided turban on his head, and danced in the *malik's chauk* while the village *dum* played a *rebab*. Mullah Darweza would dearly have liked the luxury of stabbing the *malik* himself some dark night, but his profession had to be considered, and what would become of his reputation for sanctity if the story got about, let alone the danger of retaliation, which would mean that he would be a prisoner in his house after dark, and would not be able to go to the mosque to say the night prayers, even if he had not to leave the village altogether?

The Mullah was leading prayers in the mosque that day when his eye fell on Chikki among the worshippers, and as they were leaving the mosque he whispered to him to come to his house that night after the night prayers had been said. What passed there is known only to those two, but Chikki bore away a bag of rupees, and a few nights later, as the *malik* had gone down to a stream to perform his ablutions before evening prayers, a shot rung out from no one knows where, and the *malik*, without a cry, fell forward into the stream, and when the villagers arrived and picked him up they found he had been shot through the heart, and no one ever knew who had done it. This windfall whetted Chikki's appetite, and he soon found this occupation even more lucrative than that of cattle lifting.

As his fame increased, secret commissions came to him from many quarters—from men who had life enemies, but who feared to risk their own lives in ridding themselves of them. With success, however, came danger. Chikki was a marked man, and had to take unusually strict precautions for the preservation of his own life; his repeating rifle was never out of his hand, and no one ever saw him off his guard. He built himself a strong tower, and at night-time retired into this by means of a rope ladder to the upper window (it had no lower windows), then, drawing up the ladder after him, he secured the window. Then came the opportunity of his life. There were two factions in the tribe, the Gur and the Samil, and these had been on bad terms for a long time, but hostilities had so far been confined to a few murders and thefts. Then one day a prominent *malik* of the Gur faction was shot while on a visit to a Samil village. This could not be atoned for without war, and within twenty-four hours the tocsin of war was beating in every Gur village all over the hills. The Samil replied by burning a Gur village, and soon the whole mountain-side was in arms on one side or the other; desultory warfare was carried on for some time, and much blood had been shed on both sides, but the Samil party lacked a leader. Then they bethought them of Chikki, and sent a deputation, asking him to take their lead. He consented on condition of their recognizing him as paramount chief of the Zaimukhts in the event of success attending his arms. They agreed, and he, collecting together some other soldiers of fortune who had thrown in their lot with him, took the field against the Gur faction. The latter were defeated in several engagements, and finally both sides tired of the fray, and they were all the more ready to come to terms as the harvest was ripe and would spoil if not rapidly gathered in.

Both sides agreed to call a *jirgah*, which met, drew up conditions of peace acceptable to both sides, and smoked the pipe of peace. The agreement was ratified by a big feast, in which twenty fat *dumbas* were slain and cooked, with immeasurable quantities of *ghi*, and a dance, in which the men of the two sides, which had so recently been moving heaven and earth to shoot each other, danced together as though they had never been anything but the greatest of friends all their lives.

Chikki was now at the zenith of his power. Eight thousand riflemen, all armed with weapons of precision and all good shots, obeyed his call, and he was able to build a strong fort at Chinarak, in the Zaimukht Mountains, which he garrisoned with his bodyguard of outlaws, while acres of rich land all round brought him supplies of grain and other produce, which enabled him to offer to all who came that open-handed, unstinting hospitality which is the surest path to popularity in Afghanistan. Yet withal he maintained his simple mode of life and plain hillman's costume ; and once when he came down into Sadda, a town in British territory, to meet the great Political Officer there, he formed a marked contrast to the gay clothes and coloured shawls and gold-banded turbans of the Sahib's satellites. He wore simply shirt and trousers of plain homespun, and a black turban, ornamented only by a fringe with a few beads on, and had on his feet a pair of palm-leaf sandals, such as could be bought in any bazaar for the sum of one anna. But his rifle was the best there, and the well-filled cartridge-belt and the six-chambered revolver buckled on excited the envy of many a man round him, while the firm tread and the thick-set frame and the determined features displayed the commanding and reckless character of the man. Yet in society that he cared for he would unbend and display a boisterous good-humour, though of a kind which would make a jest of acts of cruelty involving human suffering and even death.

As may be supposed, Chikki had many enemies who were seeking his life, and he would not allow anyone not known to him to approach him at night or even in the day, and rarely had his fingers off his revolver or the trigger of his rifle. Once he was being shaved by his barber when the foolish man said to him: "Muhammad Anim" (one of Chikki's sworn enemies) "offered me five hundred rupees the other day if, while I was shaving you, I should slip the razor and cut your throat; but *Ma'uzbillah!* I seek refuge in God; I am your sacrifice, and refused the son of a pig." Chikki said nothing then, but when the shaving was over he whipped out his revolver, and said to the luckless barber: "You refused this time, but next time the temptation may be too great for you, so I had better be first in." The tongue of that barber wagged no more, and Chikki got a new and probably more discreet practitioner.

It fell on a day that there was illness in Chikki's household, and someone brought him word that the Bannu doctor was in camp not far off at Thal; so it came about that while I was seeing patients by my tent that afternoon four of Chikki's stalwarts, armed cap-à-pie, appeared with a polite and urgent request that I would accompany them back to his stronghold, Chinarak, and use my medical skill on the sick ones. As soon as the day's work was over we started off. There was a thunderstorm on the mountains above us, and a mountain-torrent had to be crossed which would not be fordable in flood, so we urged on to a point whence a view could be got of the river-bed. On reaching it we saw the turbid waters of the flood sweeping down about a mile higher up the valley from the place where we had to cross, while we had considerably over a mile of rough ground to traverse before we could reach the ford. All pressed forward, the footmen running at the horses' stirrups, and we just managed to get through the rising stream before the flood reached us, thus saving what would have been some hours of waiting for the flood to subside.

Chinarak is a mud fort, with towers and an intricate maze of yards, houses, and passages within; but its strength lies more in its inaccessibility, for the narrow gorge, with high, overhanging cliffs, by which we approached might easily be defended by a few marksmen. On the north side, however, the approach to it is easier. After the sick had been seen, Chikki informed me that, as he had heard that I was a preacher of the *Injil*, he wished to hear me, so that he might judge of the comparative merits of Christianity and Muhammadanism; and to that purpose he had called his Mullah, and we two should sit on either side and speak in turn, while he judged. His men collected round us, truly a motley crew, nearly all of them men who had fled across the border from British justice for some murder or other crime, and had found congenial employment in his bodyguard. I had just been visiting some of their houses professionally, and found representatives of all the tribes down the frontier, and even a few Hindustanis. There they were, with a devil-may-care look in their truculent faces, which made you feel that they would take half a dozen lives, to rob a cottage, with as little compunction as if they were cutting sugar-cane. Perhaps Chikki thought I was eyeing my congregation suspiciously, for he turned to me with a twinkle, and said: "Do not alarm yourself about all these fellows round. They may be all rascals, no doubt; but I have my Martini-Henry here, and if anyone molests you, I will send a bullet through him." No doubt with a good aim, too, for he was reputed the best marksman in the tribe, a fact which I may illustrate by an anecdote.

Like most Afghans, he was very punctilious in the performance of the prescribed Muhammadan prayers, and beyond the regular five times used to indulge in those prayers of supererogation which Muhammad appointed for the devout, or for those who had sins which might be expiated by their performance. Chikki, too, appeared to believe that he kept a credit and debit account of this kind, and that some particularly unwarranted murder would be suitably balanced by the repetition of a number of extra prayers. He had a little book of Arabic prayers called the "Ganj-el-Arus" hung round his neck, and, when at leisure from his more warlike pursuits, would employ himself in the repletion of his credit account therefrom. He handed the book to me, and showed me with some little pride a prayer in it which he said he had composed himself, and which he said was always heard. It was in his own vernacular Pashtu, for he did not know Arabic; and the prayer was that, whenever he raised his rifle to his shoulder to shoot, the bullet might not miss its mark.

Before I came away I left some Pashtu Testaments and other literature with Chikki, and I have reason to believe that he studied them with interest. He, at least, gave up some of his predatory and warlike habits, and devoted himself to more peaceful avocations. When the frontier war of 1897 broke out, not long after, and the tribes all round him were flocking round the standards of *jehad*, and the tocsin of war resounded from the valleys of Swat in the north to the Suliman Mountains of Waziristan in the south, he resisted all the allurements of the Mullahs to take part in the campaign against the *Kafirs*, the English, and restrained the men of his own tribe from any participation in the warfare. It can be seen by a reference to the map that this abstention of the Zaimukht tribe, which numbers about eight thousand fighting men, made a considerable difference to the troops acting in the Miranzai and Kurram Valleys, in the angle between which their territory is situate.

He pressed me to begin medical mission work in his own territory, and promised me support, both material and influential, if I would do so. It was a tempting field, and, no doubt, it would have exerted a widespread influence for peace on the neighbourhood ; but there were insurmountable difficulties of another nature, and the project had to be abandoned.

A few years ago I heard with regret that my old friend Chikki had been ambuscaded by a section of the Khujjal Khel Wazirs, with whom he had an old-standing quarrel He and the men with him fell riddled with bullets, and the victors exultingly cut out his heart and bore it off in triumph, boasting that it weighed ten *seers* (twenty pounds).

CHAPTER XXIII

ROUGH DIAMONDS

A novel inquirer—Attends the bazaar preaching—Attacked by his countrymen—In the police-station—Before the English magistrate—Declares he is a Christian—Arrival of his mother—Tied up in his village—Escape—Takes refuge in the hills—A murder case—Circumstantial evidence—Condemned—A last struggle for liberty—Qazi Abdul Karim—His origin—Eccentricities—Enthusiasm—Crosses the frontier——Captured—Confesses his faith—Torture—Martyrdom.

I WILL recount shortly in this chapter the stories of two Afghan converts, to show what strange cases we have to deal with, and how difficult it is to discover the motives at work, even if we ever do discover them.

Seronai was one of the Marwat clan of Pathans, which inhabits the southern part of the Bannu district.

One afternoon in the year 1899 I had been conducting the open-air preaching in the Bannu bazaar, and was returning home, when I noticed that I was being followed by a stalwart Afghan, over six feet high and broad in proportion. I had noticed him among the crowd at the preaching, as he was quite the biggest man there.

"What is it I can do for you?" I said to him.

"I am going to join your religion," was the reply.

I took him home, found that he was a farmer in a small way, possessed a few acres of land in a very criminal village right at the base of the frontier hills, could not read or write, and knew very little indeed of the Muhammadan religion beyond the prayers. Yet when I asked him, "Why do you wish to join our religion?" the only answer I could obtain was, "Because it is my wish."

"But you do not know anything about either religion."

"You can teach me; I will learn."

So importunate a pupil it was impossible to refuse. He was willing enough to learn, but proved very slow of comprehension. It is our rule not to let inquirers idle away their time, but to give them work, whereby they may at least prove that they do not intend to become burdens on the mission. Seronai was willing enough to work, and had the appetite of an ox; but, unless watched, his strength was far in excess of his discrimination. Given a field to dig up, and he dug up the flower-beds round, too. Given a tree to cut down, and he brought it down quick enough, crashing through a verandah, till finally we found that if we kept him at all it was most economical not to let him do anything.

About his zeal there was no doubt. Not only did he attend all the Christian services, but insisted on accompanying us to the bazaar preaching, and letting all and sundry know that he intended to—in fact, had already—become a Christian. This naturally roused the ire of the people in the bazaar, and when one day there were some of his fellow-countrymen in the audience, I could see that they meant ill, though, from Seronai's great size and strength, they would no doubt be careful in their tactics. The next day, the bazaar preaching being over, Seronai returned towards the mission, while I stopped behind a few moments conversing with a questioner in the crowd. I had gone a little way up the street when I saw an excited mob and heard much shouting, and out of the crowd burst Seronai, tearing himself away from his captors with clothes torn, turban off, and his long locks dishevelled about his face. He ran towards me, calling out, "Save me from these men!"

It did not seem likely when he had been unable to save himself. However, I did my best to enable him to escape, but we were at once surrounded by the crowd, and though no violence was intentionally done to me, Seronai was torn away and mercilessly beaten. Before long, however, the police appeared and dispersed the crowd, and marched off Seronai to the lock-up. As that seemed the safest place for the time being, I told him to keep up his spirits, and that the next day arrangements would be made for him.

The next day he was brought before the civil officer of the district, who also called for the chief man of the section of the tribe which had been creating the disturbance the day before. Seronai was then asked whether he wished to be a Muhammadan or Christian.

"I wish to become a Christian and to remain with the *Padre Sahib*," he said decidedly.

"Very well, you shall," said the officer, and told the chief to explain to his people that they must not resort to further violence.

The next week an old lady in a great state of excitement appeared in the mission compound. With her was a lad of about fourteen summers. They were Seronai's mother and younger brother. She had been told that her son had become a Hindu. As to what a Christian was, she had no idea. She had never heard of such a thing. All she knew was that her son had disgraced her, and when Seronai came she wept on him, and called him reproachful names, and caressed him, all in turns and all together. Seronai was very quiet, and he was genuinely sorry for the old lady's trouble, and came to me and said: "I must go back to my village with my mother to comfort her, and then I will return to you."

It was about a week later. We were sitting in church at evening service, when in came Seronai, looking very hot and dishevelled. He said that the people in his village had seized him, and tied him down to a bed, and set a guard over him night and day. It was impossible to escape till one day a raiding party of Wazirs came down suddenly on the village grazing grounds and carried off about twenty camels. A *chigah* was sounded, and all the able-bodied men of the village started off in pursuit. His mother came and untied him, and he had escaped to us, doing the forty-five miles that lay between his village and the mission without a stop Seronai's condition pointed to the truth of his story, which was, indeed, a very credible one. We heard afterwards that the camel raid had taken place in the way he related.

Seronai went on now learning about the Christian religion, but making very little visible progress. He was zealous, and did not for a moment try to avoid persecution by hiding his light—in fact, he seemed to delight in courting it. Some suggested that he was becoming a Christian in order to spite some relation. This does occasionally happen; but there were no grounds for supposing it to be the case here. Others suggested that he had made a bet that he would become one, but this would hardly account for his carrying the rôle so far at such great personal suffering. In short, though his spiritual aspirations were not, *as far as we could see*, sufficient to account for it, we were quite at a loss to find any other satisfactory explanation.

About a month later he disappeared once again, and then I did not hear of him for two years. At the end of that time, I was seated one day in school teaching one of the classes, when I got a message from the head of the gaol saying there was a prisoner who professed to be a Christian, and desired to see me. On responding to the call, imagine my surprise to find Seronai. He said that on leaving us he had intended to work his land, but, owing to the enmity of the people, had been obliged to seek refuge in the mountains, where a certain *malik* had befriended him and given him shelter. He had remained there till a few weeks back, when he wished to pay a visit to his mother and his village. On arrival there, he found that a tragedy had just been enacted. He had a sister there married to a farmer in the village; this lady had accepted the advances of another swain from the next village, and had prepared to elope with him. They had, however, been frustrated in their intentions, for the corpses of the two had been found—the woman shot through the head, her lover through the heart.

Suspicion would most naturally fall on the husband, but the arrival of Seronai at this moment suggested an alternative: the people of the village would be glad to get an apostate, such as they considered him to be, into trouble; circumstantial evidence was not difficult to arrange, and witnesses in support might be had for the asking. Besides, by making a scapegoat of Seronai, the rest of the village would escape the harrying of the police myrmidons, who might otherwise settle on their village like a swarm of locusts, for no one knew how long. Thus it came about that Seronai was in gaol on the charge of double murder. It was not much that I could do for him beyond giving him the consolations of religion; circumstantial evidence was very black against him, and it was not a matter of surprise when the judge found him guilty and awarded him the extreme penalty of hanging.

Two days yet remained to the carrying out of the sentence, when there was a great uproar in the gaol. Seronai and another prisoner, also under sentence of death, had broken loose from cells, but, unable to scale the outer wall of the prison, had clambered on to the roof of one of the buildings, from which they bade defiance to all who ventured near. They tore up the cornice, and if anyone came near he ran the risk of having his head smashed with a well-directed brick. This siege went on for two and a half hours; the two defenders were so alert that if a ladder was put up at one side while a feint was made at the other, they ran from side to side, aiming bricks at anyone within reach. This could not be allowed to go on, so the superintendent of police made the guard fall in with loaded rifles, and then took out his watch, and, addressing the two men, told them that if they did not surrender in four minutes the guard would fire. There was breathless suspense among the spectators, who by this time numbered several hundreds, as the minutes passed and the men were still defiant. Half a minute remained when the two men surrendered to the guard, and were marched back to the cells. Two days later the extreme penalty of the law was enforced.

Qazi Abdul Karim was altogether a different type of man to Seronai; he came of a good Afghan family and was a very learned man, being, as his name denotes, a *Qazi*, or one entitled to adjudicate Muhammadan law. He was well versed in the Quran, the Hadis, and Muhammadan theology and literature, and held a position of honour in the towns of Quetta and Kandahar. He was a man of property, too, so that no one could taunt him with having become a Christian for the sake of bread. He was converted many years ago at Quetta, where he was baptized by the medical missionary, Dr. Sutton; he passed through many dangers and privations, but I go on at once to speak of my first acquaintance with him at Bannu. He had worked for a time at most of the frontier mission stations, but did not seem able to settle down anywhere. The Missionary Society requires those who desire to become its recognized agents to pass certain examinations, and examinations were not in his line, and he would not present himself for one; thus he never became a recognized agent of the Society. He had a repugnance to doing work in the hospital wards, so it was difficult to know how he was to gain his support. His habits, too, were rather expensive, as he had been accustomed to entertain freely in his Muhammadan days, and could not realize that he must not ask all and any into meals when he had not the wherewithal to pay for them. He had given up almost everything to become a Christian, and he could not understand why the Society would not support him to work on his own lines, without the trammels of rules and regulations.

He was very sensitive in his nature, and ready to think that he was being slighted or not wanted, so he seldom stopped long in any one station. He did not get on well, as a rule, with the other native Christians, and often imagined that schemes were being laid for poisoning his food. This led to bickerings, which the missionary often had trouble in allaying. Thus, notwithstanding his great gifts, Abdul Karim was not a *persona grata* in any of the missions, and the missionary was often glad when he realized that he had outstayed his welcome and passed on to another station. Yet, though certainly not popular with the native Christians, they all admired him for the troubles he had undergone for the sake of Christ, and for his pluck in confessing his faith before all audiences, and regardless of consequences. The last time he visited Bannu he had been undergoing great hardships in a voluntary tramp through the country, literally "despised and rejected of men," because of his uncomprising advocacy of Christianity. He was worn quite thin, and looked so haggard that I did not at first recognize him, and his clothes were reduced to a few rags. We fed him up and got him some new clothes; but even then he could not rid himself of the idea that some people were trying to poison him. This gave rise to the report that he was mad, and certainly his eccentricity in this respect was sufficient to give colour to the report. I feel sure, however—and I knew him well—that his devotion to Christ was very real, and amounted to a real passion to suffer for His sake.

In the summer of 1907 he was taken with an intense desire to enter Afghanistan, and preach the Gospel there. He crossed over the frontier at Chaman, and was seized by some Afghan soldiers. These finally brought him before the Governor of Kandahar. He was offered rewards and honours if he would recant and accept Muhammadanism, and, when he refused, he was cast into prison loaded with eighty pounds of chains. He was examined by H.M. the Amir and the Amir's brother, Nasirullah, but remained firm in his confession of Christianity.

Finally, he was marched off to Kabul under very painful conditions. As far as could be gathered from the reports that filtered down to India, he had to walk loaded with chains and with a bit and bridle in his mouth from Kandahar to Kabul, while any Muhammadan who met him on the way was to smite him on the cheek and pull a hair from his beard. After reaching Kabul, it was reported that he died in prison there; but another report, which purported to be that of an eyewitness, and seemed worthy of credence, related that he had been set at liberty in Kabul, and had set out alone for India.

On the way the people in a village where he was resting found out who he was—probably one of them had heard him preaching in India—and they carried him off to their mosque to force him to repeat the Muhammadan *Kalimah*, "There is no God but God, and Muhammad is the Prophet of God." This is the accepted formula of accepting Islam, and if a convert can be persuaded to say this publicly, it is regarded as his recantation.

Abdul Karim refused. A sword was then produced, and his right arm cut off, and he was again ordered to repeat it, but again refused. The left arm was then severed in the same way, and, on his refusing the third time, his throat was cut. There is no doubt that, whatever the details of his martyrdom may be, Abdul Karim witnessed faithfully up to the last for his Saviour Christ, and died because he would not deny Him.

There are many secret disciples in Afghanistan who honour Christ as we do, and make His teachings their daily guide, but are not yet prepared to follow Him even to the death; and there is no doubt that, at the present time, a public acknowledgment of Christianity would mean death, and probably a cruel death. At the same time, I believe that the Church in Afghanistan will not be established till there have been many such martyrs, who will seal their faith with their blood.

When the news of the death of Abdul Karim reached Bannu, more than one of our Afghan Christians offered to go over into Afghanistan and take his place as herald of the Cross, and bear the consequences, but I pointed out to them that the time was not yet.

CHAPTER XXIV

DEDUCTIONS

Number of converts not a reliable estimate of mission work—Spurious converts *versus* ndigenous Christianity—Latitude should be allowed to the Indian Church—We should introduce Christ to India rather than Occidental Christianity—Christianizing sects among Hindus and Muhammadans—Missionary work not restricted to missionaries—Influence of the best of Hindu and Muhammadan thought should be welcomed—The conversion of the nation requires our attention more than that of the individual—Christian Friars adapted to modern missions—A true representation of Christ to India—Misconceptions that must be removed.

I HAVE completed these sketches of mission work, and I wish to summarize in this chapter some of the conclusions that I have been led to draw from the experiences of the last sixteen years, and then in a concluding chapter to point out what I think to be the most promising lines of advance.

It has too long been the habit to gauge the results of mission work by the number of converts or baptisms, but this is wrong both by omission and by commission: by omission, because it takes no count of what is the larger portion of mission work—the gradual permeation of the country with the teachings and example of Christ; by commission, because it encourages missionaries to baptize and register numbers, chiefly of the lower classes, who have no right to it, because they come from egregiously unworthy motives. Such converts not only are a dead weight on the mission to which they are attached, but too often utterly discredit Christianity in the eyes of the non-Christians around them by their greed and unworthy conduct. It is well that we should sometimes stop and think what it is that we are desirous of doing, and then face the question: "Are we really accomplishing that, or doing something altogether different?"

Are we desirous of planting in India a Christian Church on the lines which we see developed in England or America? If so, I sincerely hope that we shall never succeed. Are we desirous of binding on Eastern converts the same burden of dogmas which has disrupted and still distresses the Western Church? Again, I sincerely hope not Are we desirous of giving India the life and teaching of our Lord Jesus Christ, and of living Him before the people? There we have a worthy object—to compass which no sacrifice is too great—worthy of the best and most devoted of our men and women, and claiming the spiritual and material support of the whole Western Church.

Now, it is quite possible—in fact, we have seen it enacted before our eyes—that, having given India Christ and the Bible, India's sons and sages may not interpret everything as we have done, but may do so in their own mystical and transcendental way. We may not always be able to admit such by baptism into the fold of the Christian Church—they may not themselves desire it—but are we to say that our mission has not been accomplished? Accomplished it assuredly has been, but perhaps not on the lines which we desired or imagined. If, again, after studying the life and words of Christ, and comparing them with the Christianity which they see practised in the West, or in the Westerns who reside among them, they are not drawn to Western Christianity while yet having a devotion to Christ; if they do not feel they can consistently join any of our Western Churches; and if they form a Church of India, are we then to be disappointed and think we have failed of our mission? A thousand times, no! Let us rather praise God that, instead of a number of hothouse plants requiring careful watering and tending lest they sicken and wither, we have a harvest of indigenous growth nurtured on the native soil of India, and ripening to a fruitful maturity under its own sun, and fed by the natural showers of heaven without the aid of the missionaries of a foreign clime.

We see, therefore, that the gathering in of converts is not the first or most important work of the missionary. His work is rather, first, to live Christ before the people of the country; secondly, to give them the teachings of Christ by giving them the Scriptures in their own tongue, and preaching and explaining the same to them. We often find in practice that when some Indian has been captivated by the Gospel, he is hurried on to baptism, and thereby cut off prematurely from his old stock and grafted on the new—prematurely because he is often insufficiently grounded in the Christian faith to withstand the torrent of persecution which is his lot the moment he is baptized, and because the leavening influence which he would otherwise be exerting on a wide circle of his relations and acquaintances is at once destroyed.

Christians at home encourage the missionary to think that nothing has been accomplished till the inquirer is baptized, and that, once baptized and recorded in the church register and the mission report, the work, as far as that individual is concerned, is completed, and the missionary may leave him and turn his attention to someone else. Fatal mistake! Injurious to the convert because, left only half grounded in the faith, he falls into worldly and covetous habits, or may even apostatize outright; injurious to the unevangelized remainder because, instead of being attracted for a time longer to the study of Christianity by the influence of the inquirer, they are thrown into a position of violent antagonism by the secession of the convert, and are no longer willing to give the claims of Christ any hearing at all.

Herein lies the inestimable value of the much-maligned

mission schools and colleges. They do not produce a great crop of immediate baptisms, and so are belittled by some as barren agencies; but nothing else is more surely permeating the great mass of Muhammadan and Hindu thought with Christian thoughts, Christian ideals, and Christian aspirations

We see all around us in present-day India attempts to reclothe Islam and Hinduism in Christian habiliments, or else ardent reformers, hopeless of that Augean task, creating new little sects and offshoots, in which Christian ideas are served up for Muhammadan and Hindu consumers thinly disguised in a dressing of their own religions. These sects sometimes affect a display of hostility to Christianity, lest those whom they wish to draw should mistake them for being only missionary ruses for catching them with guile; but, all the same, they are steps, and I think inevitable steps, in the gradual permeation of the country with the religion of Christ. India has been surfeited with philosophies and dogmas and rites and ceremonies from the hoary Vedic ages down, but she is hungering and thirsting for a living power to draw her God-ward, and such a power is Christ. She cannot have too much of Him, whether this life be set forth in the devoted service of Christian men and women, in hospitals, and schools, and zenanas, and plague camps, and leper asylums, or in the daily preaching and teaching of Him in town and village, in the crowded bazaars, or in the hermitages of the *sadhus* and faqirs.

This is not a work restricted to those who have been set apart as missionaries, but one which claims every professed Christian in the land. Every European Christian, be he in civil or military service, in trade or profession, or merely a temporary visitant for pleasure-seeking, can and should be doing this essentially Christian missionary work if he is living honestly and purely up to the tenets of his religion; and many of the best converts in the land have been first drawn to Christ by watching the consistent private and public Christian life of some such unobtrusive Englishman or Englishwoman, who never was or tried to be a missionary in the usual sense of the term.

On the other hand, the Christianizing of the country has been made all the more remote and difficult by those Englishmen who contemn or discredit the religion they profess, or live lives openly and flagrantly at variance with its ethics.

We do not gain anything from a missionary point of view, and we dishonour God, when we speak of everything in Islam or Hinduism as evil. The Mussulman has given a witness to the Unity of God and the folly of idolatry which has been unsurpassed in the religious history of the world, and he has qualities of devotion and self-abnegation which the Christian Church may well desire to enlist in her service rather than to ignore or decry. The Hindu has evolved philosophies on the enigmas of life, and sin, and pain, and death, which have for ages been the solace and guide of the myriad inhabitants of India, and he has attained heights of self-abnegation and austerity in the pursuit of his religious ideals which would have made the Christian ascetics of the early centuries of our era envious. Religion has been to them a pervading force which has coloured the most commonplace acts of daily life. Here we have qualities which have prepared the soil for the implanting of the Christian faith, and which, when imbued and enlightened with the love of Christ, will reach a luxuriance of Christian energy worthy of the religious East, in which so many of the religions of the world have had their birth. India, indeed, wants Christ, but the future Christianity of India will not be that Occidental form which we have been accustomed to, but something that will have incorporated all the best God-given qualities and capacities and thoughts of the Muhammadans and Hindus.

It is a great pity that missionary energy is still largely

destructive rather than constructive. In the earlier days of mission work it was popularly supposed that missionaries were to attack the citadels of Islam and Hinduism, which were considered to be the great obstacles to the acceptance of Christianity by the people of India, and it was thought that, those once overthrown, we should find a Christian country. Much more probably we should find an atheistic and materialistic India, in which Mammon, Wealth, Industrial Success, and Worldliness had become the new gods. The real and most deadly enemies with which the missionary has to contend are infidelity and mammon worship. We may well try to enlist the religious spirit of all the Indian creeds in the struggle against these, the common enemies of all faiths, or we may find, when too late, that we have destroyed the fabric of faith, and set up nothing in its place. The old Islam, the old Hinduism, are already doomed, not by the efforts of the missionaries, but by the contact with the West, by the growth of commerce, by the spread of education, by the thirst for wealth and luxury which the West has implanted in the East. All the power of Christianity is required to give India a new and living and robust faith, which shall be able to withstand these disrupting forces.

Some of the Christian attacks on Eastern religions are painful to read, because one cannot help seeing that the same weapons have been used in the West, and often with success, against belief in the Christian Scriptures, and the missionaries are only preparing tools which will one day be used against themselves. They may for the moment win a Byrrhic victory against the forces of Islam and Hinduism, but they are at the same time undermining the religious spirit, the ardent faith, the unquestioning devotion, which have been the crown and glory of India for ages. Let it rather be their endeavour to present a real, living, pulsating Christianity, capable of enlisting all these divine forces in its own service without weakening or destroying one of them, and all that is best in Islam and Hinduism will be drawn into it. The product will be nearer to the mind of Christ than much that passes by the name of Christianity in the West, yet has lost the power of the living Christ. Do not destroy, but give something worthy of acceptance, and be careful of the type.

Converts will come right enough when we work on these lines, but they will not so often be the man-made converts which have been drawn by the outward attractions which missions sometimes offer. They will more often be those who have been drawn of the Spirit, and become converts in spite of us and our little faith. And they will inherit the blessing of Isaac as assuredly as the first class partake of the waywardness of Ishmael.

The East has long possessed and developed in a myriad different ways the idea of sacrifice, while the more practical West has been tending more and more towards a philanthropic Christianity which makes a life of service its ideal. The best will be when we bring about a union of the religious devotion of the East with the altruism of the West.

So far the asceticism and devotion of the Orient has been rendered nugatory and disappointing by its uselessness—by, if we may use a paradoxical expression, its very selfishness—for it was directed to the emancipation of the individual soul rather than to the salvation of the race. But when the sacrifice of the Orient and the service of the Occident join hands and go forth in the name of Christ to mitigate and remove the ills and sorrows of this sad, sad world, then indeed will the spirit of Christ be fulfilled in His Church.

A recent writer, whose missionary enthusiasm had caught a spark from the mystic fires of the East, writes: "The thing which is lacking (in mission work) I believe to be the vision of the homeless, suffering, serving Jesus—the Jesus who came to serve, and laid down His life for the sheep."* He then goes on to enunciate the need for Christian Friars, who may bring a knowledge of Christ to India in the only way to which her people have ever been accustomed. From time immemorial all the religions that have occupied the arena of the Indian stage, and compelled the adherence and devotion of her people, have been promulgated by peripatetic ascetics, who have shown by their devotion to their ideals the intensity of their convictions, and have not wearied of journeying from end to end of the land, through heat and through cold, through privations and hunger and nakedness, that they might make known to the people how they were to obtain salvation.

The Friars suggested by the above writer would therefore be such as India is already familiar with, and would work on a prepared soil. He writes: "The part of the Friars is to live Christ so literally before the Church and the world, that both may become conscious of Him. The Church is lacking in ideal and devotion; the Friars must, therefore, lead lives of such heroism and devoted service in the face of every danger that the Church may be fired by their example. . . . If such a body of men were to act in this way, none would be so quick to cast themselves at the Master's feet as the people of India, and the high castes would lead the way."

But it must be clearly understood that these Friars are not to replace or render unnecessary any section of the existing missionary body. Every one of the various activities of the present mission work is wanted, urgently wanted. They will, however, fire their energies, enlarge their scope, and increase their usefulness. Two misconceptions require to be removed from the Indian mind. One is, that missionary activity is a political activity, a department of the Government artfully disguised. The other is, that the English are, after all, only

* S. E. Stokes in *The East and the West* for April, 1908.

lukewarm about their religion, and do not hesitate to disregard it if it clashes with their comfort or interest. To combat these ideas it is the lives of the missionaries that are of more importance than the organization, and the more Christ is lived and exemplified, the more spiritual and lasting will be the result.

CHAPTER XXV

A FORWARD POLICY

Frontier medical missions—Their value as outposts—Ancient Christianity in Central Asia—Kafiristan: a lost opportunity of the Christian Church—Forcible conversion to Islam—Fields for missionary enterprise beyond the North-West Frontier—The first missionaries should be medical men—An example of the power of a medical mission to overcome opposition—The need for branch dispensaries—Scheme of advance—Needs.

Down the North-West Frontier is the long line of mission outposts: Srinagar, Mardan, Peshawur, Karak and Thal in the Kohat district, Bannu, Tank, Dera Ismaïl Khan, Dera Ghazi Khan, Quetta. All of these comprise medical mission work as part of their activities. Several have educational work as well. Yet we regard them as something more than outposts: they are bases. The strength of the British military stations on that frontier is far in excess of the requirements of their immediate surroundings, because under conceivable conditions they have to act as the bases of an army acting beyond them, or they might have to stem the advance of an invading force. In a precisely similar way we must regard our frontier missions, not merely in relation to their environments, but as the means whereby we shall be able to go forward and evangelize the yet unoccupied lands to the west and the north. They should be sufficiently well equipped in both *personnel* and material, so that when need arises they might be able to supply the men and means for occupying mission stations farther on.

The countries of Central Asia to the west and north of

India are a challenge and a reproach to the Christian Church—a reproach because in the early centuries of the Christian era the zeal of the first missionaries carried the Gospel right across Turkestan and Tibet to China, and Christian Churches flourished from Asia Minor to Mongolia. Dr. Stein, in his recent work, "Buried Cities of Khotan," tells us how in those days there were fair towns and running streams and orchards, where now is only a sandy, waterless waste. The rains ceased, the water channels dried up, the people had to leave their towns and villages, and the sand was blown in and covered houses and trees and everything deep in its drifting dunes, where they have been unvisited and forgotten till the present traveller unearthed them. A similar spiritual drought seems to have fallen on the Armenian and Nestorian Churches of those parts, and, deadened and retrograde, they were unable to withstand the great Muhammadan invasions of the sixth and succeeding centuries, which swept like tornadoes right across Asia into China.

In again proclaiming the Gospel in Turkestan the Christian Church will only be reoccupying her lost territories, where at one time Christian congregations gathered in their churches, but for centuries only the Muhammadan call to prayer has been permitted to be heard.

It is a reproach, again, because on our North-West Frontier, only separated from Chitral by a range of mountains, is the interesting land known as Kafiristan. There is reason to believe that the inhabitants of this land, known as the Kafirs, are the descendants of some of the Greeks whom Alexander of Macedon brought over in his train three hundred years before Christ. Two stories are current among the Kafirs regarding their origin, but both point to their arrival about the third century before Christ. One is that a number of Greeks, expelled from the lowlands by the advance of surrounding and more powerful tribes, took refuge in these mountain fastnesses; and the other is that they are the descendants of wounded soldiers left by Alexander the Great in the neighbouring region of Bajour. They still practised till a few years ago pagan idolatrous rites, which had probably changed little for two thousand years, and they resisted the inroads of the Muhammadans, who were obliged to recoil before their inaccessible mountain fastnesses. They welcomed some Christian missionaries who visited their valleys at different times in the last century, and there is every reason to believe that, had the Christian Church accepted the task, the whole of that nation would have adopted the Christian religion. But though these travellers urged on the Church her opportunity and her responsibility, no step was taken.

Colonel Wingate, a retired frontier officer, writes:* "I had gone for a stroll one day in the summer of 1895 with another officer for a short distance outside the military camp. Though we were wearing the uniform of officers, we were without arms, when suddenly we saw a party of natives approaching. They were travelling at a rapid rate, and as they drew near we observed that they were armed with bows and arrows and spears, each carrying a coloured blanket in a roll over the shoulder, their food of dried meat and rice tied on to their girdles. The whole party were warriors, as indicated by the rows of shells sewn on to the kilts worn round their waists. They proved to be an influential deputation from Kafiristan to the headquarters camp to obtain the assurance of the British nation that they would still enjoy their protection. From time to time, commencing with the mission of Major Biddulph, interviews between headmen of the Kafiri tribes and officers of the British Government had taken place, resulting in the belief that the independence of Kafiristan would be preserved. But the unexpected and ominous answer came over the field telegraph wires: 'Tell them they are now the *subjects* of the Amir. While waiting for the answer I had some conversation with

* "Across our Indian Frontier," by Colonel G. Wingate, C.I.E.

them. They were wonderfully bright and generous-hearted, and fond of a joke. When I asked them if they were ready to embrace the Christian religion, they replied: 'We do not want to change the religion of our fathers; but if we must change, then we would far rather become Christians than Muhammadans, because we should still be Kafirs,' alluding to the common application of this word by Muhammadans to all unbelievers. . . . The unsparing proselytism of Muhammadan conquest has done its worst. Hearths and homes in their mountain fastnesses, which had been preserved inviolate for one thousand years against the hated Mussulman foe, have been ruthlessly invaded and spoiled. The bravest of their defenders have been forcibly made into Muhammadans, and the fairest of their daughters have been torn from the arms of their natural protectors and carried off as new supplies for the harims of their conquerors." Another lost opportunity to add to the account of the Christian Church!

But there are lands now in that historic region "where three empires meet" which may yet be occupied by the messengers of "peace and goodwill towards men." Is the Church going to rise to the present opportunities or let them, too, slip by?

Swat, Chitral, Baltistan, Hunza, Astor, Chilas, are each of them the home of a nation. Then the great historic cities of Bukhara, Samarcand, Tashkend, Merv, Kokan, Kashgar, have some of them been in their time the capitals of great kingdoms.

In some of these places there are already missionaries at work, most of them belonging to Swedish and German societies; but how utterly inadequate these few scattered workers are to the great problem which they have to face! What is needed at the present are medical missions. A medical man would be welcomed by the people in all these places. The time for the preacher has yet to come. It would not be wise, even were it possible, to send up clerical missionaries and evangelists into these parts at present. But the doctor will find his sphere everywhere, and will find his hands full of work as soon as he arrives. He will be able to overcome suspicion and prejudice, and his timely aid and sympathetic treatment will disarm opposition, and his life will be a better setting forth of Christianity than his words. There is a door everywhere that can be opened by love and sympathy and practical service, and no one is more in a position to have a key for every door than the doctor.

I have already said much to show how powerful an agency medical work is for overcoming prejudice, but I will cite one instance more, where the doctor was the son of a convert of the very place where he was working, and had succeeded by his loving and skilful attentions in overcoming the opposition and much of the prejudice of the people. The first branch dispensary in connection with the Bannu Medical Mission was opened at Shekh Mahmud in 1895. This is a large village near the *Tahsil* town of Isa Khel, on the right bank of the Indus River. About thirty-five years ago a landowner of this place was converted to Christianity, and, together with his family, received into the Christian Church. At first he passed through great vicissitudes: his house was burnt over his head by his fellow-villagers, and he and his family barely escaped with their lives. His enemies then tried to expatriate him by erasing his name from the village registers, and swearing in court that he was a stranger to the district. Eventually, however, their perjury was found out, and the court restored him his lands and had a new house built for him in the place of the one that had been burnt down. This man passed to his rest trusting in our Lord Jesus Christ, leaving three sons, who were all following in their father's footsteps, and have been privileged to see many of their former enemies brought to Christ themselves. The eldest son has also died, but leaving two sons, of whom the elder has obtained the Government qualification of doctor, and is destined to take charge of the branch dispensary which we are about to open at Thal. The second and third sons have received a medical training in the mission hospital, and are both engaged in medical mission work—the second at the Bannu Headquarters Hospital, and the youngest is in charge of a branch dispensary built on the very land that his Muhammadan countrymen tried to wrest from his father. On the last occasion of my visiting this branch, just before leaving India for my visit to England in 1908, this young doctor—Fazl Khan by name—had made a dinner for the poor of the village, and nearly two hundred must have come to partake of his hospitality. This custom of feeding the poor is often done in India by those undertaking a long journey or some other enterprise, so that the prayers of the poor may be a blessing on the work.

Well, after all the guests had partaken, the Christian doctor offered prayers for my safe journey to England, and for the medical mission work at Bannu and at Sheikh Mahmud, and after each petition all present raised the cry of "Allah," being their way of saying "Amen." Now, these were the sons and relatives of the very men who had burnt the house of the Christian doctor's father, and tried to oust him from his lands. This is an example of what may be accomplished in a fanatical frontier district through the agency of medical mission work carried on by an Indian Christian.

I am constantly getting requests from *maliks* (chiefs) of these trans-frontier tribes to visit them in their mountain homes, and when I have accepted I have received a cordial welcome, and been well treated, while I have had abundant opportunities of medical mission work. There is great scope for the itinerant medical missionary among them, but he requires a base to which he can send cases requiring severe operations or ward treatment. Small branch dispensaries in charge of Indian hospital assistants are of the greatest value, and there are many suitable places for such along our Indian frontier. The advantages of such dispensaries I believe to be as follows; (1) They exert an extraordinary Christianizing, civilizing, and pacifying influence on the tribes in their immediate vicinity. (2) They form subsidiary bases for the medical missionary, not only enabling him to work up that particular district, but relieving the pressure on the headquarters hospital. The assistant-in-charge sifts the cases that come to him, tells some that their disease is irremediable, thereby saving them the expense and weariness of a long journey, and recommending others to go up to headquarters for operations. (3) They form training-schools for our Indian helpers, whereby they are prepared for taking posts of even greater responsibility. This matter of efficient training of our Indian helpers is, I believe, a matter of paramount importance.

My hope is, then, in the near future to see a number of new centres of medical mission work opened in these hitherto almost untouched lands of Central Asia, and, associated with these centres, a number of village dispensaries for the more remote tracks. The central missions would have a staff of at least two European medical men, and the branches would be in the charge of Indian assistants. There is no reason, however, why an Indian of sufficient qualifications and experience should not take the place of one of the European staff when circumstances admit of it. The central hospital should be well equipped in both out- and in-patient departments, and have sanitary wards accommodating from thirty to eighty in-patients. The branches should also be able to take in from six to ten in-patients, as not only will the assistant in charge often get cases of urgency, which require immediate indoor treatment, and cannot be forwarded to the base hospital, but when the head medical missionary visits these out-stations he will be glad to be able to accommodate a few operation cases which may be waiting for him there.

This scheme would not clash with Government medical aid, because in most of these regions there are very few, if any, Government hospitals or dispensaries, and those places which already have sufficient Government medical aid might well be passed over in favour of the numberless places that have none.

Here is a grand field for young medical men who are anxious to consecrate their abilities to the service of God and man. They are not offered tempting salaries or honours, but they will have the satisfaction of knowing that they are helping to lighten the burden of mankind where that burden was weighing most heavily, and to bring the light and love of Christ into some of the darkest abodes of cruelty and superstition to be met with on the face of God's earth.

Those who help this work with the gifts in money or kind, without which it would be impossible of execution, can have the satisfaction of knowing that they are not only relieving bodily suffering which would otherwise be unrelieved, and carrying the Evangel to those who have never heard of it, but they are drawing nations together in bonds of service and sympathy, and diminishing the danger of racial conflict and devastating war.

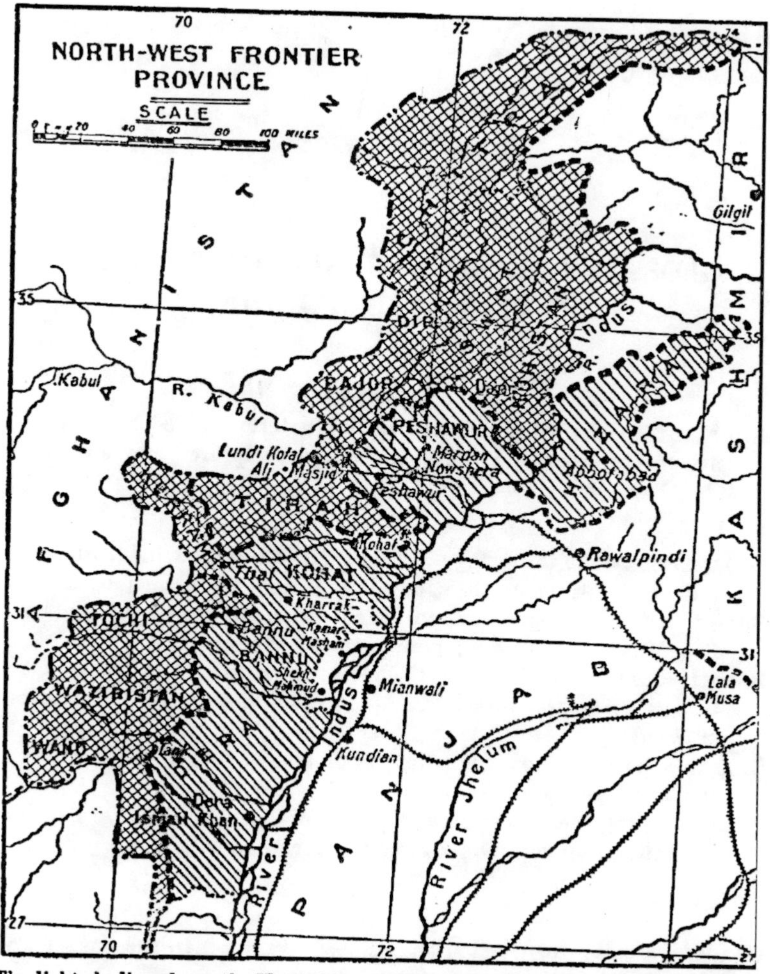

The light shading shows the North-West Frontier Province, and the darker shading (between the Durand line and the Indian Frontier) the territory of the independent and semi-independent tribes.

GLOSSARY OF WORDS NOT GENERALLY USED OUTSIDE INDIA

A.

Ahl-el-kitáb=the people of the Book: a term applied by Muhammadans to Jews, and Christians whose Scriptures they accept as the Word of God.

B.

Banaprastha=the third stage of the life of a devout Hindu, when he retires from trade or office, and lives in some forest or jungle.

Ber=a tree, very common in Afghanistán—*Zizyphus jujuba* and *Z. vulgaris*. Its fruit is largely eaten by the people.

Bhagti=devotion, faith. The Hindus contrast salvation by *bhagti* to that by *karma*, or works. Chaitanza and others were the apostles of *bhagti*.

Bhásha=the script in which the Hindi language is usually written; the language itself.

Brahmachári=the first stage of the life of a devout Hindu, when he is a celibate student under some teacher or *guru*.

C.

Chadar=a cotton or woollen shawl, used as a wrap in the day and a sheet by night.

Chapáti=flat cakes of unleavened bread, cooked over a *tauwa*, or flat piece of iron.

Chárpár="the four-legged," the plain native wooden bedstead.

Chauk=the room which the headman of a village sets apart for the use of the public. Village business and gossip is carried on here, and travellers accommodated.

Chigah=an alarm, sounded by beating a drum in a village, for the arm-bearing population to come out in pursuit of raiders or robbers.

Chilam—the Afghán term for the Indian hookah, or hubble-bubble pipe. The kind used in Afghanistán is simpler in construction, and has a shorter tube.

D.

Dáktar=the native corruption of "doctor."

Dharmsála=a Hindu temple and rest-house for travellers, these two institutions being almost invariably combined.

Dilaq=the patchwork cloak which is characteristic of the Muhammadan faqir.

Dúm=the village barber and musician, these two offices being usually combined; he also does most of the minor surgery of the village.

Dúmba=the fat-tailed Afghán sheep.

F.

Fatwá=a religious decree, promulgated by a court of Mullahs, or by one Mullah of authority.

Feringi=the name universally accorded in Afghanistán to Europeans (the Franks). In British India it has a prejudicial signification, but not so in Afghanistán.

G.

Ghazá=a religious murder, when a Muhammadan fanatic kills a Christian or Hindu for the sake of religion.

Ghází=the fanatic who commits *ghazá*.

Grihasta=the second stage in the life of a devout Hindu, when he marries a wife, begets children, and carries on his profession or trade.

Guru=a religious preceptor or guide among Hindus or Sikhs.

H.

Hákim=a ruler, an executive officer.

Hakím=a native doctor, who practises on Western or Hippocratic lines.

Halwa=a kind of sweet pudding, very popular with the Afgháns.

Hazrat 'Esa = the Muhammadan appellation for our Lord Jesus Christ.

Hujra=a guest-house, where travellers are accommodated in Afghán villages. It differs from *chauk* in that it is more specialized for the use of travellers, while the latter is more for the use of the village folk.

I.

'Íd=a Muhammadan feast-day. There are two chief feasts—the "'Id-el-fitr," or day following the fast-month of Ramazán, and the "'Id-el-zoha" or "'Id-el-bakr," which is the Feast of Sacrifice, in memory of Abraham's would-be sacrifice of his son.

Izzat=honour: a word constantly in an Afghán's thoughts and conversation, but which even he is not always able to define.

J.

Jirgah=a council of the tribal elders. This may be appointed by the tribesmen themselves to settle some dispute, or in British India it may be appointed by the civil officer to help in deciding some judicial case.

K.

Káfir=an infidel. Strictly, only one who does not believe in God and the prophets, but loosely applied to all non-Muslims.

Kalámulláh=the Word of God. Comprises, according to Muhammadan teaching, four books—the Law (Tauret), the Psalms (Zabúr), the Gospel (Injil), and the Qurán.

Kalima=the Muhammadan creed: "There is no God but God, and Muhammad is the prophet of God." The recitation of this is the recognized way of declaring one's self a Muhammadan.

Kanal=a measure of land—one-eighth of an acre.

Karmá=works. According to Hindu philosophy, a man's reincarnation depends on the character and amount of his *karmá*.

Karnal=the Afghán corruption of "colonel."

Khán=a lord, a chief; an honorific title in Afghanistán, or merely part of a man s name.

L.

Lashkar=an army; often applied in Afghanistán to a small body of men going out from a tribe for warlike purposes, but they may be going for peaceful purposes—hence the English "lascar."

M.

Málik=in Afghanistán the headman of a village or tribe.

Má'uzbilláh=a Muhammadan exclamation on hearing bad news or a calamity: "May God protect us!"

Muharram=a yearly Muhammadan feast held on the 10th of the month of Muharram.

Mullah=a Muhammadan preacher.

Munshi=a clerk or preceptor.

P.

Pagari=the Eastern head-dress or turban.

Patwári=a village bailiff, who keeps the accounts of the village lands.

Patwarkhána=the office of the bailiff.

Parda=the Eastern custom of secluding women from the public gaze.

Puláo=a popular dish in Afghanistán, consisting of meat cooked with rice, with spices, nuts, raisins, and sweetenings.

Q.

Qurbán=*lit.*, sacrifice; also used as an expression of devotion by an inferior to a superior.

Qismet=fate, destiny; an ever-present idea in the Muhammadan mind.

R.

Rebáb=an Afghán stringed instrument, resembling a guitar.

S.

Sáhib=*lit.*, gentleman; the term of respect usually applied to Englishmen.

Samádh=the posture assumed by an ascetic for contemplation of the Deity. There are a great variety of these, each possessing its own peculiar merit.

Sangar=an entrenchment. In the mountain warfare of Afghanistán these are made of short walls of stones on the hillside.

Sanyási=the fourth stage in the life of a devout Hindu, when he retires from the world, and gives himself up entirely to religious meditation.

Sardár=a chief, an Afghán nobleman.

Sarkár=the usual term for the British Government.

Sharm=shame. The Afghán idea underlying this word is a complex, in which shame, public disgrace, modesty, delicacy, sense of honour, all share in varying degree. He is always talking of it.

Shāster=a religious book of the Hindus.

Shesham=a common tree on the frontier that yields an excellent hard wood for various articles of household use—*Dalbergia sisso.*

Sowár=a horseman.

Sura=a chapter of the Qurán.

T.

Tahsíl=the subdivision of an administrative district; the centre for the collection of the revenue.

Tálib=a Muhammadan religious student; a pupil in a mosque.

Tap-jap=a recitation of religious formulæ by a Hindu.

Tauba=*lit.*, repentance; an exclamation denoting abhorrence or contrition.

U.

Ustad=a master or preceptor; a religious teacher (among Muhammadans).

W.

Wiláyati=belonging to Europe; especially applied to merchandise of European origin.

Y.

Yogsadhan=a system of contemplation, combined with religious exercises, whereby occult power is acquired.

Yunáni=pertaining to Greece. This is the word usually applied to that system of native medicine which was derived from the Greeks; in Europe it is spoken of in connection with the name of Hippocrates, who formulated it. The other, or Hindu system, is the Vedic; those who practise the former are called *hakíms*, the latter *baids*.

Z.

Zamindár=a farmer, a landowner.

Zyárat=a shrine; the grave of a holy man; a place of pilgrimage.

INDEX